Social Edge Computing

Dong Wang • Daniel 'Yue' Zhang

Social Edge Computing

Empowering Human-Centric Edge
Computing, Learning and Intelligence

 Springer

Dong Wang
Champaign, IL, USA

Daniel 'Yue' Zhang
Amazon Alexa AI
Seattle, WA, USA

ISBN 978-3-031-26938-7   ISBN 978-3-031-26936-3   (eBook)
https://doi.org/10.1007/978-3-031-26936-3

This Springer imprint is published by the registered company Springer Nature Switzerland AG
The registered company address is: Gewerbestrasse 11, 6330 Cham, Switzerland

To Na and David
                D.W.
To Qi
            D.Y.Z.

Preface

The rise of the Internet of Things (IoT) and Artificial Intelligence (AI) leads to the emergence of edge computing systems that push the training and deployment of AI to the edge of the network, so as to achieve reduced bandwidth cost, improved responsiveness, and better privacy protection. There exist several major limitations of existing research in edge computing for supporting AI applications at the edge. First, many current methods focus on a device-server offloading design while ignoring the collective computing power of devices privately owned by individuals. Second, the unique analytical skill and domain knowledge of the device owners (humans) are underutilized in existing edge computing systems. Third, the current centralized training of AI models is no longer appropriate in privacy-sensitive applications where the training data are owned by individuals. To address these knowledge gaps, this book presents a new paradigm, the Social Edge Computing (SEC), that empowers applications at the edge by revolutionizing the computing, intelligence, and learning of the human-centric systems. The integration of edge computing, humans, and AI in SEC allows machines and humans to make collaborative and optimized decisions in edge-based intelligent applications. The SEC paradigm generalizes the current machine-to-machine interactions in edge computing (e.g., mobile edge computing literature), and machine-to-AI interactions (e.g., edge intelligence literature) into a holistic human-machine-AI ecosystem.

The SEC paradigm introduces a set of critical challenges such as the rational nature of device owners, pronounced heterogeneity of the edge devices, real-time AI at the edge, human and AI interaction, and the privacy concern of the human users. This book addresses these challenges by presenting a series of principled models and system designs that enable the confluence of the computing capabilities of devices and the domain knowledge of the people, while explicitly addressing the unique concerns and constraints of humans. The book first presents a set of novel resource management frameworks that enable heterogeneous IoT devices owned by end-users to collaboratively provide computing power for executing AI models at the edge. The book then presents two human-machine interactive learning frameworks that leverage human intelligence to troubleshoot and improve the AI model performance. Finally, the book reviews a federated learning-based edge learning framework that allows device owners to contribute to the training of AI models with minimized privacy risks. The book also offers extensive evaluation of SEC in real-world edge computing applications, which shows that the proposed paradigm benefits edge intelligent applications by achieving impressive performance gains in various aspects such as service responsiveness, energy efficiency, and model accuracy. SEC enables "social interactions" between machines and humans at the edge by allowing the devices to obtain the unique domain knowledge and expertise from humans to improve the performance and transparency of the application. SEC also motivates novel AI for social good applications such as privacy-aware health monitoring, disaster damage assessment, crowd abnormal event detection, and vehicle-based criminal tracking.

Using theories, models, and techniques described in this book, the reader is familiarized with analytic and system machinery needed to explore the power of human-centric computing, learning, and intelligence at the edge of networks. These techniques will allow the use of billions of edge devices owned by individuals to tackle computing, scientific, and societal challenges that cannot be addressed by existing computing infrastructures. Much in the same way that cloud computing allows us to address the big data problems that require massive computing power while abstracting away the underlying hardware and software complexity and heterogeneity, the techniques described in this book allow us to leverage the resource constrained but ubiquitous edge computing devices owned by individuals to address the grand challenges with humans-in-the-loop while providing a privacy-sensitive, transparent, efficient, and trustworthy framework for device owners and stakeholders of the SEC ecosystem. The uniqueness of human-centric nature and integration of human and machines makes the process more challenging. The book takes the reader on a journey of discovery through the analytical and systematic underpinning of building human-centric social edge computing systems. We hope that techniques developed in this book will become part of the solution space in dealing with challenges in future human-centric computing and information systems. These techniques can help fully harness the power of devices, algorithms, and humans in the next generation of computing, intelligence, and learning applications at the edge.

Champaign, IL, USA   Dong Wang
Seattle, WA, USA   Daniel 'Yue' Zhang
September, 2022

Acknowledgments

This book would not have been possible without the encouragement, support, and hard work of many individuals who contributed in different ways to the journey of discovery described within. The authors are grateful to all the colleagues, students, and researchers who dedicated their time to developing theory, building systems, running experiments, and generally advancing the state of the art in social edge computing, as well as the agencies funding their work.[1]

In a research meeting between Dong Wang and Daniel Zhang back in 2018, the research leading to this book was started. The foundations and core ideas of this book came out from two different research communities: Social (Human-Centric) Sensing and Edge Computing. During their brainstorming session, the authors realize there exists an exciting new research direction that lies at the intersection between these two communities, which focuses on the human-centric research challenges (e.g., rationality, privacy, human-AI interactions) in edge computing. The authors later coined the term of this direction as *Social Edge Computing (SEC)*, which is the theme of this book. The authors are grateful to their colleagues in the system and networking communities who shared insights and offered advice on early directions of this research. Special thanks goes to Weisong Shi for his insightful advice and help in understanding the related research landscape in edge computing and what a new book may contribute to that landscape.

The authors would further like to acknowledge Yang Zhang, Lanyu Shang, Md Tahmid Rashid, Huimin Zeng, Zhenrui Yue, Sharon Hu, Yue Ma, YiFeng Huang, Nathan Vance, Chao Zheng for taking part in building systems, developing theory, and running experiments described in this book. Special thanks goes to Lanyu Shang who also helped proofread the book and offered suggestions for improvement.

---

[1] Research reported in this book was sponsored, in part, by the NSF grants IIS-2202481, CHE-2105005, IIS-2008228, CNS-1845639, CNS-1831669. The views and conclusions contained in this document are those of the authors and should not be interpreted as representing the official policies, either expressed or implied of the US Government. The US Government is authorized to reproduce and distribute reprints for Government purposes notwithstanding any copyright notation here on.

Finally, the book would not have been possible without the support of our friends and family, who encouraged us to complete this work, and put up with the late nights, missed promises, and rescheduled obligations it took to do so.

Contents

Acronyms

ACC	Aggregated Computation Complexity
ACT	Active Crowd Translation
AED	Abnormal Event Detection
AGUC	Adaptive Global Update Control
AHDS	Abnormal Health Detection Systems
AI	Artificial Intelligence
AL	Active Learning
ALPR	Automatic License Plate Recognition
BCAI	Budget Constrained Adaptive Incentive
CAM	Class Activation Map
CCG	Cooperative-Competitive Game
CCMB	Constrained Contextual Multi-armed Bandit
CMB	Constrained Multi-armed Bandit
CNN	Convolutional Neural Network
CoGTA	Cooperative-competitive Game-theoretic Tasks Allocation
CPD	Crowd Plate Detection
CQC	Crowd Quality Control
CTG	Crowd Task Generation
DDA	Disaster Damage Assessment
DDM	Damage Detection Map
DFPN	Decentralized Fictitious Play with Negotiation
DHR	Deadline Hit Rate
DIA	Dynamic Incentive Adjustment
DNN	Deep Neural Network
DRR	Data Reduction Ratio
E2E	End-to-End
EI	Edge Intelligence
EIDR	Extrinsic-Intrinsic Deep Reinforcement Learning
FL	Federated Learning
HI	Human Intelligence
IACNN	Interactive Attention Convolutional Neural Network

iDSA	interactive Disaster Scene Assessment
IoT	Internet of Things
IPD	Incentive Policy Design
MEC	Mobile Edge Computing
MIC	Machine Intelligence Calibration
MILP	Mixed Integer Linear Programming
ML	Machine Learning
MTurk	Amazon Mechanical Turk
OCAI	Optimal Contracting with Asymmetric Information
PNE	Pure Nash Equilibrium
QBC	Query by Committee
QoS	Quality of Service
QSS	Query Set Selection
ROC	Receiver Operating Characteristic
ROI	Region of Interest
RSU	Roadside Unit
RTM	Real-time Traffic Monitoring
SCSR	Supply Chain Selfish Routing
SEC	Social Edge Computing
SMIN	Social Media Image Normalization
SMOTE	Synthetic Minority Over-sampling Technique
SOTB	Stochastic Optimal Task Batching
SVM	Support Vector Machine
UAV	Unmanned Aerial Vehicle
WCET	Worst-Case Execution Time

Chapter 1
A New Human-Centric Computing Age at Edge

The recent advances in artificial intelligence (AI) and the Internet of Things (IoT) have given rise to a pyramid of intelligent mobile applications such as autonomous driving, smart health monitoring, and virtual reality, which are running on ubiquitous edge devices such as smartphones and vehicles. With these edge devices generating unprecedented amounts of data,[1] highly centralized computing architectures such as traditional cloud computing, are no longer suitable for processing such data due to excessive bandwidth cost, and prohibitively high latency for transmitting the data to the remote servers. The advent of edge computing pushes the frontier of computation, service, and data along the cloud-to-things continuum to the edge of the network, which is in closer proximity to IoT devices and data sources [10, 11, 22]. The physical proximity between the computing and data sources promises several benefits for intelligent applications as compared to the traditional cloud-based computing paradigm. These benefits include low latency, energy efficiency, privacy protection, reduced bandwidth consumption, and context awareness [39]. The marriage of edge computing and AI has given rise to a new research area, namely, "edge intelligence (EI)" [26]. Instead of entirely relying on the cloud, EI makes the most of the widespread edge resources, ranging from small portable smart devices to large edge servers to gain AI insight. Many research solutions have been proposed to facilitate edge intelligence by designing new resource management frameworks to allocate the training and inference tasks of AI to resources on the edge [16, 31], as well as novel hardware-software co-designs, to enable on-device analytics that run AI-driven applications on the device to process the IoT data locally [25, 38]. These efforts fuel the continuous booming of AI and enable many new edge intelligence applications such as edge video analytics [3, 11], smart health [5], augmented reality [1], and vehicular sensing [28].

---

[1] Cisco estimates that nearly 850 ZetaBytes of data will be generated by all people, machines, and things at the network edge by 2021 [12].

This book is motivated by several key limitations of existing research in EI. First, the tremendous sensing and computing power on the privately owned IoT devices are underutilized. In existing EI research, it is often assumed that the superior computing power resides in dedicated servers such as edge servers (fog nodes) and micro data centers [22]. However, we found that edge devices owned by individuals are becoming increasingly capable computing platforms with significant processing power and memory. In our new paradigm, we target at pushing computing to the last mile of the edge computing system—the edge devices, so that the processing power at the edge is fully utilized. Second, existing research mostly focuses on the capabilities of the devices (machines), while ignoring the unique analytical skill and domain knowledge of the device owners (humans). This machine-centric edge computing design ignores the fact that humans can perform inference or make decisions in the edge computing framework just as a physical device. In fact, we found that human-in-the-loop edge intelligence can benefit many mission-critical tasks by introducing the domain expertise of human. For example, humans can improve the effectiveness of physical systems in many intelligent tasks (e.g., disaster assessment and traffic abnormality detection) [31, 35].

In light of the above knowledge gaps, this book presents a new paradigm—Social Edge Computing (SEC), that leverages the collective power of billions of IoT devices owned by individuals as well as the power of humans (e.g., device owners, application users) to revolutionize the computing, learning, and intelligence at the edge of networks. We formally introduce the definition of the SEC and its core features below.

1.1   Social Edge: A Human-Centric Definition of "Edge"

In this book, we define the social edge computing (SEC) as a new edge computing paradigm that fully leverages the collective computing power, intelligence, and data from the ubiquitous and individually owned edge devices and the device owners. We also refer to the device owners who participate in the edge AI applications as edge crowd (crowd in short) in this book. The edge devices in SEC are in various forms, ranging from small devices such as video cameras and smartphones to larger powerful embedded boards such as laptops and robots. The new definition of edge keeps humans in the loop, and thus being able to leverage their unique analytical, perceptual, and reasoning capabilities, which are often absent in machine-centric edge computing paradigms. Moreover, SEC focuses on individually owned devices that are massive in number and increasingly powerful, while the existing edge computing paradigm focuses more on dedicated computing nodes at the edge, such as base stations, cloudlets, smart gateways, and micro data centers.

The SEC paradigm benefits three core aspects of edge computing applications—the model execution, the model performance, and the model training of AI and machine learning algorithms employed in these applications, by proposing novel human-centric computing, intelligence, and learning frameworks as shown in Fig. 1.1. These benefits are further elaborated below.

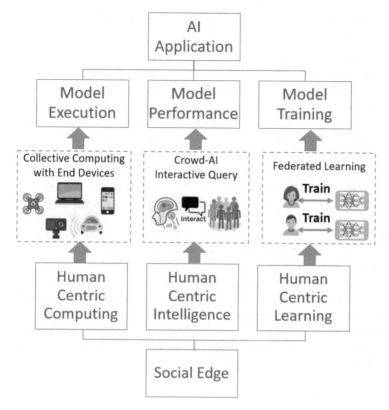

Fig. 1.1 An overview of the Social Edge Computing (SEC) paradigm

1.1.1 Human-in-the-Loop Computing at the Edge

The SEC paradigm is a unique vision of using billions of edge devices owned by individuals to perform edge computation tasks, which is in sharp contrast to the existing computing models that merely rely on dedicated edge servers and expensive cloud services [8]. By forming a global-scale collaborative edge computing infrastructure, devices that are heterogeneous in hardware and computing power can work collaboratively to process the tasks in intelligent edge applications, such as data processing, AI model execution, and data analytics. This computing paradigm is enabled by a few key technical trends: (1) the IoT devices owned by individuals are becoming increasingly powerful, and some of them even have similar computing power as the dedicated servers in traditional edge computing systems [27, 29]. Therefore, it becomes a growing trend to push the computation directly to the edge devices rather than dedicated remote servers or cloudlets [8]; (2) the popularity of mobile payment provides a more convenient way for common individuals to receive incentives by contributing the spare resources on their IoT devices for accomplishing the computational tasks [30].

1.1.2   Human-in-the-Loop Intelligence at the Edge

SEC further enables human-in-the-loop intelligence at the edge, where the artificial intelligence (AI) and human intelligence (HI) are tightly integrated at the edge of the networks to explore the collective power of both humans and machines. The concept of human-in-the-loop edge intelligence is motivated by several recent technology trends [24]. First, AI has been widely applied in many application domains, such as autonomous driving, image recognition, medical diagnosis, natural language processing, and AI for social good [9]. Second, crowdsourcing platforms (e.g., Amazon MTurk, Waze) have emerged as a popular paradigm to collect data from human sources and explore the wisdom of common individuals [24]. The merge of these technology trends unleashes an unprecedented opportunity to explore the integrated intelligence from both humans and machines to obtain the best of both worlds. While the AI-based algorithms often improve the efficiency and reduce labor costs in those applications, their performance sometimes falls short of the desired accuracy and is considered to be less reliable than domain experts [32]. The emergence of crowdsourcing brings about a new opportunity to incorporate HI into AI algorithms. Human intelligence has been shown to be superior to AI in many tasks such as relational inference, cognitive and emotion recognition, and non-structured problem-solving. The human-in-the-loop design of the SEC paradigm enables the integration of human intelligence (e.g., context-awareness, cognitive skills, reasoning ability) with the processing and sensing capability of physical devices.

1.1.3   Human-in-the-Loop Learning at the Edge

Training an optimized machine learning (ML) or AI model is a critical procedure in intelligent applications. To train the model, traditional intelligent applications require the data to be centralized in a cloud server or data center, which results in critical issues related to unacceptable latency and communication inefficiency. To overcome this limitation, edge-based training has been proposed to bring intelligence closer to the edge, where data is produced. However, conventional enabling technologies for ML at edge networks still require personal data to be shared with external parties (e.g., edge servers) which is barely practical in light of increasingly stringent data privacy legislation and growing privacy concerns [2, 20]. To address this issue, SEC revolutionizes the training process of existing centralized training approaches by leveraging the recent development in Federated Learning (FL) [17], which provides a compelling paradigm for learning ML models in a distributed and privacy-aware fashion. In particular, SEC carefully protects the privacy of the participants by enabling participants from diverse organizations to collaboratively learn a shared inference model without sharing any private personal data [14, 17]. In the SEC framework, the training is achieved through the intimate interaction of the crowd and their devices. In particular, the device constantly collects private sensory data on behalf of the user, and the training of the AI models is performed locally on the device to fully preserve the user's privacy.

1.2 Human-Centric Design: A Double-Edged Sword

While SEC brings new benefits to edge computing, it also introduces a set of fundamental challenges that are yet to be fully addressed. In this section, we review a few critical research challenges that exist in SEC.

1.2.1 The Rational Edge Challenge

We start by discussing an important challenge—rational edge, which is unique to the human-in-the-loop computing design of SEC. SEC takes full advantage of individually owned edge devices to support computational tasks of AI at the edge. However, these edge devices are usually owned by end users (which are also referred to as end devices) rather than application providers. Due to the rational nature of device owners, end devices and applications often have inconsistent or even conflicting objectives [29]. We refer to this unique feature of SEC as "rational edge". Due to the rational edge feature, two important issues prevent existing resource management schemes from being applied to SEC, namely *competing objectives* and *asymmetric information*.

Competing Objectives From the application's perspective, it is important to ensure that the end devices finish the allocated tasks in a timely fashion to meet the Quality of Service (QoS) requirements (e.g., end-to-end delays). In contrast, device owners are often less concerned about the QoS of the applications but are instead concerned about their costs in running the computational tasks allocated by the applications (e.g., the device's current utilization, energy consumption, memory usage). Thus, they are often unwilling to execute the allocated tasks until sufficient incentives are provided [7]. This is in sharp contrast to the traditional distributed computing systems where computational resources are fully cooperative and directly controlled by the application. The mismatch in objectives held by the end users and the application must be carefully addressed by developing a set of new computation allocation models that respect such discrepancies between the two parties.

Asymmetric Information Another critical challenge in SEC is that the application server and end devices usually have different degrees of information, i.e., "asymmetric information". Such asymmetric information makes resource management in SEC systems particularly challenging [29]. The asymmetric information challenge can be viewed from two aspects. On the server side, the application normally has detailed information about the tasks (e.g., the dependencies and criticality of the tasks). This information is important in understanding how tasks are related to the QoS requirements imposed by the AI application (e.g., which tasks are more important and should be prioritized; which tasks should have a tighter deadline). In contrast, the end devices are often less concerned about the details of the tasks and the servers' QoS requirements but more interested in their own device status (e.g., CPU utilization, energy consumption, memory usage). Moreover, an end device may not share its status information with the server or other end devices in the system due to various concerns (e.g., privacy, energy, bandwidth). This leads to insufficient information for the server to make optimal computation allocation decisions.

1.2.2 The Pronounced Heterogeneity Challenge

Another challenge of the human-in-the-loop computing design of SEC lies in the heterogeneity of edge resources. The heterogeneity in SEC is often more pronounced than in regular edge computing systems as the end devices in SEC often have diversified hardware, runtime environments, network interfaces, and architectures, making it difficult to orchestrate these devices to collaboratively accomplish the sensing and computational tasks. Hence, it is essential to abstract away the details of heterogeneous hardware specifications of the end devices for the ease of resource management in SEC. Moreover, the heterogeneous devices have diverse runtime environments that may not support the SEC tasks to be processed. For example, a device may have an incompatible operating system or lack the necessary dependencies to execute an SEC algorithm (e.g., a deep learning algorithm cannot run on a device without necessary libraries such as Tensorflow or CUDA [33]). Last but not least, the individually owned edge devices in SEC can also have very heterogeneous network interfaces (e.g., Bluetooth, WiFi, Zigbee) and it is essential to abstract away the networking details to allow developers to deploy SEC applications without worrying about the specific networking interfaces and protocols. The heterogeneity problem in SEC is particularly challenging because it is not possible for the application to cherry-pick the devices in a fully controlled manner given the fact the devices are owned by individuals [21]. We observe the existing resource management work in edge computing cannot sufficiently handle the pronounced heterogeneity in SEC.

1.2.3 The Human-AI Integration Challenge

SEC brings about the opportunity of leveraging human intelligence from a massive amount of crowd (e.g., device owners, participants of edge AI applications) to troubleshoot, tune, and improve the machine intelligence (AI algorithms) for intelligent edge applications. However, a particular challenge lies in integrating crowd with the AI models, that often rely on "black-box" deep neural networks [32].

In particular, the lack of interpretability of the results from AI algorithms creates a challenging case to diagnose the performance deficiency of AI, making it hard for the crowd to effectively improve the black-box AI models [18, 19]. Existing human-AI systems primarily use humans to obtain labels or features to retrain the models [4, 15]. However, these systems ignore the fact that the AI algorithms themselves are sometime problematic in which no matter how many training samples are added, the AI performance will not improve. To our knowledge, obtaining crowd intelligence to address the deficiency of AI models of intelligent edge applications has not been fully addressed in the existing literature.

1.2.4 The Human Responsiveness and Quality Assurance Challenge

Even after addressing the problem of integrating crowd intelligence with AI, two critical pitfalls still exist when leveraging crowd intelligence: (1) the crowd may not be able to provide responses that are as accurate as domain experts due to the lack of experience/expertise; (2) the delay of the crowd can be potentially too high to be acceptable for SEC applications. These two pitfalls are further exacerbated by the lack of transparency of AI algorithms, making it difficult to determine how to best incorporate external HI to improve AI. We elaborate on the challenges below. Existing solutions often assume that more incentives will lead to less response time and high response quality [15, 23]. However, we found the quality of the responses from the crowd is diversified and does not simply depend on the level of incentives provided (e.g., the quality can be high even with low incentives provided [32]). Similarly, we observe the response delay from the crowd is not simply proportional to the incentive level. With these unique features, a critical research question to tackle is: how to effectively incentivize the crowd to provide reliable and timely responses to improve AI performance? We found knowledge gaps in answering the above questions in the existing literature.

1.2.5 The Privacy and Performance Trade-Off Challenge

A key vision of SEC is human-in-the-loop learning where the crowd can interact with the edge devices to provide invaluable training data to train a powerful AI model in a distributed fashion. However, such a training process entails potential privacy risks to owners of the edge devices. During the data collection phase, the data collected from the devices can potentially reveal end users' private information. For example, in a smart health application where biological signals such as heart rates, and demographic information such as gender and race are provided by the crowd for training purposes. This information is sensitive in nature and the leakage of such information to the server/application can lead to a severe privacy infringement [34]. Existing privacy-preserving techniques, such as anonymity techniques, can effectively protect the identities of edge devices from curious entities. On the other hand, accessibility to the sensitive information of end users is quite important in assuring the accuracy of the trained AI model for the intelligent application. Such privacy-performance trade-off calls for novel designs of a privacy-aware training framework for SEC.

1.2.6   The Crowd Data Imbalance Challenge

Another critical challenge in the vision of SEC is the data imbalance: the training data collected from the crowd can be quite different in terms of the data distributions of different class labels. Take a depression detection application as an example that people's smartphones are used to detect depression in the participants based on their biological signals. We observe that not all participants are prone to depression, meaning some people can contribute more positive samples than others. Such diversified data among participants leads to the fact that the sensing data collected from the participants for training is often imbalanced (i.e., it contains significantly more negative labels than positive ones) [37]. Training with such an imbalanced dataset can lead to degraded model performance [6, 13]. Similarly, due to the demographic distribution of the crowd, it is likely to acquire more training data from some particular demographic groups (e.g., more data from males vs. females, or more data from Caucasians vs. Asians), which eventually leads to bias in the AI model performance (e.g., better detection accuracy of males than females) [36]. This is due to the fact that the majority demographic group will provide more training data, which leads to higher accuracy for the detection results of that group. In a centralized training setting, the above problems can be easily addressed by assuming the training server knows the exact class distribution and demographic information of the participants. Such an assumption is not practical in SEC due to the privacy constraints of the crowd, and the decentralized nature of the SEC's learning framework. We found little existing research has been done to address the class imbalance and model bias issues in edge intelligent applications, which are introduced by the data imbalance challenge.

1.3   Contributions and Organization

The book presents a new paradigm—Social Edge Computing (SEC), that jointly addresses the unique challenges discussed above. SEC leverages the collective power of billions of edge devices as well as the power of the crowd who own them to jointly empower intelligent applications at the edge by revolutionizing the computing, intelligence, and training of AI models.

The main contributions of this book are threefold: (1) the book reviews a set of novel resource management frameworks and task allocation algorithms that enable heterogeneous edge devices owned by end-users to collaboratively provide *computing* power for executing AI model on resource-constrained edge devices. Different from existing edge computing resource management frameworks, the reviewed solutions jointly address the rational edge and pronounced heterogeneity challenges, and can significantly improve both the responsiveness and energy efficiency of the intelligent edge applications. (2) The book presents a crowd-machine interactive learning framework that leverages the crowd at the edge to provide *intelligence* to troubleshoot, calibrate, and eventually improve AI models. The proposed solutions overcome the black-box nature of AI models and effectively leverage the crowd to assist AI with domain knowledge. Novel incentive designs are presented for ensuring the crowd responses to be both accurate and fast. (3) Finally, the book introduces several federated learning based edge learning frameworks that allow the crowd together with their devices to provide distributed *training* for AI models. The proposed solutions not only address the privacy challenge by performing training locally on the edge devices but also ensure the trained AI model is unbiased towards a certain class label or demographic group. Through extensive evaluation of real-world edge computing applications, it is shown that SEC is able to achieve impressive performance gains in various performance metrics including service responsiveness, energy efficiency, and model accuracy. In addition to the performance boost in existing applications, by keeping humans in the loop of the traditional edge-cloud continuum, unique opportunities motivate the development of novel applications that address critical social challenges. This book also presents a diverse set of killer apps that are enabled by SEC such as private-aware health monitoring, collaborative traffic monitoring, disaster damage assessment, crowd abnormal event detection, and vehicle-based criminal tracking. We summarize the challenges and our contributions in Fig. 1.2.

The rest of the book is constructed as follows. In Chap. 2, we overview the background and relevant works to the proposed social edge intelligence paradigm. In Chaps. 3–5, we present a series of new resource management frameworks, including CoGTA, HeteroEdge, and EdgeBatch to support collaborative computing using heterogeneous and privately owned end devices. In Chap. 6, we present CrowdLearn and iDSA, two interactive hybrid human-AI frameworks that allow incorporating the domain knowledge and expertise from the crowd to troubleshoot and improve AI algorithms. In Chap. 7, we present FedSens, a federated learning framework that can train AI models in a privacy-aware fashion through the interaction between the crowd and their devices. In Chap. 8, we provide the reader with further readings that are related to the work presented in this book. In Chap. 9, we summarize the techniques, theories, models, and solutions presented in the book and discuss a few remaining challenges and exciting directions for future research.

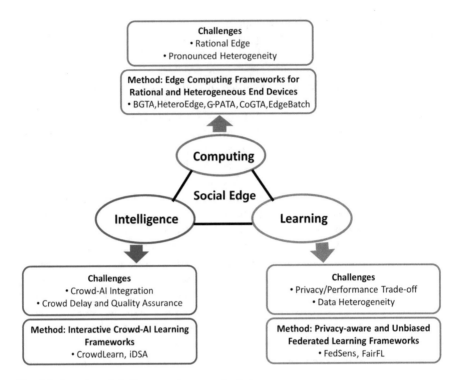

Fig. 1.2 Overview of challenges and presented solutions

References

1. A. Al-Shuwaili, O. Simeone, Energy-efficient resource allocation for mobile edge computing-based augmented reality applications. IEEE Wirel. Commun. Lett. **6**(3), 398–401 (2017)
2. C.A. Ardagna, M. Cremonini, S. De Capitani di Vimercati, P. Samarati, A privacy-aware access control system. J. Comput. Secur. **16**(4), 369–397 (2008)
3. Aws deeplens. https://aws.amazon.com/deeplens/. Accessed 23 Apr 2019
4. S. Branson, C. Wah, F. Schroff, B. Babenko, P. Welinder, P. Perona, S. Belongie, Visual recognition with humans in the loop, in *European Conference on Computer Vision* (Springer, 2010), pp 438–451
5. Y. Chen, J. Wang, C. Yu, W. Gao, X. Qin, Fedhealth: A federated transfer learning framework for wearable healthcare. Preprint. arXiv:1907.09173 (2019)
6. M. Duan, Astraea: Self-balancing federated learning for improving classification accuracy of mobile deep learning applications. Preprint. arXiv:1907.01132 (2019)
7. T. Giannetsos, S. Gisdakis, P. Papadimitratos, Trustworthy people-centric sensing: Privacy, security and user incentives road-map, in *Ad Hoc Networking Workshop (MED-HOC-NET), 2014 13th Annual Mediterranean* (IEEE, 2014), pp 39–46
8. K. Habak, M. Ammar, K.A. Harras, E. Zegura, Femto clouds: Leveraging mobile devices to provide cloud service at the edge, in *2015 IEEE 8th International Conference on Cloud Computing (CLOUD)* (IEEE, 2015), pp. 9–16
9. K. He, X. Zhang, S. Ren, J. Sun, Delving deep into rectifiers: Surpassing human-level performance on imagenet classification, in *Proceedings of the IEEE International Conference on Computer Vision* (2015), pp. 1026–1034

10. Y.C. Hu, M. Patel, D. Sabella, N. Sprecher, V. Young, Mobile edge computing—a key technology towards 5g. ETSI White Paper **11**(11), 1–16 (2015)
11. C.-C. Hung, G. Ananthanarayanan, P. Bodik, L. Golubchik, M. Yu, P. Bahl, M. Philipose, Videoedge: Processing camera streams using hierarchical clusters, in *2018 IEEE/ACM Symposium on Edge Computing (SEC)* (IEEE, 2018), pp. 115–131
12. C.G.C. Index, Forecast and methodology, 2016–2021 white paper. Updated: February, 1, 2018 (2018)
13. N. Japkowicz, S. Stephen, The class imbalance problem: A systematic study. Intelligent Data Anal. **6**(5), 429–449 (2002)
14. J. Konečný, H.B. McMahan, F.X. Yu, P. Richtárik, A.T. Suresh, D. Bacon, Federated learning: Strategies for improving communication efficiency. Preprint. arXiv:1610.05492 (2016)
15. F. Laws, C. Scheible, H. Schütze, Active learning with Amazon mechanical turk, in *Proceedings of the Conference on Empirical Methods in Natural Language Processing* (Association for Computational Linguistics, 2011), pp. 1546–1556
16. E. Li, Z. Zhou, X. Chen, Edge intelligence: On-demand deep learning model co-inference with device-edge synergy, in *Proceedings of the 2018 Workshop on Mobile Edge Communications* (ACM, 2018), pp. 31–36
17. H.B. McMahan, E. Moore, D. Ramage, S. Hampson, et al., Communication-efficient learning of deep networks from decentralized data. Preprint. arXiv:1602.05629 (2016)
18. B. Nushi, E. Kamar, E. Horvitz, D. Kossmann, On human intellect and machine failures: Troubleshooting integrative machine learning systems, in *AAAI* (2017), pp. 1017–1025
19. B. Nushi, E. Kamar, E. Horvitz, Towards accountable AI: Hybrid human-machine analyses for characterizing system failure. Preprint. arXiv:1809.07424 (2018)
20. Y. O'Connor, W. Rowan, L. Lynch, C. Heavin, Privacy by design: informed consent and internet of things for smart health. Procedia Comput. Sci. **113**, 653–658 (2017)
21. Z. Sanaei, S. Abolfazli, A. Gani, R. Buyya, Heterogeneity in mobile cloud computing: taxonomy and open challenges. IEEE Commun. Surv. Tutorials **16**(1), 369–392 (2014)
22. W. Shi, J. Cao, Q. Zhang, Y. Li, L. Xu, Edge computing: Vision and challenges. IEEE Internet Things J. **3**(5), 637–646 (2016)
23. A. Sorokin, D. Forsyth, Utility data annotation with Amazon mechanical turk, in *IEEE Computer Society Conference on Computer Vision and Pattern Recognition Workshops, 2008. CVPRW'08* (IEEE, 2008), pp. 1–8
24. D. Wang, B.K. Szymanski, T. Abdelzaher, H. Ji, L. Kaplan, The age of social sensing. Computer **52**(1), 36–45 (2019)
25. S. Wang, G. Ananthanarayanan, Y. Zeng, N. Goel, A. Pathania, T. Mitra, High-throughput CNN inference on embedded arm big. little multi-core processors. Preprint. arXiv:1903.05898 (2019)
26. X. Wang, Y. Han, C. Wang, Q. Zhao, X. Chen, M. Chen, In-edge AI: Intelligentizing mobile edge computing, caching and communication by federated learning. IEEE Netw. **33**(5), 156–165 (2019)
27. D.Y. Zhang, D. Wang, An integrated top-down and bottom-up task allocation approach in social sensing based edge computing systems, in *IEEE INFOCOM 2019-IEEE Conference on Computer Communications* (IEEE, 2019), pp. 766–774
28. Q. Zhang, X. Zhang, Q. Zhang, W. Shi, H. Zhong, Firework: Big data sharing and processing in collaborative edge environment, in *2016 Fourth IEEE Workshop on Hot Topics in Web Systems and Technologies (HotWeb)* (IEEE, 2016), pp. 20–25
29. D.Y. Zhang, Y. Ma, Y. Zhang, S. Lin, X.S. Hu, D. Wang, A real-time and non-cooperative task allocation framework for social sensing applications in edge computing systems, in *2018 IEEE Real-Time and Embedded Technology and Applications Symposium (RTAS)* (IEEE, 2018), pp. 316–326
30. D.Y. Zhang, Y. Ma, C. Zheng, Y. Zhang, X.S. Hu, D. Wang, Cooperative-competitive task allocation in edge computing for delay-sensitive social sensing, in *2018 IEEE/ACM Symposium on Edge Computing (SEC)* (IEEE, 2018), pp. 243–259

31. D. Zhang, N. Vance, D. Wang, When social sensing meets edge computing: Vision and challenges, in *2019 28th International Conference on Computer Communication and Networks (ICCCN)* (IEEE, 2019), pp. 1–9

32. D.Y. Zhang, Y. Zhang, Q. Li, T. Plummer, D. Wang, Crowdlearn: A crowd-ai hybrid system for deep learning-based damage assessment applications, in *2019 IEEE 39th International Conference on Distributed Computing Systems (ICDCS)* (IEEE, 2019), pp. 1221–1232

33. Y. Zhang, H. Wang, D.Y. Zhang, D. Wang, Deeprisk: A deep transfer learning approach to migratable traffic risk estimation in intelligent transportation using social sensing, in *2019 15th International Conference on Distributed Computing in Sensor Systems (DCOSS)* (IEEE, 2019), pp. 123–130

34. D. Zhang, Y. Ma, X.S. Hu, D. Wang, Toward privacy-aware task allocation in social sensing-based edge computing systems. IEEE Internet Things J. **7**(12), 11384–11400 (2020)

35. D.Y. Zhang, Y. Huang, Y. Zhang, D. Wang, Crowd-assisted disaster scene assessment with human-AI interactive attention, in *Proceedings of the AAAI Conference on Artificial Intelligence* (2020), pp. 2717–2724

36. D.Y. Zhang, Z. Kou, D. Wang, Fairfl: A fair federated learning approach to reducing demographic bias in privacy-sensitive classification models, in *2020 IEEE International Conference on Big Data (Big Data)* (IEEE, 2020), pp. 1051–1060

37. D.Y. Zhang, Z. Kou, D. Wang, Fedsens: A federated learning approach for smart health sensing with class imbalance in resource constrained edge computing, in *IEEE INFOCOM 2021-IEEE Conference on Computer Communications* (IEEE, 2021), pp. 1–10

38. G. Zhong, A. Dubey, C. Tan, T. Mitra. Synergy: An HW/SW framework for high throughput CNNS on embedded heterogeneous SoC. ACM Trans. Embedded Comput. Syst. (TECS) **18**(2), 13 (2019)

39. Z. Zhou, X. Chen, E. Li, L. Zeng, K. Luo, J. Zhang, Edge intelligence: Paving the last mile of artificial intelligence with edge computing. Proc. IEEE **107**(8), 1738–1762 (2019)

Chapter 2
Social Edge Trends and Applications

Abstract The advent of edge computing pushes the frontier of computation, service, and data along the cloud-to-things continuum to the edge of the network, and brings new opportunities for human-centric applications (e.g., social sensing, smart mobile computing, edge intelligence). By coupling those applications with edge computing, the individually owned edge devices form a federation of computational nodes where the data collected from them can be processed and consumed "on the spot". In this chapter, we offer a high-level view of the SEC paradigm, its background, motivation, trends, enabling technologies, and examples of applications.

2.1 Social Edge Computing: The Paradigm Shift

IoT devices owned by individuals are increasingly equipped with powerful computing and diverse sensing capabilities. The sensing data generated by these devices provides an alternative lens into physical phenomena as compared to traditional sensor networks [38]. Due to the sheer volume of data generated by these devices, it makes sense to explore opportunities for processing the data at the edge of the network. Previous work in edge computing leverage cloudlets [28, 29], micro data centers [1, 4], and fog computing [5, 42] to address the deficiency of cloud computing when the data is produced at the edge of the network. However, these solutions fail to take advantage of individually owned edge devices as SEC does, and they instead rely on infrastructures which must be provisioned ahead of time [52]. In this section, we formally define SEC and discuss how it is complementary to existing edge computing frameworks.

2.1.1 What Is Social Edge Computing?

Definition (Social Edge Computing (SEC)) A new computing paradigm that involves humans and/or devices on their behalf to sense, process, and analyze data about the physical world at the edge of the network.   □

In this definition, the devices owned by individuals not only collect data about the physical world, but also actively participate in the application by performing computations and analytic tasks. These individually owned edge devices can be quite heterogeneous, ranging from a GPS sensor, a Raspberry Pi, or a robot, to a powerful multi-processor server. SEC has two important features: (1) it is human-centric and (2) it has the flexibility to support various applications with different system architectures. We elaborate on these features below.

2.1.1.1 Human-Centric Nature of SEC

SEC is human-centric. On one hand, the owners of the edge devices are freelance users and their unique concerns must be carefully considered in the SEC paradigm. Examples of these human concerns include privacy and security, compliance and churn, and incentives. On the other hand, we envision that not only can devices engage in the sensing and computational tasks, but device owners can directly participate as well. In fact, many social (human-centric) sensing applications require input directly from a human participant, such as reporting traffic congestion [2], or taking videos of an emergency event [49]. Also, SEC considers the potential of people serving as "SEC nodes" where they directly make inferences using the data. For example, consider an abnormal event detection scenario where the edge devices are used to collect video data and infer abnormal events such as an intrusion [20]. Instead of using machine learning algorithms to perform such data analytic tasks, humans can directly identify the abnormal events from the video with a high accuracy [7]. We explore the possibility of leveraging humans as computing nodes in a pioneer work [54]. This unique feature of SEC where human's input and intelligence complement the existing edge/cloud computing paradigm enables new human-centric edge computing applications, which will be elaborated later in this chapter.

2.1.1.2 Flexibility of SEC to Support System Variations

Like traditional edge computing systems that come in many different architectures [21], SEC has diverse system variations as well (Fig. 2.1). While SEC focuses more on the individually owned edge devices, it by no means intends to drastically replace the existing cloud or edge computing paradigm by diminishing the existing infrastructure such as cloud servers, large data centers, cloudlets, or near-edge micro data centers. In fact, SEC fully takes advantage of existing system infrastructures.

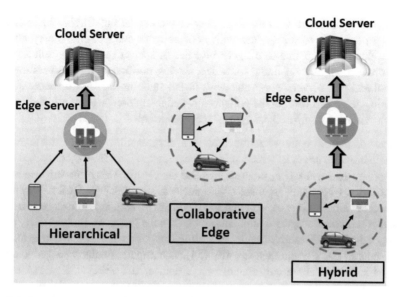

Fig. 2.1 Example SEC system variations

The choice of the system architecture is application specific. We summarize a few representative architectures below.

Hierarchical A typical cloud-edge hierarchical SEC system architecture is shown in Fig. 2.1. It follows the hierarchical structure where a remote cloud server, which is often powerful and has a massive storage capacity, manages the application and provides a global interface to the users. The application governs a set of spatially distributed edge clusters, where an edge cluster consists of a local edge server (e.g., a micro data center or a Roadside Unit (RSU)) and the nearby edge devices that connect to it. In [11, 13, 25], typical edge clusters are illustrated, including a set of devices in a coffee shop connected to a small in-house server owned by the shop; a set of vehicles connected to a Roadside Unit on the same street; and a set of mobile phones connected to the nearest base station. The key characteristic of this hierarchical structure is that the data flow is static: edge devices process the data locally and offload further computational tasks to the edge servers, and the edge servers further process the data and send the results to the cloud server for data aggregation tasks and storage.

Collaborative Edge In a collaborative edge architecture, edge devices in close proximity self-organize into a computing cluster and provide peer-to-peer services such as content delivery and computation offloading. This architecture is particularly suitable for application scenarios where edge or cloud servers are not readily available, or to avoid periodic costs by using these infrastructures. Consider a crowd video sharing application example where a set of spectators at a sporting event (e.g., a soccer game) can take videos of the game highlights and stream them to people in the audience who miss the play or who sit in undesirable locations. To improve performance for devices with poor network connections, the system can encode the video streams to a lower bit rate. In such a scenario, a remote cloud can introduce significant delay for video sharing and local edge servers may not be available (the servers/smart gateways at the stadium may not be accessible by the audience). Therefore, in the collaborative edge architecture, individually owned edge devices can perform these typical server-side roles.

Hybrid A hybrid system architecture is a combination of both a hierarchical and collaborative edge, in which self-organized edge devices are connected to the available infrastructure (i.e., edge servers and the cloud). This infrastructure is ideal for scenarios where self-organized edge devices cannot satisfy QoS requirements, so readily available edge servers and the cloud are leveraged to boost performance. Consider a disaster response application where edge devices collaboratively report damages during a disaster, often by executing image analysis and machine learning algorithms to classify damage severity [54]. A computationally weak edge device such as a video camera can collect image data of the affected area and offload the damage assessment task to a powerful edge device nearby via Bluetooth. The assessment result is further reported to all nearby edge devices in the form of alerts. In the case where edge devices are underperforming due to the lack of high-end processors, the collaborative edge can offload tasks to nearby edge servers, such as base stations, or cloud servers for further processing.

2.1.2 Why We Need Social Edge Computing?

Social Edge Computing (SEC) is motivated by a few key technical trends: (1) the edge devices owned by individuals are becoming increasingly powerful and some of them even have similar computing power as the dedicated servers in traditional edge computing systems [44, 49]. Therefore, it becomes a growing trend to push the computation to the edge devices rather than dedicated remote servers or edge servers [11]; (2) the popularity of mobile payments provides a more convenient way for individuals to receive incentives by contributing the spare resources on their edge devices for accomplishing social sensing tasks [37]. We summarize a few advantages of SEC below.

Coverage and Availability One of SEC's main advantages is its coverage and the availability of edge devices. There are billions of individually owned edge devices worldwide that can collect and process data at a global scale. This natural mobile network is clearly advantageous in terms of coverage as compared to static infrastructures such as data centers or surveillance cameras. Furthermore, SEC provides mobility as the sensing and computing resources move geographically with their users, which makes SEC ideal for human-centric sensing and computing tasks where the availability of resources is closely correlated with the prevalence of noteworthy events.

Delay Reduction Social sensing applications can process the sensing data on the edge devices where the data has been collected on devices in close proximity, which could significantly reduce the communication costs (e.g., bandwidth) and improve the Quality of Service (QoS) (e.g., delay) of the applications. This makes SEC ideal for real-time or time-sensitive applications at the edge.

Utilization SEC fully leverages the sensing and computing power of the edge devices. Compared to traditional edge computing frameworks that offload computational tasks to edge servers or cloud servers, SEC envisions that tasks can be executed on smart devices owned by individuals. By pushing the tasks to the edge, the SEC architecture removes the single point of failure and alleviates the performance bottleneck of the "back-end" solution. This enables SEC to avoid high deployment costs for sensing tasks, and to be economic on the back-end infrastructure.

Reward Earnings In SEC, participants can obtain rewards by contributing the idle resources of their devices to execute computing tasks for the SEC application. Similar to how unused computing cycles are sold in cloud environments, this creates a new market where the idle resources of edge devices can now be fully utilized. This benefit is further facilitated by the popularity of mobile payments (e.g., ApplePay, Xoom) which provide a convenient way for individuals to receive incentives/rewards on their mobile devices [37].

2.2 Enabling Technologies for Social Edge Computing

The SEC paradigm is enabled by the recent development of a few advanced technologies presented below.

2.2.1 Edge Computing

A comprehensive survey of edge computing is given by Shi et al. [31]. A critical challenge in edge computing is *computation offloading* where heavy data analytic tasks are transferred to external servers from edge devices with limited memory, battery, and computation power [24]. Pushing all the computation tasks to the remote servers can be rather ineffective, particularly for delay-sensitive applications [31]. Various efforts have focused on offloading computation tasks to the edge devices to reduce communication costs and application latency [17]. For example, Satyanarayanan et al. introduced an intermediate layer (i.e., "Cloudlet") located between the cloud and mobile devices to address the high latency issue between edge devices and servers [29]. Gao et al. proposed a probabilistic computation offloading framework that offloads the computation tasks to the mobile devices [10]. Kosta et al. proposed an energy-aware code offloading framework to dynamically switch between edge devices and cloud servers to improve the energy efficiency of the system [16]. Recently, Saurez et al. proposed a programming infrastructure "Foglet" to jointly address resource discovery, incremental deployment, and live task migration commensurate with application dynamism and resource availability [30]. SEC is complementary to the above solutions in that it explicitly considers the *rational* and *heterogeneous* nature of the crowd and edge devices.

2.2.2 Social Sensing

Social sensing refers to an emerging human-centric sensing paradigm where sensing measurements from humans or devices on their behalf are used to reconstruct the state of the world, both physical and social [36]. It has received a significant amount of attention due to the proliferation of low-cost mobile sensors and smart devices (e.g., smartphones), the ubiquitous Internet connectivity (e.g., 5G), and the mass data dissemination opportunities (e.g., social media) [38]. A large set of social sensing applications are sensitive to delay, i.e., have real-time requirements [35]. Examples of such applications include intelligent transportation systems [50], environmental sensing [22], and disaster and emergency response [19]. A key limitation in the current social sensing solution space is that data processing and analytic tasks are often done on a "back-end" system (e.g., on dedicated servers or commercial clouds) [26, 34, 46, 51]. Unfortunately, this scheme ignores the rich processing capability of increasingly powerful edge devices owned by individuals (e.g., mobile phones, tablets, smart wearables, and the Internet of Things). For example, the emerging AI accelerators (commonly called "AI Chip") on smartphones are capable of finishing complex deep learning tasks that are traditionally done on large server racks [43]. The advent of edge computing pushes the frontier of computation, service, and data to the edge of the network [13, 14, 31], and brings new opportunities for social sensing applications. In SEC, by combining social sensing with edge computing, the individually owned edge devices not only serve as pervasive sensors, but also form a federation of computational nodes where the data collected from them can be processed and consumed at the edge [32, 48, 49, 53].

2.2.3 Edge AI

The real-time response requirement of modern IoT applications, in conjunction with data privacy and network connectivity issues, call for *intelligent* edge devices that are able to support delay-sensitive computation for deep learning on-site [18, 52]. Many solutions have been developed to promote deep learning using IoT devices. One common technique is "neural network compression" which can significantly reduce the complexity of the neural network so that it can be run on resource-constrained IoT devices efficiently. For example, Han et al. developed Deep Compression—a pipeline of pruning, quantization, and Huffman coding techniques to reduce both the storage and energy consumption of deep neural networks [12]. Many hardware solutions have also been proposed. For example, AI-enabled chips and dedicated hardware have been developed and integrated into video cameras, hand-held devices, and vehicles to allow edge devices to run deep learning tasks efficiently. Typical hardware include EdgeBox from Microsoft [56], DeepLens from AWS [3], and TPU from Google [15]. In addition, some hardware accelerators have been proposed to further speed up the computation at the edge with a low energy cost [39, 55]. There are also several recent software-hardware co-design approaches that extract both the data and control flow parallelism [41]. SEC extends the Edge AI by incorporating the crowd (e.g., device owners) into the training and learning processes of AI.

2.2.4 Federated Learning

A key enabler for SEC to acquire private training data from humans is the federated learning framework. Federated learning allows edge devices to collaboratively learn a shared global machine learning model while keeping all the private training data on the devices [23]. Such a framework is a nice fit for privacy-sensitive applications such as smart health where the training data often contains sensitive health conditions and biological signals of participants. For example, FedHealth develops a federated learning framework to aggregate locally trained health monitoring models from different organizations and generates a personalized model through transfer learning [6]. Several efforts have been made to address resource constraints and data imbalance issues. For example, Wang et al. recently proposed an adaptive federated learning framework that dynamically tunes the global model update frequency to meet the resource constraints of heterogeneous edge devices [40]. Duan et al. [9] developed Astraea, a self-balancing data sampling scheme that is dedicated to addressing the class imbalance problem to improve the model accuracy in federated learning. In SEC, we address several key limitations in the existing federated learning frameworks, including energy constraints, bias and class imbalance to ensure the learned AI model is unbiased and accurate.

2.3 Emerging Social Edge Computing Applications

After introducing the definition, motivation and technical enablers of SEC, we will discuss a few representative SEC applications in real-world scenarios.

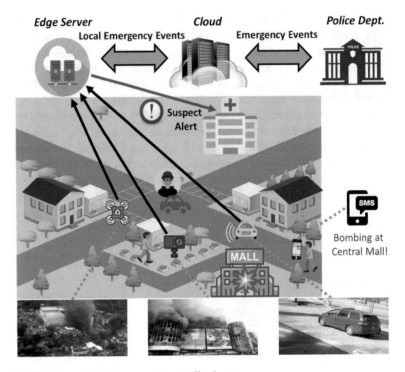

Fig. 2.2 Disaster and emergency response application

2.3.1 *Disaster and Emergency Response*

An important application of SEC is to provide real-time situation awareness during disasters and emergency events (e.g., forest fire, robbery, terrorist attacks) [46]. During such events, human sensors (e.g., citizens, first responders, news reporters) often spontaneously report a massive amount of sensing information that describes the unfolding of the event. SEC provides a suitable architecture for this category of applications: (1) the edge devices, with close proximity to the human sensors, can collect and extract useful features about the event without sending all data streams back to the cloud; (2) the edge server layer in SEC can gather processed data and exacted features from edge devices to provide real-time event updates for local citizens; (3) the cloud server aggregates all information collected and provides it to relevant agencies and/or the general public. Figure 2.2 illustrates a scenario where people use mobile phones and cameras to provide first-hand footage of a terrorist attack at a shopping center. These data can be helpful in tracking a suspect's escape path. The edge server layer provides time-critical alerts for potential threats and offers safety recommendations.

2.3.2 Collaborative Traffic Monitoring

Collaborative traffic monitoring aims at collecting timely information about traffic conditions (e.g., congestion, accidents, and events) of an area of interest (e.g., a city) by exploring the power of social sensing. Such applications are useful for many transportation services such as route planning, traffic management, and fuel-efficient navigation [25]. Traditionally, traffic monitoring has been performed by analyzing data from statically installed traffic cameras, which suffer from poor coverage [8]. Moreover, the data generated by these traffic cameras were processed at a remote cloud server, which introduces significant delay and bandwidth costs. SEC can address this problem by fully leveraging social sensing and the edge devices owned by people. In particular, the individually owned sensing devices on vehicles (e.g., cameras, accelerometers, GPS sensors) offer opportunities to collect a large amount of traffic data in real time. For example, a typical traffic monitoring application can task a set of drivers to use their dashboard cameras to record traffic in front of their vehicles. The processed data (e.g., extracted features) are offloaded to nearby edge servers (i.e., RSU) for further analysis of traffic conditions. Additionally, human sensors are also capable of reporting high-level descriptions of the traffic context using their smartphones. An example of such a social sensing application is Waze[1] where drivers collectively report their observations of accidents, road hazards, and traffic jams in real time. In Fig. 2.3, pedestrians and drivers collaboratively contribute traffic data using their edge devices. The edge server infers the traffic conditions of local streets from the social sensing data and sends accident alerts to the drivers. Transportation agencies can also query the cloud for road conditions and accidents in their regions of jurisdiction and prioritize accident response, road repair, or traffic control accordingly.

2.3.3 Crowd Abnormal Event Detection

The goal of crowd abnormal event detection is to generate alerts for abnormal events from data contributed by human sensors and their portable devices (e.g., mobile phones). Traditional abnormal event detection solutions largely depend on video data collected from installed surveillance cameras and utilize image processing techniques to identify these events [27]. Those solutions fail in situations where installed cameras are not available (e.g., due to deployment costs). The prevalence of camera-enabled portable devices has enabled the collection of geo-tagged pictures, videos, and user-reported textual data through social sensing applications. Such multi-modal data can be exploited for enhanced situation awareness during abnormal activities (e.g., providing insights for investigating the severity and causes

---

[1] https://www.waze.com/.

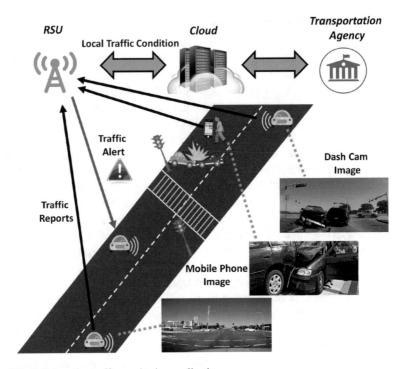

Fig. 2.3 Collaborative traffic monitoring application

of events). For example, during a soccer game, events such as the sudden appearance of an unexpected object or malicious behavior of people (e.g., throwing a signal flare into the field) can pose great threats to the safety of players and interrupt the normal course of the game (Fig. 2.4). In our SEC framework, the audience (as human sensors) can contribute videos, images, and texts to report their observations about abnormal events. Upon detection of abnormal events during the game, the cloud-hosted service will send alerts to the fans and the police department for emergency response.

2.3.4   Automatic License Plate Recognition

The plate recognition application (Fig. 2.5) was first introduced in an effort to leverage private vehicles to collaboratively track down suspects of AMBER alerts [45]. In this application, vehicles equipped with dash cameras form a city-wide video surveillance network that tracks moving vehicles using the automatic license plate recognition (ALPR) technique. This system can be used to effectively track down criminal suspects who are on the run in vehicles. It complements existing vehicle searching processes that heavily rely on reports from witnesses who might

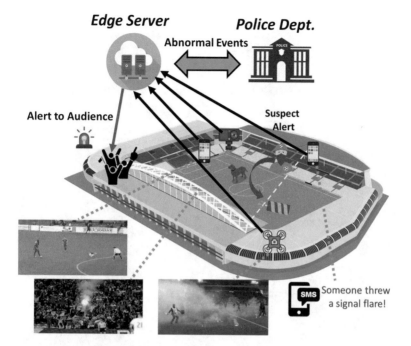

Fig. 2.4 Crowd abnormal event detection application

miss alerts and cannot search enough areas of the city [47]. Collecting surveillance video footage can expand coverage. However, analyzing huge amounts of video data in the cloud leads to unreasonable data transmission costs and high response latency. SEC can significantly reduce the cost of data transmission and response latency by offloading the data to nearby RSUs for real-time processing. SEC also pushes local processing to be done on these private vehicles to extract features from the raw images and send the processed data to the RSUs instead. This is because the video data collected from the vehicles can also reveal private information of the drivers (e.g., residence location) or the faces of the citizens. Upon detecting the suspect's vehicle, the cloud-hosted service will send alerts to the police department for an immediate response.

2.3.5   Crowd Video Sharing

The crowd video sharing application (Fig. 2.6) uses self-organized edge devices to perform peer-to-peer video content delivery. This application is most suitable for events where people take interesting videos and want to share them with one another [33]. For example, if a spectator at a soccer match has a good view of some action, then other spectators in less favorable locations may desire to view the footage

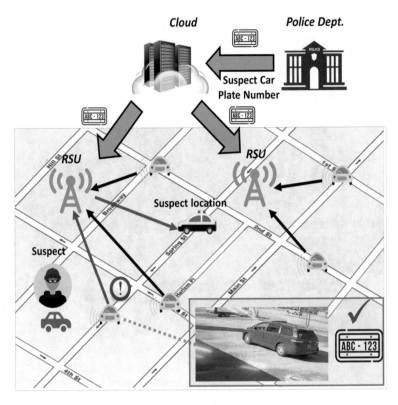

Fig. 2.5 Automatic license plate recognition application

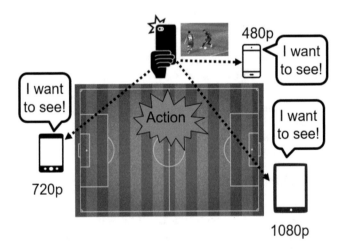

Fig. 2.6 Crowd video sharing application

from a better perspective. In order to facilitate this application, the system must (1) employ the participating edge computing resources to avoid bottlenecks as the system scales, and (2) perform video encoding so that devices with poor network connections can be sent with smaller video files, thus avoiding network delays. This problem can be solved using SEC by coordinating edge devices to perform computation and communication tasks, thus providing a source of computing power and bandwidth which scales with the number of participating devices, i.e., demand. A bottom-up game theoretic decision-making process optimizes the encoding and transmission of the videos in order to minimize delay in the system [48].

References

1. M. Aazam, E.-N. Huh, Fog computing micro datacenter based dynamic resource estimation and pricing model for IoT, in *2015 IEEE 29th International Conference on Advanced Information Networking and Applications* (IEEE, 2015), pp. 687–694
2. A. Artikis, M. Weidlich, F. Schnitzler, I. Boutsis, T. Liebig, N. Piatkowski, C. Bockermann, K. Morik, V. Kalogeraki, J. Marecek et al., Heterogeneous stream processing and crowdsourcing for urban traffic management, in *EDBT* (2014), pp. 712–723
3. Aws deeplens. https://aws.amazon.com/deeplens/. Accessed 23 Apr 2019
4. K. Bilal, O. Khalid, A. Erbad, S.U. Khan, Potentials, trends, and prospects in edge technologies: Fog, cloudlet, mobile edge, and micro data centers. Comput. Netw. **130**, 94–120 (2018)
5. F. Bonomi, R. Milito, J. Zhu, S. Addepalli, Fog computing and its role in the internet of things, in *Proceedings of the First Edition of the MCC Workshop on Mobile Cloud Computing, MCC '12*, New York (ACM, 2012), pp. 13–16
6. Y. Chen, J. Wang, C. Yu, W. Gao, X. Qin, Fedhealth: A federated transfer learning framework for wearable healthcare. Preprint. arXiv:1907.09173 (2019)
7. Y. Cong, J. Yuan, J. Liu, Abnormal event detection in crowded scenes using sparse representation. Pattern Recogn. **46**(7), 1851–1864 (2013)
8. E. D'Andrea, P. Ducange, B. Lazzerini, F. Marcelloni, Real-time detection of traffic from twitter stream analysis. IEEE Trans. Intell. Transp. Syst. **16**(4), 2269–2283 (2015)
9. M. Duan, Astraea: Self-balancing federated learning for improving classification accuracy of mobile deep learning applications. Preprint. arXiv:1907.01132 (2019)
10. W. Gao, Opportunistic peer-to-peer mobile cloud computing at the tactical edge, in *Military Communications Conference (MILCOM), 2014 IEEE* (IEEE, 2014), pp. 1614–1620
11. K. Habak, M. Ammar, K.A. Harras, E. Zegura, Femto clouds: Leveraging mobile devices to provide cloud service at the edge, in *2015 IEEE 8th International Conference on Cloud Computing (CLOUD)* (IEEE, 2015), pp. 9–16
12. S. Han, H. Mao, W.J. Dally, Deep compression: Compressing deep neural networks with pruning, trained quantization and Huffman coding. Preprint. arXiv:1510.00149 (2015)
13. Y.C. Hu, M. Patel, D. Sabella, N. Sprecher, V. Young, Mobile edge computing—a key technology towards 5g. ETSI White Paper **11**(11), 1–16 (2015)
14. C.-C. Hung, G. Ananthanarayanan, P. Bodik, L. Golubchik, M. Yu, P. Bahl, M. Philipose, Videoedge: Processing camera streams using hierarchical clusters, in *2018 IEEE/ACM Symposium on Edge Computing (SEC)* (IEEE, 2018), pp. 115–131
15. N.P. Jouppi, C. Young, N. Patil, D. Patterson, G. Agrawal, R. Bajwa, S. Bates, S. Bhatia, N. Boden, A. Borchers et al., In-datacenter performance analysis of a tensor processing unit, in *2017 ACM/IEEE 44th Annual International Symposium on Computer Architecture (ISCA)* (IEEE, 2017), pp. 1–12

16. S. Kosta, A. Aucinas, P. Hui, R. Mortier, X. Zhang, Thinkair: Dynamic resource allocation and parallel execution in the cloud for mobile code offloading, in *Infocom, 2012 Proceedings IEEE* (IEEE, 2012), pp. 945–953
17. K. Kumar, Y.-H. Lu, Cloud computing for mobile users: Can offloading computation save energy? Computer **43**(4), 51–56 (2010)
18. E. Li, Z. Zhou, X. Chen, Edge intelligence: On-demand deep learning model co-inference with device-edge synergy, in *Proceedings of the 2018 Workshop on Mobile Edge Communications* (ACM, 2018), pp. 31–36
19. X. Li, D. Caragea, H. Zhang, M. Imran, Localizing and quantifying damage in social media images, in *2018 IEEE/ACM International Conference on Advances in Social Networks Analysis and Mining (ASONAM)* (IEEE, 2018)
20. C. Lu, J. Shi, J. Jia, Abnormal event detection at 150 fps in matlab, in *Proceedings of the IEEE International Conference on Computer Vision* (2013), pp. 2720–2727
21. P. Mach, Z. Becvar, Mobile edge computing: A survey on architecture and computation offloading. Preprint. arXiv:1702.05309 (2017)
22. X. Mao, X. Miao, Y. He, X.-Y. Li, Y. Liu, Citysee: Urban co 2 monitoring with sensors, in *2012 Proceedings IEEE INFOCOM* (IEEE, 2012), pp. 1611–1619
23. H.B. McMahan, E. Moore, D. Ramage, S. Hampson, et al., Communication-efficient learning of deep networks from decentralized data. Preprint. arXiv:1602.05629 (2016)
24. A. Mtibaa, K.A. Harras, A. Fahim, Towards computational offloading in mobile device clouds, in *2013 IEEE 5th International Conference on Cloud Computing Technology and Science (CloudCom)*, vol. 1 (IEEE, 2013), pp. 331–338
25. J. Ni, A. Zhang, X. Lin, X.S. Shen, Security, privacy, and fairness in fog-based vehicular crowdsensing. IEEE Commun. Mag. **55**(6), 146–152 (2017)
26. R.W. Ouyang, L.M. Kaplan, A. Toniolo, M. Srivastava, T.J. Norman, Parallel and streaming truth discovery in large-scale quantitative crowdsourcing. IEEE Trans. Parallel Distribut. Syst. **27**(10), 2984–2997 (2016)
27. T. Sakaki, M. Okazaki, Y. Matsuo, Earthquake shakes twitter users: real-time event detection by social sensors, in *Proceedings of the 19th International Conference on World Wide Web* (ACM, 2010), pp. 851–860
28. M. Satyanarayanan, The emergence of edge computing. Computer **50**(1), 30–39 (2017)
29. M. Satyanarayanan, P. Bahl, R. Caceres, N. Davies, The case for VM-based cloudlets in mobile computing. IEEE Pervasive Comput. **8**(4), 14 (2009)
30. E. Saurez, K. Hong, D. Lillethun, U. Ramachandran, B. Ottenwälder, Incremental deployment and migration of geo-distributed situation awareness applications in the fog, in *Proceedings of the 10th ACM International Conference on Distributed and Event-based Systems* (ACM, 2016), pp. 258–269
31. W. Shi, J. Cao, Q. Zhang, Y. Li, L. Xu, Edge computing: Vision and challenges. IEEE Internet Things J. **3**(5), 637–646 (2016)
32. N. Vance, D.Y. Zhang, Y. Zhang, D. Wang, Privacy-aware edge computing in social sensing applications using ring signatures, in *2018 IEEE 24th International Conference on Parallel and Distributed Systems (ICPADS)* (IEEE, 2018), pp. 755–762
33. N. Vance, D. Zhang, D. Wang, Edgecache: a game-theoretic edge-based content caching system for crowd video sharing, in *2019 IEEE 21st International Conference on High Performance Computing and Communications; IEEE 17th International Conference on Smart City; IEEE 5th International Conference on Data Science and Systems (HPCC/SmartCity/DSS)* (IEEE, 2019), pp. 750–757
34. D. Wang, L. Kaplan, H. Le, T. Abdelzaher, On truth discovery in social sensing: A maximum likelihood estimation approach, in *Proc. ACM/IEEE 11th Int Information Processing in Sensor Networks (IPSN) Conf* (2012), pp. 233–244
35. D. Wang, T. Abdelzaher, L. Kaplan, C.C. Aggarwal, Recursive fact-finding: A streaming approach to truth estimation in crowdsourcing applications, in *2013 IEEE 33rd International Conference on Distributed Computing Systems* (IEEE, 2013), pp. 530–539

36. D. Wang, T. Abdelzaher, L. Kaplan, *Social Sensing: Building Reliable Systems on Unreliable Data* (Morgan Kaufmann, 2015)
37. J. Wang, M. Li, Y. He, H. Li, K. Xiao, C. Wang, A blockchain based privacy-preserving incentive mechanism in crowdsensing applications. IEEE Access **6**, 17545–17556 (2018)
38. D. Wang, B.K. Szymanski, T. Abdelzaher, H. Ji, L. Kaplan, The age of social sensing. Computer **52**(1), 36–45 (2019)
39. S. Wang, G. Ananthanarayanan, Y. Zeng, N. Goel, A. Pathania, T. Mitra, High-throughput cnn inference on embedded arm big. little multi-core processors. Preprint. arXiv:1903.05898 (2019)
40. S. Wang, T. Tuor, T. Salonidis, K.K. Leung, C. Makaya, T. He, K. Chan, Adaptive federated learning in resource constrained edge computing systems. IEEE J. Sel. Areas Commun. **37**(6), 1205–1221 (2019)
41. Y. Xiao, S. Nazarian, P. Bogdan, Self-optimizing and self-programming computing systems: A combined compiler, complex networks, and machine learning approach. IEEE Trans. Very Large Scale Integration (VLSI) Syst. **27**(6), 1416–1427 (2019)
42. S. Yi, Z. Hao, Z. Qin, Q. Li, Fog computing: Platform and applications, in *2015 Third IEEE Workshop on Hot Topics in Web Systems and Technologies (HotWeb)* (IEEE, 2015), pp. 73–78
43. X. You, C. Zhang, X. Tan, S. Jin, H. Wu, Ai for 5g: research directions and paradigms. Sci. China Inf. Sci. **62**(2), 21301 (2019)
44. D.Y. Zhang, D. Wang, An integrated top-down and bottom-up task allocation approach in social sensing based edge computing systems, in *IEEE INFOCOM 2019-IEEE Conference on Computer Communications* (IEEE, 2019), pp. 766–774
45. Q. Zhang, X. Zhang, Q. Zhang, W. Shi, H. Zhong, Firework: Big data sharing and processing in collaborative edge environment, in *2016 Fourth IEEE Workshop on Hot Topics in Web Systems and Technologies (HotWeb)* (IEEE, 2016), pp. 20–25
46. D.Y. Zhang, C. Zheng, D. Wang, D. Thain, X. Mu, G. Madey, C. Huang, Towards scalable and dynamic social sensing using a distributed computing framework, in *2017 IEEE 37th International Conference on Distributed Computing Systems (ICDCS)* (IEEE, 2017), pp. 966–976
47. Q. Zhang, Q. Zhang, W. Shi, H. Zhong, Enhancing amber alert using collaborative edges: Poster, in *Proceedings of the Second ACM/IEEE Symposium on Edge Computing* (ACM, 2017), pp. 27
48. D.Y. Zhang, Y. Ma, Y. Zhang, S. Lin, X.S. Hu, D. Wang, A real-time and non-cooperative task allocation framework for social sensing applications in edge computing systems, in *2018 IEEE Real-Time and Embedded Technology and Applications Symposium (RTAS)* (IEEE, 2018), pp. 316–326
49. D.Y. Zhang, Y. Ma, C. Zheng, Y. Zhang, X.S. Hu, D. Wang, Cooperative-competitive task allocation in edge computing for delay-sensitive social sensing, in *2018 IEEE/ACM Symposium on Edge Computing (SEC)* (IEEE, 2018), pp. 243–259
50. Y. Zhang, Y. Lu, D.Y. Zhang, L. Shang, D. Wang, Risksens: A multi-view learning approach to identifying risky traffic locations in intelligent transportation systems using social and remote sensing, in *2018 IEEE International Conference on Big Data (Big Data)* (IEEE, 2018), pp. 1544–1553
51. Y. Zhang, D. Zhang, N. Vance, Q. Li, D. Wang, A light-weight and quality-aware online adaptive sampling approach for streaming social sensing in cloud computing, in *2018 IEEE 24th International Conference on Parallel and Distributed Systems (ICPADS)* (IEEE, 2018), pp. 1–8
52. D. Zhang, N. Vance, D. Wang, When social sensing meets edge computing: Vision and challenges, in *2019 28th International Conference on Computer Communication and Networks (ICCCN)* (IEEE, 2019), pp. 1–9
53. D.Y. Zhang, T. Rashid, X. Li, N. Vance, D. Wang, Heteroedge: Taming the heterogeneity of edge computing system in social sensing, in *Proceedings of the International Conference on Internet of Things Design and Implementation (IoTDI)* (ACM, 2019), pp. 37–48. https://doi.org/10.1145/3302505.3310067

54. D.Y. Zhang, Y. Zhang, Q. Li, T. Plummer, D. Wang, Crowdlearn: A crowd-ai hybrid system for deep learning-based damage assessment applications, in *2019 IEEE 39th International Conference on Distributed Computing Systems (ICDCS)* (IEEE, 2019), pp. 1221–1232
55. G. Zhong, A. Dubey, C. Tan, T. Mitra, Synergy: An HW/SW framework for high throughput CNNS on embedded heterogeneous SoC. ACM Trans. Embedded Comput. Syst. (TECS) **18**(2), 13 (2019)
56. C.L. Zitnick, P. Dollár, Edge boxes: Locating object proposals from edges, in *European Conference on Computer Vision* (Springer, 2014), pp. 391–405

Chapter 3
Rational Social Edge Computing

Abstract With the ever-increasing computing power of edge devices and the growing acceptance of running human-centric learning and intelligence applications on such edge systems, effectively allocating computation tasks to the edge devices has emerged as a critical undertaking for maximizing the performance of SEC systems. Task allocation in SEC faces several unique challenges (e.g., conflicting interests, constrained cooperativeness, dynamic compliance) that are centered around the "rational actor" nature of edge devices. To overcome these challenges, this chapter reviews a novel game-theoretic task allocation framework: Cooperative-Competitive Game-theoretic Task Allocation (CoGTA). The CoGTA framework includes a dynamic feedback incentive scheme, a decentralized fictitious play design with a new negotiation scheme, and a judiciously designed private payoff function.

3.1 The Rational Social Edge Computing Problem

In this section, we focus on a critical problem in running an intelligent application on edge devices, i.e., allocating real-time tasks to non-cooperative edge computing nodes. We assume edge nodes (i.e., edge devices owned by individuals) are in general non-cooperative and selfish (e.g., they are not interested in executing the sensing/computation tasks or sharing their private device status unless incentives/payoffs are provided) [20]. This assumption is unique in the edge computing system and in sharp contrast to the assumption made in the "backend" based solutions where all computational nodes are fully cooperative, and the information is shared among all nodes [28]. While many works have been proposed to address the task allocation problem in real-time systems [24, 28], four major challenges that are unique to running intelligent applications in the edge computing systems have not been well addressed: *conflicting interests, asymmetric and incomplete information, constrained cooperativeness,* and *dynamic compliance.*

Conflicting Interests The first challenge is conflicting interests where the application and edge users have different and potentially conflicting objectives. For example, from the application's perspective, it is important to ensure the edge nodes finish the allocated SEC tasks within a certain period of time (e.g., deadline) to meet the QoS requirements. Current SEC task allocation schemes are often "top-down" based by assuming that a centralized decision maker (e.g., project manager or a server level allocation algorithm) makes the decision on which node should take on which tasks and when the tasks should be executed [25]. However, these "top-down" based methods do not fit well with the edge computing paradigm where edge nodes can be personal mobile devices owned by end-users who are not necessarily willing to execute the tasks allocated on their devices [15]. For example, a smartphone user may refuse to execute tasks which would possibly affect the experience of using the phone.

Asymmetric and Incomplete Information The second challenge is the asymmetric and incomplete information where the application (server) and edge nodes usually have different degrees of information in the edge computing paradigm. The server normally has detailed information about the tasks (e.g., the dependency and criticality of the tasks) but knows little about the edge nodes. In contrast, edge nodes are often less concerned about the details of the tasks and more concerned about their own device status (e.g., node's current utilization, energy consumption, memory usage). Furthermore, an edge node may not share its status information with the server or other edge nodes in the system due to various concerns (e.g., privacy, energy, bandwidth) [23]. Such asymmetric and incomplete information at both server and edge nodes make the task allocation problem of SEC applications in edge computing systems more challenging.

Constrained Cooperativeness The third challenge is related to developing collaboration schemes among edge devices. Previous studies showed that collaboration among computation nodes can significantly improve the efficiency of resource utilization in distributed systems [6, 21]. However, collaboration among edge devices is especially challenging because: (1) edge devices are rational actors unwilling to collaborate with others unless potential incentives are provided; (2) various constraints may also prohibit collaboration among edge devices (e.g., latency constraints imposed by the physical distance between devices or trust constraints imposed by the trusts between devices); (3) collaboration over task allocation requires explicit consideration of *task dependencies* of an application.

Dynamic Compliance The fourth challenge refers to the fact that the cost of an edge device and its willingness to execute SEC tasks can change over time. For example, consider a traffic monitoring application where edge devices (e.g. dashcams, mobile phones owned by people) are used to monitor real-time traffic conditions (vehicle count, traffic speed, etc.). Each edge device is tasked to monitor a particular street. An edge device (or its end user) may change the compliance of task execution due to (1) changes in the battery status of the device, or (2) changes in its physical location with respect to the monitored street. Failure to capture such dynamics in compliance may lead to significantly inferior task allocations where the cost of edge devices to complete a task is too high or against its will. This problem has not been well addressed by existing work due to the difficulty in modeling compliance of edge devices and requires a deep understanding of devices' dynamic status and willingness to participate.

3.2 A Cooperative-Competitive Game-theoretic Tasks Allocation Framework

In a sense, unlike traditional task allocation problems studied for a centralized computing scheme, the rational edge for social computing requires careful coordination among private user-owned devices that are not fully controlled by a single party. We also observe that in the real-world scenario, tasks can have dependencies and SEC application jobs often consist of many interdependent and heterogeneous tasks. Such dependency not only makes the task allocation more challenging, but also raises an interesting research question: can we guide the privately owned edge devices to collaboratively finish a job by picking the tasks they can handle most efficiently, even they are selfish in nature? To answer this research question and to jointly address the above challenges in rational social computing, we present a Cooperative-Competitive Game-theoretic Tasks Allocation (CoGTA) framework [27].

3.2.1 Problem Definition

Figure 3.1 depicts a high-level view of the CoGTA framework in SEC paradigm. In this framework, a project manager (resides on the server) launches a delay-sensitive social computing application that constantly collects and processes sensor data about the physical world via edge devices (e.g., laptops, drones, smartphones, automobiles). These edge devices may not be constantly connected to the network and often have a limited battery, bandwidth, memory and computation power [18]. Let $EN = \{E_1, E_2 \ldots E_X\}$ denote the set of all edge devices in the application. These edge devices are not only able to collect sensor data but also perform some computation tasks to reduce the burden of the back-end servers. The *back-end server* is a remote processing unit responsible for task distribution and data processing/analytics. A back-end server is often a powerful and controlled system (e.g., dedicated virtual machines, cloud platforms) that is directly managed by the project manager. We assume the edge devices have constantly changing device status and do not share the dynamic status of the server due to the privacy concerns and synchronization overhead.

We assume that communication among edge devices is constrained due to trust and privacy concerns. We describe such constraints as a *Trust Graph*:

Definition (**Trust Graph $\mathbf{G}_{dev}$**) An undirected graph $\mathbf{G}_{dev} = (\mathbf{V}_{dev}, \mathbf{L}_{dev})$. If there is a link $(x, y) \in \mathbf{L}_{dev}$ between E_x and E_y, it means that device E_x and E_y trust

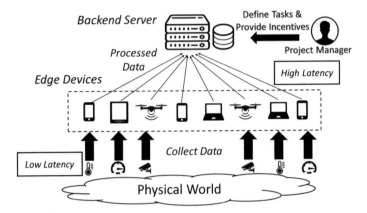

Fig. 3.1 CoGTA in social edge computing

each other. For example, edge devices that belong to users who are friends or from the same institution may trust each other. We assume untrusted edge devices cannot communicate with each other.   □

The task model considers task dependencies. In specific, an SEC application is assumed to have a set of Z jobs, $Job = \{J_1, J_2, \ldots J_Z\}$, which are initialized by the server at the beginning of each sensing cycle (i.e., sampling period). Each job converts the raw sensor input data to the final analysis results.

We adopt a frame-based task model [2] commonly used in the real-time system community where jobs are periodically initialized and have the same deadline.[1] We use Δ to denote the common deadline of all the jobs in an application. Δ captures the user desired QoS in terms of when the jobs should be finished.

To accomplish the data processing function, each job consists of one or more tasks that have dependencies among one another [8]. Each task is associated with a 3-tuple: $\tau_i = \{VI_i, VO_i, c_{i,x}\}$ where VI_i is the data volume to be processed by task τ_i and VO_i is the size of the output. $c_{i,x}$ is the estimated worst-case execution time (WCET) if τ_i is assigned to edge device $E_x, 1 \leq x \leq X$. The dependencies among the tasks in an application are modeled by a *task dependency graph* defined below.

Definition (Task Dependency Graph ($\mathbf{G}_{task}$)) A directed graph $\mathbf{G}_{task} = (\mathbf{V}_{task}, \mathbf{L}_{task})$ where vertex $V_i \in \mathbf{V}_{task}$ represents task τ_i; link $(\tau_i \rightarrow \tau_j) \in \mathbf{L}_{task}$ signifies that the input of task τ_j depends on the output of task τ_i (Fig. 3.2).   □

For a given application, we assume that a total of N tasks (from all Z jobs) are to be processed in each sensing cycle, i.e., $T = \{\tau_1, \tau_2, \ldots, \tau_N\}$. Energy consumption

---

[1] Note that in the real-time system community, *tasks* are periodically initialized while *jobs* are instances of tasks. We choose to follow the nomenclature used in the distributed system community for the words *job* and *task*, i.e., *jobs* are entities containing *tasks*. Thus, we say that jobs (and the tasks in the jobs) are periodically initialized.

is a major concern for most edge devices. We adopt a relatively simple energy model since it is sufficient for demonstrating how CoGTA can take energy into consideration during the task allocation process.[2] Given the WCET of task τ_i, $c_{i,x}$, the energy consumed by executing τ_i on edge device E_x is computed as

$$e_{i,x} = Power_x * c_{i,x}. \tag{3.1}$$

$Power_x$ is the average power consumption of edge device E_x and is calculated by

$$Power_x = Power_{comp,x} + Power_{trans,x} \tag{3.2}$$

where $Power_{comp}$ is the power consumption for computation and P_{trans} is power for data transmission via wireless network and is proportional to the data size transferred.

Based on the definitions, assumptions and system models, we formally define the objectives of CoGTA. As pointed out in the previous subsection, the application (server) and edge devices have competing objectives. That is, the application tries to optimize the QoS by minimizing the deadline miss rate of all jobs while the edge devices are interested in maximizing their own payoffs. Therefore, our goal is to develop a co-opetitive task allocation scheme that can best meet the objectives of both sides. To model the QoS requirement, we define end-to-end delay (E2E delay) of a job as:

Definition (End-to-End Delay of Job ($\mathcal{L}_z$)) The total amount of time taken for a unit of sensor measurement data (e.g., a video frame) to be processed by all tasks in J_z.   □

Our task allocation problem can be formulated as a multi-objective constrained optimization problem that targets at finding a task allocation scheme to

$$\text{maximize:} \quad u_x, \forall 1 \le x \le X \text{ (edge device's objective)}$$

$$\text{minimize:} \quad \sum_{z=1}^{Z} \delta_z, \forall 1 \le z \le Z \text{ (application's objective)} \tag{3.3}$$

$$\text{s.t.:} \quad \mathbf{G}_{task}, \mathbf{G}_{dev} \text{ are satisfied (dependent and trust constraints)}$$

$$\text{s.t.:} \quad \mathcal{L}_z \le \Delta, \forall 1 \le z \le Z \quad \text{(deadline constraints)}$$

Here u_x is the payoff that edge device E_x receives by executing tasks. It defines the individual gain of an edge device and more details on u_x are given in Sect. 5.2.2. δ_z is a binary variable, $\delta_z = 1$ if job J_z misses the deadline and $\delta_z = 0$ otherwise.

---

[2] The CoGTA framework can be readily extended to more complicated energy models, e.g., supporting multiple voltage/frequency levels. The details are omitted due to the page limit.

3.2.2   The CoGTA Framework

An overview of the CoGTA framework is given in Fig. 3.2. The framework consists
of three major components: (1) a novel Cooperative-Competitive Game (CCG)
that models the competing objectives between edge devices and applications; (2)
a Decentralized Fictitious Play with Negotiation (DFPN) scheme followed by edge
devices to make local decisions and autonomously form collaborations to maximize
individual payoffs while obeying the task dependency and trust constraints; (3) a
Dynamic Incentive Adjustment (DIA) scheme that dynamically tunes the incentives
to address the dynamic compliance of end-users while ensuring QoS of the
application. We present these components in detail below.

3.2.2.1   Cooperative-Competitive Game for Task Allocation

Our CCG is designed to tackle the specific challenge of the competing objectives between the application and edge nodes. A CCG is described by a tuple
$(H, EN, J, T, S, \Psi, \pi, R)$ where H is the game host (i.e., the server) and EN
is a set of X players (i.e., edge devices). J is a set of Z jobs and T is a set
of N tasks. Ψ represents the task allocation strategy space for all players, i.e.,
$\Psi = \Psi_1 \times \Psi_2 \times \ldots \times \Psi_X$ where Ψ_x represents the strategy space of player E_x.
We define a Strategy Profile S as a set of individual task allocation strategies, i.e.,
$S = \{s_1, s_2, \ldots, s_X\} \in \Psi$, where s_x denotes the strategy (i.e., which tasks to
execute) on edge device E_x. π is a cost function vector $\pi = \{\pi_1, \pi_2, .., \pi_X\}$ where
element π_x represents the cost of edge device E_x to execute the allocated tasks based
on strategy s_x. Finally, $R = \{R_1, R_2 \ldots, R_N\}$ is the set of rewards provided by the
application and R_i is the reward for task τ_i.

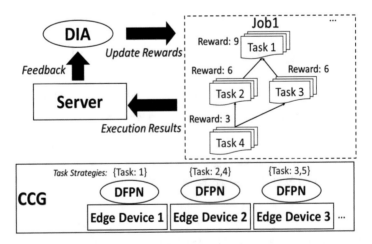

Fig. 3.2 Overview of CoGTA

Cost function π_x specifically captures the concerns and dynamic compliance of edge device E_x and is defined as:

$$\pi_x = \begin{cases} e_x = c_{i,x} * (Power_{comp,x} + Power_{trans,x}), \\ \infty, \eta_{b,x} \le thres_b \ or \ \eta_{d,x} \ge thres_d \end{cases} \tag{3.4}$$

where e_x is the energy consumed by running task τ_x on E_x, $\eta_{d,x}$ is the physical distance between E_x and the device that produces the input data for τ_x, and $\eta_{b,x}$ is the remaining battery of E_x.

3.2.2.2   Game Protocol and Payoff Function

We introduce our game protocol of CCG below.

- At the beginning of a sensing cycle, the server defines Z jobs, the task dependencies and the reward for each task.
- Each edge device picks a strategy that has the best payoff for itself via a fictitious play with the negotiation process (refer to the next subsection for details).
- If multiple devices choose the same task, for fairness, we randomly assign this task to one of the competing devices (*tie-breaking*). We refer to one round of this task allocation process as an "iteration".
- Within each iteration, we assume each edge device is myopic and only picks one task at a time.
- Keep iterating until all tasks are picked. Then each device starts to process the tasks it picked.
- Devices send outputs of executed tasks to the server to claim rewards, the server observes QoS performance loss, and then updates rewards for the next sensing cycle.

The above protocol follows the rule of *singleton weighted congestion game* where the Pure Strategy Nash Equilibrium is *guaranteed* to exist [1]. This is crucial for edge devices to make mutually satisfactory task allocation decisions.

The above protocol does not explicitly consider task dependencies and the potential benefit of "co-opetition" among devices. Task dependencies described by $\mathbf{G}_{task}$ and the trust constraints among devices given by $\mathbf{G}_{dev}$ introduce additional challenges to CCG. To tackle these challenges, we first define a key term below.

Definition (Task Delegation and Collaboration) Task delegation refers to the process where an edge device transfers the output of a task to another edge device for further processing. Collaboration between two devices happens when a device (referred to as "producer") is delegating its task to another device (referred to as "consumer"). □

We solve the co-opetitive task allocation problem with task and trust constraints using a modified "supply chain" model. Specifically, the output of a task is

considered as a piece of "raw material" and the subsequent tasks in the job continue
to process this "raw material" until the job finishes computation to generate the
"final product" (i.e., end results). An edge device can choose to process all materials
by itself or, at a certain stage, "sell" (i.e., by performing task delegation) the
output of a task to other edge devices or the server to get immediate rewards.
Therefore, we provide a reward for each task based on the "difficulty" to process
it and how "valuable" the task output is. We discuss reward assignment in details in
Sect. 3.2.2.4.

To impose QoS constraints (e.g., end-to-end delay) of the application, we define
a *penalty function* $l_{i,x,y}$ as:

$$
l_{i,x,y} = \begin{cases} \dfrac{\Delta}{\Delta - (td(x, y) + c_{i,x})}, & td(x, y) + c_{i,x} < \Delta \\[2mm] \infty, & td(x, y) + c_{i,x} \geq \Delta \end{cases} \tag{3.5}
$$

where $td(x, y)$ denotes the transmission delay from E_x to E_y or Server ($y = H$)
and $c_{i,x}$ is the WCET of τ_i. The intuition of this penalty function is to penalize "lazy
but greedy" edge devices who want to get high rewards for picking many tasks but
fail to process them efficiently. Specifically, the closer the execution time of a task
is to the deadline, the higher the penalty is.

Given the above definitions, we formally derive the payoff functions, a key
element in CCG. The payoff functions are associated with each edge device's
strategy and contain several different forms to capture the various execution
scenarios. Assume that device E_x picks task τ_i in an iteration and $d(i)$ is the number
of devices that pick τ_i. Based on the reward, penalty and cost, we define the *payoff
function* $u_{i,x}^H$ of edge device E_x for finishing task τ_i and offloading the rest of the
job to the server as:

$$
u_{i,x}^H = \begin{cases} E\left(\dfrac{R_i}{\pi_x * l_{i,x,H}}\right) = \dfrac{R_i * (\Delta - (td(x, H) + c_{i,x}))}{\Delta * d(i) * e_x} \\[3mm] 0, \quad l_{i,x,H} = \infty \ or \ \pi_x = \infty \end{cases} \tag{3.6}
$$

where $E(\cdot)$ finds the expected payoff, which is simply the original payoff divided
by the number of devices that pick the tasks due to the tie-breaking process.

We further derive the payoff of performing collaboration between devices. For
a task delegation, we assume E_x is the producer of task τ_i's output and $E_{x'}$ is the
consumer of this output by picking a subsequent task $\tau_{i'}$. The *collaboration payoff
function* for producer E_x with respect to τ_i is:

$$
u_{i,x}^p = \begin{cases} \dfrac{R_i * (\Delta - (0.5 * td(x, x') + c_{i,x}))}{\Delta * d(i) * \pi_x}, & x' \neq x \ or \ H \\[3mm] 0, & (x' \to x) \notin \mathbf{L}_{dev} \ or \ x' = x \end{cases} \tag{3.7}
$$

We allow the producer and the consumer to share the penalty due to the transmission delay between them (i.e., $0.5*td(x, x')$). The above payoff function definition takes into consideration the trust constraints by setting the payoff to 0 if E_x and $E_{x'}$ are not connected in $\mathbf{G}_{dev}$.

Now assume an edge device E_x is receiving output from a set of tasks $\{\tau_{i'}|(i' \to i) \in \mathbf{L}_{task}\}$. Let $x(i')$ denote the device that picks a task $\tau_{i'}$. We design the *collaboration payoff function for consumer* E_x with respect to τ_i as below.

$$u_{i,x}^c = \begin{cases} \dfrac{u_{i,x}^H}{d(i)} - \sum_{i'}^{(i' \to i) \in \mathbf{L}_{task}} \dfrac{u_{i',x(i')}^p}{d(i)}, \\ \\ 0, \qquad \exists i', x(i') = null \text{ or } (x(i'), x) \notin \mathbf{L}_{dev} \end{cases} \tag{3.8}$$

where the term $\exists i', x(i') = null$ or $(x(i'), x) \notin \mathbf{L}_{dev}$ denotes some of those previous tasks of τ_i have not been picked or picked by untrusted devices. Hence, picking τ_i will not have sufficient data input for execution, which yields no actual payoff for E_x. This design is to ensure that edge devices only take tasks whose previous tasks have already been picked.

With the CCG setup given here, we are now ready to introduce the scheme for "playing" the game in the following two subsections.

3.2.2.3   Decentralized Fictitious Play with Negotiation

Here, we present an efficient learning scheme to find the optimal task allocation based on Fictitious Play (FP) and negotiation heuristics to significantly reduce both the search space and convergence time. The algorithm is described as:

- *Initial Step:* Each edge device initializes a local empirical histogram ($histo$) [4] as a basis to "guess" the strategies other players might employ based on their historical strategies, where $histo_{i,x}$ denotes the frequency of E_x picking τ_i. We initialize $histo$ at the beginning of the game as: $histo_{i,x} = \frac{R_i}{\sum_{i=1}^{N} R_i}$
- *Best Response:* Each edge device then picks the task with the highest payoff (defined in Eq. (3.6)) based on the guess of all other players' strategies.
- *Negotiation:* After picking a task, each edge device decides whether to send the output of the task to the server or "sell" it to other devices. An edge device labels the task as "on sale" if it is willing to perform task delegation. Each edge device also decides whether to "buy" a task on sale. Each device performs this negotiation with the goal of maximizing $u_{i,x}^p$ and $u_{i,x}^c$ (defined in Eqs. (3.7) and (3.8)), respectively.
- *Coordination:* After all the devices make decisions, a local edge server collects all the decisions and shares them with all the devices.
- *Update Belief:* Each device observes the strategies of others, and then updates its empirical histogram by increasing the corresponding strategy count by 1. Then

the estimation on the future strategies is derived as the most frequent strategy of each device, recorded by $histo$.

The above steps are repeated until convergence. The negotiation step allows edge devices to be co-opetitive. In particular, we assume a device is always willing to invite collaboration if (1) it cannot consume the output of a task; and (2) the increased reward of the collaboration is non-negative. Specifically, we derive the reward increase as $u_{i,x}^{p} - u_{i,x}^{H}$. If another device is willing to accept the task delegation (via $u_{i,x}^{c}$), the collaboration is formed.

Note that traditional FP algorithms assume that a centralized entity has the payoff information of all devices in the system. This assumption does not hold in the edge computing scenarios where neither the server or the edge devices know the private payoffs of all devices [3]. In our solution, each device runs the above enhanced FP algorithm locally without disclosing its individual payoff function.

3.2.2.4 Dynamic Incentive Adjustment

Our CCG and DFPN approaches discussed in the previous subsections ensure that the edge devices achieve maximum payoff through a co-opetitive gameplay. As shown in the payoff functions (Eqs. (3.6) and (3.7)), the definition of the rewards plays a critical role with respect to whether a task is picked by edge devices for execution. Due to the dynamic compliance issues, static reward functions are generally not optimal for the server to satisfy QoS requirements. We introduce a Dynamic Incentive Adjustment scheme for the server to dynamically update task rewards in order to meet the QoS objective of the application. Below, we first present the general reward function and then discuss how it is dynamically adjusted.

The design of the task reward function is based on the following two considerations. First, if a task must transfer a large amount of input data to the server for processing, it would be "more valuable" to execute the task on an edge device. Second, if a task is at later stages of a job (i.e., close to the final output), it would be more "valuable" in general so as not to waste the computation that has already been done for the job. Now, let VO_i and VI_i be the size of output and input of τ_i, respectively, and $drr_i = \frac{VO_i}{VI_i}$ be the data reduction ratio (DRR). Thus DRR represents how much reduction of data communication is achieved by accomplishing a task. Furthermore, let the aggregated computation complexity (ACC) acc_i be recursively defined as $acc_i = \sum_{(i' \to i) \in \mathbf{L}_{task}} acc_{i'} + c_{i,H}$. ACC represents the total computational effort to finish a task. Finally, we define task reward R_i for τ_i as a linear combination of drr_i and acc_i:

$$R_i = \frac{\alpha_1}{\alpha_1 + \alpha_2} drr_i + \frac{\alpha_2}{\alpha_1 + \alpha_2} acc_i \qquad (3.9)$$

where α_1 and α_2 are the weighting factors. To ensure that it is meaningful to add DRR and ACC, we normalize both DRR and ACC scores. Therefore, the reward of each individual task is bounded.

The dynamic tuning of rewards is accomplished by adopting the exponential weights algorithm [5] as a feedback control mechanism. The intuition of this tuning process is that the server assumes there exist two "experts" who vote for the importance of the two factors ("DRR" and "ACC") in the reward function. Each expert's vote is associated with the corresponding weight (α_1 or α_2). Based on the experts' votes, the server calculates the reward according to Eq. (3.9). After the jobs are executed, the server can observe which jobs missed the deadlines and re-attribute the performance feedback to each expert as a loss function and adjust their weights accordingly. Specifically, we update the weights (α_1 and α_2):

$$\alpha_k^{new} = \alpha_k^{old} * e^{-\eta \lambda_k}, \quad 1 \le k \le 2. \tag{3.10}$$

η is a learning parameter, λ_k is a loss function for α_k, and

$$\lambda_1 = \frac{\sum_{z=1}^{Z} o_z^t * \delta_z}{\sum_{z=1}^{Z} \delta_z} - \frac{\sum_{z=1}^{Z} o_z^t * (1 - \delta_z)}{\sum_{z=1}^{Z} (1 - \delta_z)}, \sum_{z=1}^{Z} \delta_z \ne 0 \text{ or } Z$$

$$\lambda_2 = \frac{\sum_{z=1}^{Z} o_z^c * \delta_z}{\sum_{z=1}^{Z} \delta_z} - \frac{\sum_{z=1}^{Z} o_z^c * (1 - \delta_z)}{\sum_{z=1}^{Z} (1 - \delta_z)}, \sum_{z=1}^{Z} \delta_z \ne 0 \text{ or } Z, \tag{3.11}$$

where δ_z signifies whether job J_z missed the deadline or not. In the above equation, we use the average transmission overhead o_z^t (edge to server) of the tasks that meet the deadlines (i.e., $\frac{\sum_{z=1}^{Z} o_z^t * (1 - \delta_z)}{\sum_{z=1}^{Z} (1 - \delta_z)}$) as a set point and compare it with the average transmission overhead of the tasks that missed the deadlines ($\frac{\sum_{z=1}^{Z} o_z^t * \delta_z}{\sum_{z=1}^{Z} \delta_z}$).

The same idea applies for the ACC factor (using computation overhead o_z^c). The parameters α_1 and α_2 are tuned to minimize the loss functions. If all jobs meet their deadlines (i.e., $\sum_{z=1}^{Z} \delta_z = 0$), we keep the current reward function. In the rare case where all jobs miss their deadlines (i.e., $\sum_{z=1}^{Z} \delta_z = Z$), we resort to admission control and decrease the number of assigned jobs.

3.3   Real-World Case Studies

We evaluate the CoGTA framework using two real-world case studies. We choose the following representative task allocation schemes from recent literature as baselines.

- **Congestion (COG)**: a congestion game based edge computing task allocation scheme where tasks are modeled as resources and the reward of a task is monotonically decreasing as more edge devices claiming that task [13].

- **Bottom-up Game-Theoretic Task Allocation (BGTA)**: a bottom-up task allocation scheme that does not allow cooperation among edge devices [26].
- **Greedy-Max Reward (GMXR)**: A greedy task allocation scheme where an edge device greedily picks the tasks with the highest reward [22].
- **Centralized Server-based Allocation (CSA)**: a centralized task allocation scheme where an edge device sends all its computation tasks to the cloud servers.
- **Mixed Integer Linear Programming (MILP)**: a top-down task allocation scheme with cooperative distributed computing resources using MILP to minimize the deadline miss rate [7].

The first case study is *Abnormal Event Detection (AED)* in SEC where the goal is to generate alerts of abnormal events from video data contributed by camera-enabled sensors (e.g., mobile phones, drones, etc.). For example, in a mobile SEC project, the participants are tasked to take videos/images of a location assigned by the application to help identify abnormal events such as trespassing, sudden movements, and the appearance of unusual objects. Upon detection of abnormal events, the application provides alerts to its subscribed users or the general public.

We use the UCSD Anomaly Detection Dataset [14] which consists of 98 (50 training, 48 testing) video footages collected from surveillance cameras that monitor pedestrian walkways around the UCSD campus. The dataset provides ground truth labels for two abnormal events: (1) detection of non-pedestrian objects; (2) anomalous pedestrian motion patterns. We treat this dataset as the video data collected from the edge devices since our edge devices do not have cameras. We assume that each edge device generates one sensor data stream. Each run of the experiment contains a total of 100 sensing cycles. Within each sensing cycle, the edge devices are tasked to process a total of 8 s of video clips (with each video source sampled at 20 image frames per cycle).

Jobs for Abnormal Activity Detection We adopt the abnormal activity detection framework proposed in [19] to define the set of tasks for a job in this application: (1) data collection of video signals as image frames; (2) image prepossessing (i.e., converting images to grayscale); (3) motion feature extraction (i.e., optical flow); (4) object detection using YOLO framework[16]; (5) feature classification using a sparse combination classifier [19]. All jobs have the same set of tasks but process different video clips. The results from different jobs are sent back to the server for the aggregation and final decision.

To impose trust constraints, we design two trust groups and each device is randomly assigned to one of the two groups in an experiment. We assume devices within each group can communicate with each other but inter-group communication is not allowed due to trust constraints. The evaluation results are averaged over 100 experiments.

Quality of Service (Application (Server) Side) In the first set of experiments, we focus on how the objective is achieved from the application side. In particular, we evaluate the deadline hit rate (DHR) and end-to-end (E2E) delay of all the compared task allocation schemes. The DHR results are shown in Fig. 3.3. Here we use all

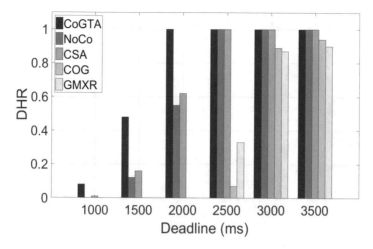

Fig. 3.3 DHR in AED

15 edge devices and gradually increase the deadline constraints. We observe that CoGTA has significantly higher DHRs than all the baselines and is the first one that reaches 100% DHR as the deadline increases. We attribute such performance gain to our deadline-driven dynamic incentive adjustment that guides the edge devices' decisions towards minimizing deadline miss rate by providing dynamic incentives.

Figure 3.7 summarizes the E2E delays of all the schemes as the number of video sources varies. We show the average delays and the 90% confidence bounds. Clearly, our CoGTA scheme has the least E2E delay and the tightest confidence bounds compared to all the baselines. The results further demonstrate the effectiveness of CoGTA for meeting the real-time QoS requirements of the application. The performance gain of the CoGTA is achieved by explicitly modeling the dynamic status of the edge devices (e.g., computation capability and energy profile) and allocating tasks according to the current device status.

Payoff and Energy Consumption (Edge Device Side) In the second set of experiments, we focus on how the objectives of edge devices are achieved. In particular, we study the payoff and energy consumption of edge devices. Figure 3.4 shows the results of the payoff gained by the edge devices. We normalize DRR and ACC to a 0–100 scale and cost π_x to a 1–5 scale. We observe that CoGTA has the highest payoff compared to all the baselines. This is because CoGTA can most efficiently finish the jobs by pushing the computation to the edge, thus avoiding communication latency of sending tasks to the server. This results in the least penalty for the rewards gained. Also, CoGTA allows edge devices to obtain their rewards effectively via achieving the Nash Equilibrium.

The results of energy consumption by edge devices are shown in Table 3.1. Here we use all 15 edge devices, and set the number of video sources to 10 and deadline to 3 s. The number of video sources being less than the number of edge devices

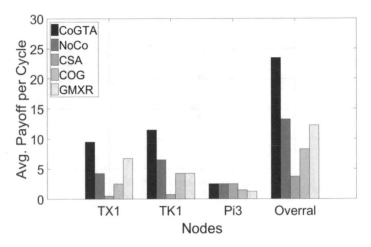

Fig. 3.4 Average payoff in AED

Table 3.1 Average energy (mJ) per frame in AED

	CoGTA	NoCo	CSA	COG	GMXR
Jetson TX1	167.71	160.84	127.99	163.88	161.39
Jetson TK1	162.73	161.45	122.17	162.03	158.20
Raspberry Pi3	64.89	65.72	64.03	67.10	69.64
All	1472.51	1463.23	1262.79	1484.85	1493.78

emulates the scenarios that the number of devices can be much larger than the number of jobs required by the application in many real-world applications [10]. We can observe that the CSA and NoCo baselines consume the least energy due to the fact that they push most of the computation tasks to the back-end servers. However, CoGTA consumes a similar amount of energy as compared to CSA and NoCo but achieves much higher DHR and lower E2E delay since CoTGA adopts an energy-aware payoff function and thus uses energy more efficiently.

Communication Overhead (Edge to Server) We further investigate the communication overhead from edge devices to the server. Figure 3.5 shows the percentage of tasks (within a sensing cycle) that are accomplished by the edge devices. We observe that CoGTA finishes the highest percentage of the tasks at the edge devices among all the schemes, which greatly alleviates the computation burden of the server. The results on the communication overhead (in terms of the amount of data sent from edge devices to the server) are shown in Fig. 3.6. We observe that CoGTA incurs the least communication overhead compared to the baselines. The reduced communication overhead also explains the E2E delay reduction achieved by CoGTA shown in Fig. 3.7.

The second case study is *Real-time Traffic Monitoring (RTM)* where participants in an SEC application use personal mobile devices (e.g., mobile phones, dashcams)

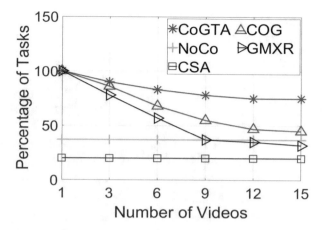

Fig. 3.5 Percentage of tasks finished by edge devices per cycle

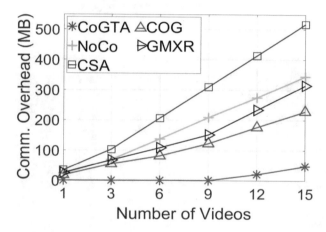

Fig. 3.6 Communication costs in AED

to record and analyze the current traffic conditions. For example, a traffic monitoring application can task a set of drivers to use their dashcams to take videos of the traffic in front of their vehicles and then infer the congestion rate of the road.

We collected the video data using dashcams from two vehicles. The data contains a total of 30 video clips and 15 of them are used for training. We divided the application into 100 sensing cycles and each sensing cycle processes video clips of 6 s (with each video source sampled at 15 image frames per cycle).

Jobs for Traffic Monitoring (1) data collection of traffic video signals as image frames; (2) image prepossessing; (3) feature extraction (optical flow and Histogram of Oriented Gradients); (4) feature classification using trained Support Vector Machine (SVM) to identify vehicles and traffic counts. The final result of each job is further processed by the server to infer the overall traffic condition.

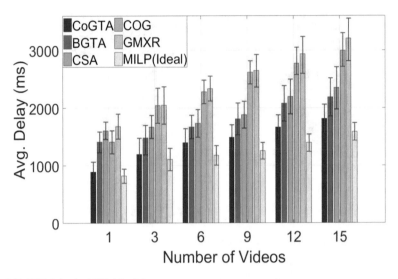

Fig. 3.7 E2E delay in AED ($\Delta = 3$s)

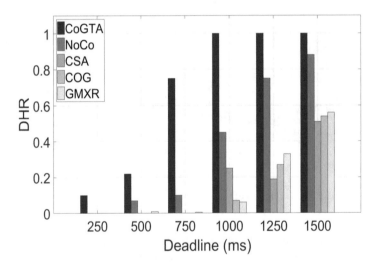

Fig. 3.8 Deadline hit rate in RTM

Similar trends as the first case study are observed (see Figs. 3.8, 3.9, 3.10, 3.11, and 3.12): CoGTA outperforms all the baselines in both meeting the QoS of the application and maximizing the payoffs of edge devices with reasonable energy consumption. We omit the detailed discussions due to space limit.

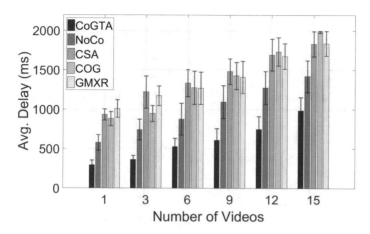

Fig. 3.9 E2E delay in RTM ($\Delta = 2$s)

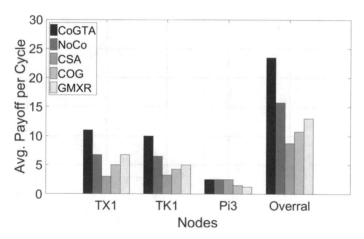

Fig. 3.10 Average payoff in RTM

3.4   Discussion

Finally, we discuss a unique vision of using private edge devices owned by individuals to perform edge computation tasks (i.e., rational edge), which is in sharp contrast to existing models that assume edge devices are collaborative [9, 17]. We discussed a novel task allocation framework—CoGTA, that addresses the rationality of edge devices while achieving desired quality of service of SEC-based applications.

One potential limitation of CoGTA is that, neither approach considers the dynamic churn rate of end users. We assume the availability of devices does not change within each sensing cycle. In practice, such availability could change at

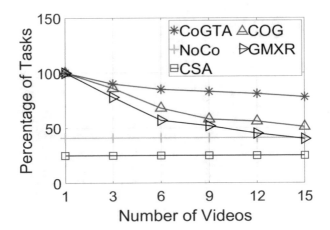

Fig. 3.11 Percentage of tasks finished by edge devices per cycle

Fig. 3.12 Edge to server communication overhead per cycle

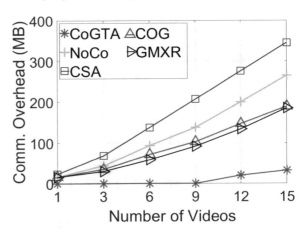

any point in time, which may lead to unfinished or partially finished tasks. This issue has initially been discussed in [11], in which task re-assignment and adaptive workload management mechanisms have been developed to mask device churn. We can address this problem by allocating important tasks to more than one edge device so the task will be finished unless all devices associated with the task decide to quit simultaneously [12]. Alternatively, CoGTA can also specify that the edge devices could only join and quit at the beginning of each sensing cycle by imposing a high penalty cost for the devices who quit without finishing their tasks. We leave these extensions for future work.

Moreover, though our approaches bring the benefit of exploring the massive amount of privately owned computational resources at the edge, it introduces many challenges to be solved as well. One particular challenge is user privacy. For example, the data collected from edge devices can potentially reveal the private information of end users. We discuss how to address the privacy issue in Chap. 7.

References

1. H. Ackermann, H. Röglin, B. Vöcking, Pure Nash equilibria in player-specific and weighted congestion games, in *WINE* (Springer, 2006), pp. 50–61
2. A. Allavena, D. Mossé, Scheduling of frame-based embedded systems with rechargeable batteries, in *Workshop on Power Management for Real-time and Embedded systems (in conjunction with RTAS 2001)* (2001)
3. U. Berger, Brown's original fictitious play. J. Econ. Theory **135**(1), 572–578 (2007)
4. E. Campos-Nañez, A. Garcia, C. Li, A game-theoretic approach to efficient power management in sensor networks. Oper. Res. **56**(3), 552–561 (2008)
5. N. Cesa-Bianchi, G. Lugosi, *Prediction, Learning, and Games* (Cambridge University Press, 2006)
6. L. Chen, S. Zhou, J. Xu, Computation peer offloading for energy-constrained mobile edge computing in small-cell networks. Preprint. arXiv:1703.06058 (2017)
7. A. Davare, J. Chong, Q. Zhu, D.M. Densmore, A.L. Sangiovanni-Vincentelli, Classification, customization, and characterization: Using milp for task allocation and scheduling. *Systems Research* (2006)
8. J. Dean, S. Ghemawat, Mapreduce: simplified data processing on large clusters. Commun. ACM **51**(1), 107–113 (2008)
9. W. Gao, Opportunistic peer-to-peer mobile cloud computing at the tactical edge, in *Military Communications Conference (MILCOM), 2014 IEEE* (IEEE, 2014), pp. 1614–1620
10. A. Ghasemi, E.S. Sousa, Opportunistic spectrum access in fading channels through collaborative sensing. JCM **2**(2), 71–82 (2007)
11. K. Habak, M. Ammar, K.A. Harras, E. Zegura, Femto clouds: Leveraging mobile devices to provide cloud service at the edge, in *2015 IEEE 8th International Conference on Cloud Computing (CLOUD)* (IEEE, 2015), pp. 9–16
12. A. Kulkarni, M. Can, B. Hartmann, Collaboratively crowdsourcing workflows with turkomatic, in *Proceedings of the ACM 2012 Conference on Computer Supported Cooperative Work* (2012), pp. 1003–1012
13. D. Liu, L. Khoukhi, A. Hafid, Decentralized data offloading for mobile cloud computing based on game theory, in *2017 Second International Conference on Fog and Mobile Edge Computing (FMEC)* (IEEE, 2017), pp. 20–24
14. V. Mahadevan, W. Li, V. Bhalodia, N. Vasconcelos, Anomaly detection in crowded scenes, in *2010 IEEE Conference on Computer Vision and Pattern Recognition (CVPR)* (IEEE, 2010), pp. 1975–1981
15. M.-A. Messous, H. Sedjelmaci, N. Houari, S.-M. Senouci, Computation offloading game for an UAV network in mobile edge computing, in *2017 IEEE International Conference on Communications (ICC)* (IEEE, 2017), pp. 1–6
16. J. Redmon, S. Divvala, R. Girshick, A. Farhadi, You only look once: Unified, real-time object detection, in *Proceedings of the IEEE Conference on Computer Vision and Pattern Recognition* (2016), pp. 779–788
17. M. Satyanarayanan, P. Bahl, R. Caceres, N. Davies, The case for VM-based cloudlets in mobile computing. IEEE Pervasive Comput. **8**(4), 14 (2009)
18. W. Shi, J. Cao, Q. Zhang, Y. Li, L. Xu, Edge computing: Vision and challenges. IEEE Internet of J. **3**(5), 637–646 (2016)
19. H. Tan, Y. Zhai, Y. Liu, M. Zhang, Fast anomaly detection in traffic surveillance video based on robust sparse optical flow, in *2016 IEEE International Conference on Acoustics, Speech and Signal Processing (ICASSP)* (IEEE, 2016), pp. 1976–1980
20. W.E. Walsh, M.P. Wellman, A market protocol for decentralized task allocation, in *International Conference on Multi Agent Systems, 1998. Proceedings* (IEEE, 1998), pp. 325–332
21. G. Wei, A.V. Vasilakos, Y. Zheng, N. Xiong, A game-theoretic method of fair resource allocation for cloud computing services. J. Supercomput. **54**(2), 252–269 (2010)

22. D. Wicke, D. Freelan, S. Luke, Bounty hunters and multiagent task allocation, in *Proceedings of the 2015 International Conference on Autonomous Agents and Multiagent Systems* (International Foundation for Autonomous Agents and Multiagent Systems, 2015), pp. 387–394
23. Y. Zhang, A cross-site study of user behavior and privacy perception in social networks. Master's thesis, Purdue University, 2014
24. W. Zhang, E. Bai, H. He, A.M. Cheng, Solving energy-aware real-time tasks scheduling problem with shuffled frog leaping algorithm on heterogeneous platforms. Sensors **15**(6), 13778–13804 (2015)
25. D.Y. Zhang, C. Zheng, D. Wang, D. Thain, X. Mu, G. Madey, C. Huang, Towards scalable and dynamic social sensing using a distributed computing framework, in *2017 IEEE 37th International Conference on Distributed Computing Systems (ICDCS)* (IEEE, 2017), pp. 966–976
26. D.Y. Zhang, Y. Ma, Y. Zhang, S. Lin, X.S. Hu, D. Wang, A real-time and non-cooperative task allocation framework for social sensing applications in edge computing systems, in *2018 IEEE Real-Time and Embedded Technology and Applications Symposium (RTAS)* (IEEE, 2018), pp. 316–326
27. D.Y. Zhang, Y. Ma, C. Zheng, Y. Zhang, X.S. Hu, D. Wang, Cooperative-competitive task allocation in edge computing for delay-sensitive social sensing, in *2018 IEEE/ACM Symposium on Edge Computing (SEC)* (IEEE, 2018), pp. 243–259
28. Q. Zhu, H. Zeng, W. Zheng, M.D. Natale, A. Sangiovanni-Vincentelli, Optimization of task allocation and priority assignment in hard real-time distributed systems. ACM Trans. Embedded Comput. Syst. (TECS) **11**(4), 85 (2012)

Chapter 4
Taming Heterogeneity in Social Edge Computing

Abstract One critical challenge in SEC is the *pronounced heterogeneity* of the edge where the edge devices owned by individuals often have heterogeneous computational power, runtime environments, network interfaces, and hardware equipment. Such heterogeneity imposes significant challenges in the SEC paradigm such as masking the pronounced heterogeneity across diverse edge platforms, allocating computation tasks with complex interdependence and requirements on devices with different resources, and adapting to the dynamic and diversified context of the edge devices. In this chapter, we present a new resource management framework, HeteroEdge, to address the heterogeneity of SEC by providing a uniform interface to abstract the device details and allocating the computation tasks to the heterogeneous edge devices.

4.1 The Heterogeneous Social Edge

The edge devices in SEC often have diversified computational power, runtime environments, and hardware equipment, making it hard to orchestrate these devices to collaboratively accomplish the tasks in an SEC application. Previous efforts were made to accommodate heterogeneous devices in a computing cluster. Examples include HTCondor [12] and FemtoCloud [6]. However, these solutions cannot address the heterogeneity problem in SEC due to several unique technical challenges elaborated below.

First, the heterogeneity in SEC is more pronounced than in regular distributed/cloud based systems because (1) it is not possible for the application to cherry-pick the devices in a fully controlled manner given the fact that the devices are owned by individuals [19]; (2) the degree of heterogeneity of SEC devices is much more significant than the distributed or cloud computing systems that assume homogeneous tasks [6] or homogeneous architecture [12]. With pronounced heterogeneity, existing resource management techniques must be re-designed to cater for heterogeneous SEC. In particular, traditional backend-based edge computing applications are often designed for specific hardware or operating system environments and may not be directly applicable in a heterogeneous system. For instance, the application written for X86 is not executable on ARM processors due to architectural and hardware differences. Similarly, the applications developed for the Windows OS cannot be executed on the Android OS without code modification and re-configuration. The privilege of "write once run anywhere" is often divested from SEC developers [3]. Therefore, the pronounced heterogeneity requires resource management in SEC to support diverse application tasks to maximize resource utilization while relieving the burden of the developers.

Second, efficiently allocating interdependent application tasks with diversified resource requirements to heterogeneous devices with the complex delay-energy tradeoff is quite complex in SEC. In particular, the application tasks are often complicated and require heterogeneous hardware resources (e.g., some tasks require sensors, some tasks require GPUs) [21]. Moreover, edge devices often have diversified configurations of hardware components (e.g., GPU, single core CPU, multi-core CPU, sensors). Third, it is difficult to orchestrate the heterogeneous edge devices in accomplishing collaborative application tasks with non-trivial task dependencies. Finally, various task allocation strategies may yield complex tradeoffs between energy cost and delay overhead (e.g., assigning a task to a GPU may incur less delay but higher energy cost as compared to assigning the task to a CPU). Given the above unique complexities, we found existing resource management schemes that leverage heterogeneous devices (e.g., HTCondor [12], CoGTA [23], and FemtoCloud [6]) cannot solve the complex task mapping problem in SEC.

Third, edge devices may have different and dynamic contextual environments in SEC. The contextual environment refers to the detailed status of edge devices (e.g., the location of the device, the CPU/memory utilization, and the battery status), which often changes over time as the system runs. It is important to keep track of the contextual information in SEC to optimize many run-time decisions (e.g., task allocation, incentive adjustment) [2]. Existing edge computing systems often assume that a central controller in the system has full knowledge about the context information of all edge devices [4], which is not practical in SEC for two reasons. First, the end users have ultimate control of their edge devices, and they will decide what type of context should be visible to the application. For example, a user who chooses to share the GPU resource in an SEC application might change his/her mind if the battery of the device becomes low. Second, it also introduces a significant synchronization overhead by tracking the exact CPU usage and other context environments in real time (e.g., the edge devices have to constantly update their status to the server) [22]. Therefore, there lacks an approach that allows end users to self-configure and provides the useful dynamic context to the application.

4.2 A Heterogeneous Social Edge System: HeteroEdge

To address the above challenges, we present a new resource management framework called *HeteroEdge* to tame the heterogeneity of SEC [24]. In particular, we develop a novel supply chain based task mapping model that allows heterogeneous edge devices to collaboratively finish complicated and interdependent application tasks with an optimized delay-energy tradeoff. HeteroEdge addresses the pronounced heterogeneity of SEC devices and dynamic context challenges by developing hardware and runtime abstraction modules. We implemented a system prototype of HeteroEdge on a real-world SEC testbed that consists of Raspberry Pi3, Nvidia Jetson TX2, Jetson TK1 boards, and personal computers. HeteroEdge was evaluated using a real-world SEC applications: *Disaster Damage Assessment (DDA)*. We compared HeteroEdge with the state-of-the-art resource management schemes used in edge computing systems. The results show that our scheme achieves a significant performance gain in terms of delay and energy consumption: our scheme achieved up to 42% decrease in the end-to-end delay for the application and 22% more energy savings for edge devices compared to the baselines.

4.2.1   Problem Definition

We first formally define the resource management problem in SEC with hetero-geneous edge devices. Figure 4.1 shows a high-level overview of SEC system. The SEC system incorporates a set of edge devices, $ED = \{E_1, E_2 \ldots E_X\}$, and a local edge server ES. These edge devices can perform sensing tasks (e.g., collecting image data using camera sensors), computation tasks (e.g., running image classification algorithms), or perform data transmission over the wireless network interface. The edge devices are assumed to be heterogeneous by having different system architecture (e.g., X86, ARM), operating systems (e.g., Windows, Linux), hardware (e.g., with/without GPU, sensors), and networking interfaces (e.g., WiFi, Bluetooth). The local edge server serves as a general networking hub with various network interfaces, and all the edge devices can communicate with the local edge server.

We first discuss the task model in our framework. An SEC application is assumed to have a set of Z jobs, $Job = \{J_1, J_2, \ldots J_Z\}$, which are initialized by the server at the beginning of each sensing cycle (i.e., sampling period). Each job converts the raw sensor input data to the final analysis results. We adopt a frame-based task model [23] commonly used in the real-time system community where jobs are periodically initialized and have the same period and deadline. We use Δ to denote the common deadline of all the jobs in an application. Δ captures the user desired QoS in terms of when the jobs should be finished.

To accomplish the data processing function, each job consists of M pipeline tasks that have task dependencies. Each task is associated with a 4-tuple: $\tau_i = \{VI_i, VO_i, WCET_{i,x}, R_i\}$ where VI_i is the data volume to be processed by task τ_i and VO_i is the size of the output. $WCET_{i,x}$ is the estimated worst-case execution time (WCET) if τ_i is assigned to edge device $E_x, 1 \leq x \leq X$. R_i is the reward of completing τ_i to motivate the edge devices to participate the HeteroEdge framework. The dependencies among the tasks in an application are modeled by a *task dependency graph* defined below.

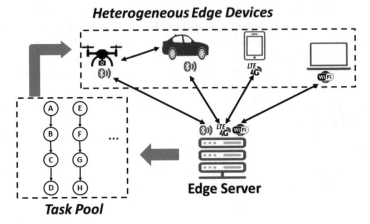

Fig. 4.1 Illustration of SEC with heterogeneous edge devices. The devices are connected via an edge server. A pool of SEC computational tasks are to be assigned to the edge devices

Definition (Task Dependency Graph (G_{task})) A directed graph $G_{task} = (V_{task}, L_{task})$ where vertex $V_i \in V_{task}$ represents task τ_i; link $(\tau_i \rightarrow \tau_j) \in L_{task}$ signifies that the input of task τ_j depends on the output of task τ_i (Fig. 4.1).   □

For a given application, we assume that a total of N tasks (from all Z jobs) are to be processed in each sensing cycle, i.e., $\{\tau_1, \tau_2, \ldots, \tau_N\}$.

To illustrate the task model of SEC, we show an example application called Disaster Damage Assessment (DDA) of SEC where a set of edge devices are tasked to provide reports of the damage severity during a natural disaster (Fig. 4.2). In this application, a job is defined as the inference of the damage severity of a specific location of interest (i.e., location A or B in the figure). Each job can then be broken down into a task pipeline, including (1) collecting the raw image data of the scene (via camera sensors), (2) pre-processing the images, and (3) inferring the severity of the damage from the images. Due to the heterogeneous nature of SEC, a single device may not be capable of processing all tasks in an SEC job. In the above example, a smartphone device that picks Job 2 collects the raw image but cannot efficiently process the image for the final results due to insufficient GPU power. Therefore, it offloads the image to a nearby device (a laptop) for further processing. Under such a scenario, the laptop and the smartphone complement each other and collectively finish an application task that cannot be accomplished by either of them alone (the laptop has no image sensors and the smartphone does not have enough computing power).

We model the communication channels in the edge as a *Communication Graph*:

Definition (Communication Graph G_{com}) An undirected graph $G_{com} = (V_{com}, L_{com})$. V_{com} is the set of all edge devices and the edge server ES. L_{com} defines the communication channels where $(E_x, E_y) \in L_{com}$ denotes E_x and E_y can directly communicate with each other. We also have $(E_x, ES) \in L_{com}, \forall 1 \leq x \leq X$ □

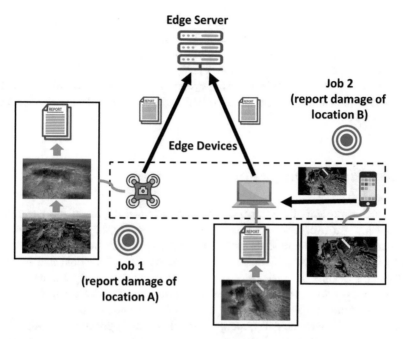

Fig. 4.2 A social edge computing application example: Disaster Damage Assessment (DDA)

Given a set of tasks from SEC application, and a set of heterogeneous edge devices from the end users, the design goal of HeteroEdge is to orchestrate the edge devices in the SEC system to perform sensing and computation tasks in an optimized way that minimizes the End-to-End (E2E) delay of the application and maximizes energy savings of the edge devices. We formally define E2E delay below:

Definition (End-to-end Delay of a Job ($\mathcal{D}_z$)) The total amount of time taken for a unit of sensor measurement data (e.g., a video frame) to be processed by all tasks in J_z. It includes the total computation time of J_z and the total communication overhead.   □

The above objective can be formulated as a multi-objective constrained optimization problem:

$$\text{minimize:} \quad \sum_{x=1}^{X} e_x \text{ (energy minimization objective)}$$

$$\text{minimize:} \quad \mathcal{D}_z, \forall 1 \leq z \leq Z \text{ (application's QoS objective)} \qquad (4.1)$$

$$\text{s.t.:} \quad \mathbf{G}_{task}, \mathbf{G}_{com} \text{ are satisfied}$$

$$\text{(task and communication constraints)}$$

where e_x is the energy consumption of edge device E_x in a sensing cycle.

Finally, we summarize a few additional assumptions we made in our model: (1) we assume edge devices are not malicious (e.g., give fake outputs) or lazy (i.e., intentionally postpone task executions) [22]; (2) we assume edge devices do not quit or join the system within a sensing cycle; (3) we assume end users are willing to provide their computation resource and energy of their devices by receiving incentives [13].

4.2.2   The HeteroEdge Framework

This section presents the system design and technical details of the HeteroEdge framework. An overview of HeteroEdge is given in Fig. 4.3. It consists of three main modules: (1) a runtime abstraction module, (2) a hardware abstraction module, and (3) a task mapping module. The runtime abstraction module and hardware abstraction module abstract away the heterogeneous details of edge devices and provide a uniform resource pool for SEC applications. The task mapping module allocates interdependent application tasks to heterogeneous hardware resources in a way that optimizes the delay-energy tradeoff for the application. We discuss the details of these components below.

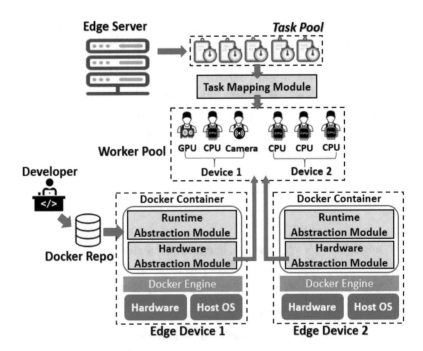

Fig. 4.3 Overview of HeteroEdge architecture

4.2.2.1 Runtime and Hardware Abstraction

A critical issue in heterogeneous SEC is that the devices have different hardware and runtime environments that may not support the application tasks to be processed. For example, a device may have an incompatible operating system or lack the necessary dependencies to execute an SEC algorithm (e.g., a deep learning algorithm cannot run on a device without necessary libraries such as Tensorflow or CUDA). To address this issue, we leverage the Docker containerization technique [16] which is a computer program that performs operating-system-level virtualization. It abstracts away the hardware details of the devices and provides a virtual environment that offers a lightweight, portable and high-performance sandbox to host various applications [14]. In particular, the SEC application developers can "wrap" all necessary dependencies and the OS itself into a Docker container for each SEC application and then upload the container image to a Docker repository. Any edge device that has a Docker engine installed can pull the image from the repository and run the SEC application. Since the Docker container is self-contained, neither the application developers nor the device owners need to worry about its own hardware, OS or runtime environment. The task execution module in HeteroEdge, therefore, allows the edge devices in SEC to provide the same interface to the SEC application developers and offers them the "write once and run anyway" feature despite the heterogeneity of SEC devices.

HeteroEdge further performs hardware-level abstraction of the computing resources available on the edge device by developing a hardware abstraction module. The hardware abstraction module abstracts away the details of heterogeneous hardware specifications from the edge devices. We are inspired by the idea from the Work Queue framework [25] where the hardware capability of a device can be represented as a set of workers. In particular, we consider three types of workers that are essential in finishing application tasks in SEC—CPU, GPU, and Sensor workers. Each worker is associated with a capability descriptor in terms of the estimated WCET of processing application tasks and a visibility flag. We formally define the workers as follows.

Definition (CPU Worker) A CPU worker represents an idle computation thread (we assume one thread per core for simplicity) of an edge device. The number of workers reflects the capability of a device to handle multiple application tasks simultaneously.   □

Definition (GPU Worker) A GPU worker represents an idle GPU of an edge device.   □

Definition (Sensor Worker) A sensor worker represents an available sensor on an edge device. The sensor worker has various types e.g., GPS/ Video/ Camera/ Accelerometer.   □

The workers of an edge device jointly define the context of the device at any given time. We assume the edge devices have constantly changing sets of workers as the system runs or when the users change their system configurations. An example worker pool of a device E_1 at a sensing cycle is {1, CPU, visible, *Alg1*: 500 ms, *Alg2*: 1500 ms}, {1, GPU, invisible, Alg1: 500 ms, Alg2: 100 ms}, {1, Sensor-Camera, visible, *Sens*: 10 ms}, {1, Sensor-GPS, visible, NA}, where *Sens*, *Alg1* and *Alg2* are the task pipelines of an SEC job. The *visible* and *invisible* are the flags set by users to denote their willingness to disclose the worker to the application.

The benefits of the hardware abstraction module are threefold: (1) the set of heterogeneous edge devices form a unified homogeneous worker pool for the SEC application by mapping the devices to workers; (2) the end users can register and control the workers they would like to provide for a particular SEC application in a way that preserves their privacy; (3) the edge devices can easily keep track of their own dynamic status and provide necessary context information for the runtime decision and optimization in SEC.

4.2.2.2 Supply Chain-Based Resource Management

The above runtime and hardware abstraction modules are designed to provide a "homogeneous" resource pool and execution interface to the SEC application. However, performing task mapping in SEC is still challenging because (1) tasks are heterogeneous and have complex execution requirements (e.g., sensing tasks can only be done on devices with compatible sensors and computational tasks may require specific computational resources such as a GPU); (2) the computing resources in our model are also heterogeneous (e.g., some devices have sensors while others do not; some devices are equipped with GPU while others are not); (3) various task allocation strategies may yield complex tradeoffs between energy cost and delay overhead.

To this end, we develop our supply chain based task mapping model to address the above challenges. In order to adapt the supply chain model to solve the task mapping problem, we develop several novel technical components. In particular, we present a novel *supply chain graph mapping* technique and a *node decomposition* component to jointly model the heterogeneous tasks, computing resources, and the tradeoff between energy and delay using a directed supply chain graph. The combination of the two techniques reduced the complex problem of finding the optimal task mapping strategy that optimizes the delay-energy tradeoff to finding the shortest path in the supply chain graph. We also design a new game-theoretic selfish routing algorithm to find the optimal task mapping strategy with a bounded performance guarantee. We elaborate these components in detail below.

Supply Chain Graph Mapping Our solution is motivated by the observation of an interesting mapping between our problem and the *supply chain* model in economics. The supply chain problem involves the transformation of natural resources, raw materials, and components into a finished product that is delivered to the end customer. To become the end product, the raw material has to be transported and processed at different factories/facilities with different capabilities (e.g., sourcing, manufacturing, packaging, assembly). In HeteroEdge, we consider the raw sensing measurements as "raw material" and the sensing devices as the "suppliers" of the raw material. The raw material has to be processed through a set of factories (i.e., edge devices) to become the final product (i.e., the end results). We refer to the series of factories/devices that the raw material travels through till reaching the consumer as a *supply chain path*. The factories have to work collaboratively by sending the processed material to one another for further processing. The edge server can be considered as the "consumer" of the final product. In particular, the chain of raw sensing data $\rightarrow$ computation nodes $\rightarrow$ edge server is an exact mapping of raw material $\rightarrow$ factories $\rightarrow$ consumer in the supply chain model.

Formally, we can map the task mapping problem into a *supply chain graph* $G_{sc} = (V_{sc}, L_{sc})$. The supply chain graph consists of a set of "device nodes" that represent the heterogeneous edge devices. Each device node is associated with the computation delay and energy cost for processing the tasks. Besides the device nodes, we also add some "source nodes" and a "destination node". The source nodes represent the locations that "supply" the raw sensing data decided by the SEC application. The destination node represents the edge server who receives the end results (i.e., the consumer of the supply chain). We also define a set of links to represent the communication channels between edge devices. A link $l \in L_{sc}$ is associated with a transmission delay and energy cost.

An example of a supply chain graph is illustrated in Fig. 4.4. It involves an SEC job of three tasks (one sensing task, two computation tasks) and three edge devices. The device capability table shows the tasks the edge devices can execute. To model the task dependency, we divide the supply chain into multiple stages. At each stage, we list all the devices that can execute the corresponding task. For example, stage 1 represents the "sensing task" to collect raw data from two locations. All devices are listed because device A is able to collect data from location 1 and devices B and C are capable of collecting data from location 2. In the next stage, devices B and C can perform the computation task (A1). In the final stage, device C can perform the final

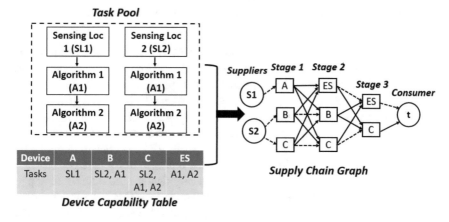

Fig. 4.4 Supply chain graph setup for HeteroEdge

task (A2). Note that the edge server ES is added to all stages of computation tasks because the edge devices can always choose to offload the computation tasks to the edge server. We use dashed lines to represent "no cost" link (e.g., communication on the same device) and use solid lines to represent a communication associated with delay and energy cost.

Given the supply chain graph, our goal is to find the best route (i.e., supply chain path) from each source to the destination that minimizes overall delay and energy consumption. Let P_z denote a supply chain path from a source node s_z to the destination node t. π_z is the total cost of P_z (including the delay and energy cost during data transmission and processing on the device nodes of P_z). The goal is to find:

$$\underset{P_z}{\text{argmin}} \ \pi_z, \forall 1 \leq z \leq Z \qquad (4.2)$$

To solve the objective function above, we perform (1) a node decomposition that unifies the *computation* cost and the *data transmission* cost of the links. This step translates the supply chain problem into a multi-source shortest-path problem; (2) a selfish routing algorithm that allows jobs to selfishly pick their paths to solve the multi-source shortest-path problem.

Node Decomposition For the supply chain graph problem shown in Fig. 4.4, the goal of the task mapping is to find the optimal path (with minimal delay and energy cost) for suppliers s_1 and s_2. To solve this problem, we first transform the supply chain graph into a uniform graph by associating all the cost with the links and expanding the device nodes to model the heterogeneous workers of the devices. The transformation considers the following scenarios.

Device with a Single CPU Worker We transform a device node into two virtual nodes: v^{IN} denotes the "entry" of a factory (edge device) and v^{OUT} denotes the "exit". We create a "virtual link" between v^{IN} and v^{OUT} and the link is associated with the delay and energy cost of performing a task on the CPU worker. The node decomposition of this scenario is illustrated in Fig. 4.5.

Device with Multiple CPU Workers Multiple CPU workers represent the multi-threading capability of an edge device, which adds more complexities to modeling the energy cost. We use a linear energy model *power* = *base energy* + *extra energy consumption* × *# of threads* [1] where the *base energy* represents the default energy consumption of a CPU independent of the number of cores being used. To model this, we introduce an extra intermediate virtual node v^{MID} in addition to v^{IN} and v^{OUT}. The link from v^{IN} to v^{MID} is created to model the base energy consumption (with no delay). This link also has a *capacity* l^{cap} that is equal to the number of cores. The link capacity denotes the number of supply chain paths that can go through the link simultaneously without causing any extra base energy cost. For example, a three-core device has the capacity of 3 where three tasks can be run on the device at the same time with only 1 unit of base energy

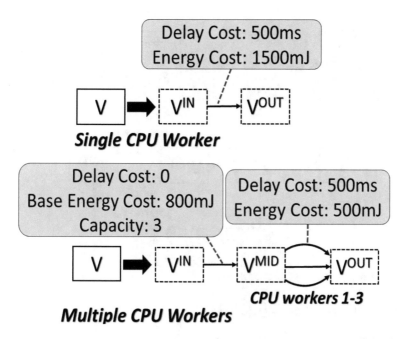

Fig. 4.5 Node decomposition scenario—without GPU

consumption plus three extra units per worker energy consumption. We also created virtual links from v^{MID} to v^{OUT} and the number of the virtual links is the same as the number of workers of the edge device v. Multiple virtual links mean the device can handle multiple tasks at the same time. The node decomposition of this scenario is illustrated in Fig. 4.5.

Device with a GPU Worker The node decomposition for a device with a GPU and 3 CPU cores is illustrated in Fig. 4.6. Note that in many scenarios, a GPU requires at least one extra CPU core to run programs [9]. Therefore, we dedicate one CPU worker to the device with the GPU worker while the rest of the CPU workers can process other tasks.

After the above node decomposition, our problem becomes a multi-source shortest path problem where the goal is to find the best supply chain path from the source to the destination that minimizes the cost of the *links* on the path. In particular, a supply chain path P_z consists of a set of links where each link $l \in P_z$ is associated with two types of cost: delay and energy consumption.

For simplicity, we use π_l^{delay} to denote the delay cost of a link l, and π_l^{energy} to denote the energy cost of l. Then we have the objective:

$$\text{minimize:}\quad \sum^{l \in P_z} \pi_l^{energy} + \lambda \times \pi_l^{delay}, \forall 1 \leq z \leq Z \qquad (4.3)$$

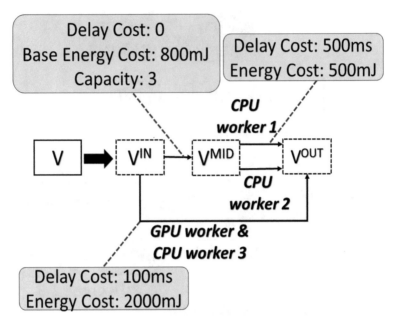

Fig. 4.6 Node decomposition scenario—with GPU

where λ is a scalar to tune the importance of energy consumption of edge devices versus the overall delay of the application.

One issue with the above objective is that the minimization of energy cost depends heavily on the energy profile of the edge devices and tends to be unfair to low-power devices. For example, consider a scenario where the edge is composed of a low-power mobile device (e.g., 5 W) and a high-power laptop (e.g., 300 W). The above objective function will try to push as many computation tasks as possible to the mobile devices to save energy on the laptop, creating an undesirable situation for mobile phone users. To address this issue, we normalize the energy consumption as follows:

$$normalized(e_x) = \frac{e_x}{power_{max} \times \Delta}, 1 \leq x \leq X \qquad (4.4)$$

where e_x is the energy consumption of a device E_x in a sensing cycle with the length of Δ and $power_{x,max}$ denotes the maximum power consumption of the device.

A Selfish Routing Algorithm for Optimal Supply Chain The objective in Eq. (4.3) is a non-trivial problem. Intuitively, each supplier (i.e., job) can selfishly pick a path that minimizes its own cost. However, the path can be congested if both suppliers pick the same route, which would introduce extra delay and energy cost. We develop a new Supply Chain Selfish Routing (SCSR) scheme to solve this problem. The SCSR scheme is based on a game-theoretic framework that allows each job to selfishly pick the route to maximize its own utility while taking into account the other players' strategies. The benefits of the SCSR scheme are threefold: (1) it is simple and effective; (2) it provides the theoretical guarantee on the convergence and execution overhead, which is crucial for delay-sensitive applications; (3) it can nicely coordinate a large number of tasks to simultaneously identify the optimal devices for execution. We first define a few terms in SCSR.

Let $\mathcal{P} = \{P_1, P_2, \ldots P_Z\}$ denote the supply chain paths of all jobs and P_z is the task mapping strategy (i.e., supply chain path) for job J_z. We use P_{-z} to denote the strategies picked by all jobs other than J_z. For the job J_z, we define a weight w_z to represent its workload which is assumed to be proportional to the size of the raw sensing data. We also define $d(l), l \in \mathbf{L}_{sc}$ as all the jobs that pick link l in their strategies. From $d(l)$, we define the *weighted congestion rate* $\mathcal{N}(l)$ of l as the sum of weights of all paths in $d(l)$, i.e., $\mathcal{N}(l) = \sum^{z \in d(l)} (w_z - (l^{cap} - 1))$. The *utility* of a strategy P_z can then be calculated as:

$$u_z(P_z) = \sum_{}^{l \in P_z} \sum_{}^{z \in d(l)} (w_z - l^{cap} + 1) \times (\pi_l^{energy} + \lambda \times \pi_l^{delay}) \tag{4.5}$$

Based on the utility function, we say a job is *satisfied* with its path if it cannot further decrease the cost by ϵ through the unilateral change of its path from P_z, i.e., $u_z(P_z) \leq u_z(P_z') + \epsilon$. If every job is *satisfied*, we say a ϵ-Nash Equilibrium is reached. When $\epsilon = 0$, the equilibrium is referred to as Pure Nash Equilibrium (PNE). The Nash Equilibrium can be found using a greedy algorithm based on the Best Response Dynamics [15]. We summarize the algorithm in Algorithm 1.

SCSR is an iterative algorithm and the quick convergence is critical for delay-sensitive SEC applications. In this subsection, we derive the upper bound of the iterations till convergence and prove SCSR converges to PNE in polynomial time. We first map SCSR into an *atomic network congestion game* where each link has the same cost. This can be achieved by breaking a link $l \in \mathbf{L}_{sc}$ into multiple sub-links where each sub-link $l' \in l$ has a unit cost. For example, assuming the original link cost has a maximum normalized cost of K, and a unit cost of 1. Then the cost can be normalized as K+1 integer values, i.e., [0, 1, 2, ... K], the link can be broken into at most K sub-links.

It is known that in the atomic network congestion game, a *potential function* exists according to [17]:

$$\Phi(\mathcal{P}) = \sum_{}^{l' \in \mathbf{L}_{sc}} \mathcal{N}(l') + \sum_{z=1}^{Z} w_z \times \sum_{}^{l' \in P_z} w_z \tag{4.6}$$

and the potential function has the following property:

$$\Phi(P_z, P_{-z}) - \Phi(P_z', P_{-z}) = 2 \times w_z \times (u_z(P_z) - u_z(P_z')) \tag{4.7}$$

Algorithm 1 SCSR Algorithm

Require: Supply Chain Graph $\mathbf{G}_{sc}$, ϵ
Ensure: Supply chain for all jobs, i.e., $P_1, P_2 \ldots, P_Z$
1: **function** SCSR($\mathbf{G}_{sc}$)
2:     Perform node decomposition, get transformed graph $\mathbf{G}'_{sc}$
3:     **Initialize:** $convergence = False$, $\mathcal{P} = NewArray[Z]$, $\mathcal{P}' = NewArray[Z]$
4:     **for all** $z \in [1, Z]$ **do**
5:         Randomly set initial strategy P_z for J_z
6:         $\mathcal{P}[z] = P[z]$, $\mathcal{P}'[z] = P[z]$
7:     **end for**
8:     **while** $converge == False$ **do**
9:         **for all** $z \in [1, Z]$ **do**
10:             run $P'_z = ShortestPath(s_z, t, \mathbf{G}'_{sc})$ for J_z
11:             **if** $u_z(P'_z) - u_z(p_z) > \epsilon$ **then**
12:                 $\mathcal{P}'[z] = P'_z$
13:             **end if**
14:         **end for**
15:         **if** $\mathcal{P}' == \mathcal{P}$ **then**
16:             Return $\mathcal{P}$
17:         **end if**
18:         $\mathcal{P} = \mathcal{P}'$
19:     **end while**
20: **end function**

In game theory, the potential function decreases each time a job makes an improvement step, namely switching to another strategy to improve its utilization (i.e., line 10–12 in Algorithm 1). The above property shows that every time a job makes an improvement step of ϵ by changing from P_z to P'_z, the potential function decreases by $2 \times w_z \times \epsilon$. We prove the convergence and upper bound of SCSR algorithm as follows.

Theorem *The SCSR algorithm converges to ϵ-Nash Equilibrium in polynomial time and bounded by $O(\frac{M \times K \times n^{2C}}{\epsilon})$, where C is a constant.*

Proof Note that in Eq. (4.6), we have

$$\Phi(\mathcal{P}) \leq M \times K \times (w^{max})^2, \forall z \in [1, Z] \tag{4.8}$$

where w_z^{max} is the maximum of w_z, $1 \leq z \leq Z$. Suppose that $w_z^{max}/w_z^{min} = O(n^C)$, where w_z^{min} is the minimum of w_z, $1 \leq z \leq Z$. We have the potential function $\Phi(\mathcal{P})$ takes at most $O(\frac{M \times K \times n^{2C}}{\epsilon})$ steps to become zero. Hence the SCSR algorithm requires at most $O(\frac{M \times K \times n^{2C}}{\epsilon})$ steps to converge to Nash Equilibrium.

$\square$

The above proof shows the efficiency of the SCSR algorithm. Note that ϵ is a key parameter that affects the convergence time of the SCSR algorithm. The selection of ϵ really depends on the size of the participation pool and the nature of the application: it controls the tradeoff between the optimality of the task mapping and the efficiency of SCSR algorithm. In our experiment, we chose ϵ pragmatically that gives the best delay. We provide a more detailed analysis of the convergence and scalability of the SCSR algorithm w.r.t ϵ in Sect. 4.3.

4.3   Real-World Case Studies

In this section, we present an extensive evaluation of HeteroEdge on a real-world edge computing test platform. We implement the HeteroEdge framework on a real-world SEC platform that consists of a set of 10 edge devices and 1 local edge server. In particular, we use a PC workstation with Intel E5-2600 V4 processor and 16GB of DDR4 memory as the local edge server. The edge consists of 10 heterogeneous devices: 2 Jetson TX2 and 2 Jetson TK1 boards from Nvidia (commonly used in portable computers, UAVs, and autonomous vehicles), and 5 Raspberry Pi3 Model B boards, and 1 personal computer. Figure 4.7 shows the implemented hardware platform for the edge devices. These edge devices represent different system architectures, operating systems and hardware capabilities. All devices and the edge server are connected via a local wireless router. The HeteroEdge system was implemented using Python. We leverage TCP socket programming for reliable data communication among edge devices.

Baseline   The proposed HeteroEdge framework is compared against the following representative baselines: (1) a random assignment scheme (**Rand**) where the social computing tasks are randomly assigned to edge devices, (2) A greedy shortest path (**GSP**) resource allocation scheme where each job greedily picks the shortest path of the supply chain graph to minimize the energy and delay cost [8]; (3) a centralized resource management scheme (**CES**) where an edge device sends all its computation

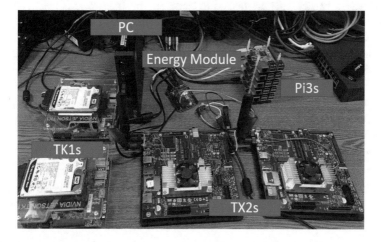

Fig. 4.7 Heterogeneous edge computing testbed

Fig. 4.8 Power monitoring module

tasks to the local edge server [20]; and the game-theoretic edge computing resource allocation scheme (**BGTA**) for non-cooperative edge devices [22].

Energy Measurement Monitoring energy expenditure is a critical performance benchmark in our evaluation. To measure the energy consumption, we used an INA219 Current Sensor IC, as shown in Fig. 4.8, interfaced to an Arduino Uno Micro-controller board via I^2C bus. The mechanism of power calculation in the INA219 involves measuring the voltage drop U_{sense} across a sense resistor connected in series to the main power rail of the device whose energy consumption is to be monitored. The INA219 amplifies the voltage drop U_{sense}, converts the analog reading to digital using an on-board ADC and computes the power consumption at any given instant P_{load} as $P_{load} = \frac{U_{sense}}{R_{sense}} \times U_{load}$ where U_{load} is the main bus voltage and R_{sense} is the electrical resistance of the sense resistor.

We evaluate HeteroEdge on a real-world usecase of *Disaster Damage Assessment (DDA)* where participants are tasked to sense and evaluate whether damages (e.g., potholes and collapsed houses caused by an earthquake) have happened and to what extent to the assigned locations during a natural disaster. The output of this application offers real-time situation awareness and timely alerts to citizens in the affected areas of disasters.

We collected 2000 images related to the Ecuador Earthquake in 2016 from Instagram and Twitter. We run the application over 100 sensing cycles. The images are organized by the timestamp and are split into 100 subsets and each of which is processed in a sensing cycle. The SEC jobs in this application consist of 3 pipeline tasks summarized below.

Tasks for DDA (1) edge devices equipped with cameras (e.g., dashcams, UAVs) are tasked to capture live images of locations of interest; (2) extracting Damage Detection Map (DDM) features using Convolutional Neural Network (CNN) model from raw images; (3) assessing the damage severity from DDM using the algorithm in [11].

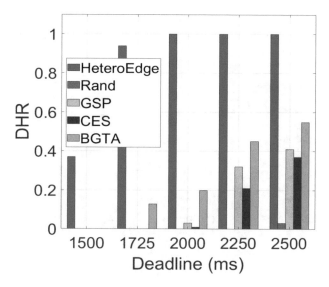

Fig. 4.9 Deadline hit rate in DDA

Quality of Service In the first set of experiments, we focus on how the objective is achieved from the application side. In particular, we evaluate the deadline hit rate (DHR) and end-to-end (E2E) delay of all the compared schemes. The DHR is defined as the ratio of tasks that are completed within the deadline. The results are shown in Fig. 4.9. We use all 10 edge devices and gradually increase the deadline constraints. We observe that HeteroEdge has significantly higher DHRs than all the baselines and is the first one that reaches 100% DHR as the deadline increases. We attribute such performance gain to our SCSR algorithm that finds the optimal "supply chain path" that allows the edge devices to search for the most efficient way to collaboratively finish SEC jobs.

Figure 4.10 summarizes the E2E delays of all the schemes as the number of jobs varies. We show both the average delay and the 90% confidence bounds of the results. We observe that our HeteroEdge scheme has the least E2E delay and tightest confidence bounds compared to the baselines. The results further demonstrate the effectiveness of HeteroEdge for meeting real-time QoS requirements of the application. The performance gain of the HeteroEdge is achieved by explicitly modeling the dynamic context of the edge devices (i.e., the dynamic worker pool) and allocating tasks according to the current device status.

We found HeteroEdge outperforms CES in the above experiments. This is because the CES encountered a significant transmission delay by offloading the raw sensing data from edge devices to the server. Such data transmission delay is independent of the computing power available at the server. In contrast, HeteroEdge performs the computation tasks on the edge devices where the data is collected. Therefore, HeteroEdge does not require significant resource provisioning on dedicated servers to outperform the centralized solution. Instead, it achieves a better QoS

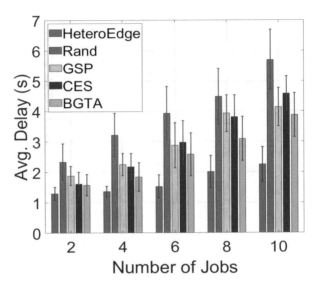

Fig. 4.10 E2E delay in DDA

performance of the applications by fully exploring the massive computing power of the privately owned IoT devices at the edge.

Energy Consumption In the second set of experiments, we focus on the energy consumption of edge devices. As mentioned in Sect. 4.2.2.2, the energy consumption is normalized to reflect the proportion of battery that is consumed by a scheme to accomplish all SEC jobs. The reason for this normalization is to avoid the unfair scenario where minimizing the absolute energy would end up with a strategy that always pushes heavy computation from high-power devices to low-power ones. The results of the average normalized energy consumption on edge devices are shown in Table 4.1. We use all 10 edge devices and set the number of jobs to 10 and deadline to 3 s. We can observe that HeteroEdge consumes significantly less energy as compared to all other baselines except CES. CES consumes the least amount of energy on every edge device because it simply pushes all the computation tasks to the local edge server. In another word, the CES scheme under-utilizes the diverse resources on the edge devices and pushes the extra burden to the server. The results illustrate that the edge devices can achieve the longest battery life under HeteroEdge, which is particularly important for edge devices with limited power supply.

Convergence and Scalability Finally, we study the convergence and computation overhead of the resource management scheme (i.e., SCSR) in HeteroEdge. We set $K = 1$ and the unit cost as 0.1 to normalize the link costs. Figure 4.11 shows the average number of iterations of SCSR till convergence when we change the number

Table 4.1 Normalized energy consumption in DDA

	HeteroEdge	RAND	GSP	CES	BGTA
Jetson TX2	0.913	0.915	0.897	0.572	0.901
Jetson TK1	0.824	0.985	0.904	0.754	0.877
Raspberry Pi3	0.613	0.952	0.803	0.589	0.724
PC	0.798	0.844	0.831	0.766	0.825
All	7.337	9.404	8.448	6.363	8.001

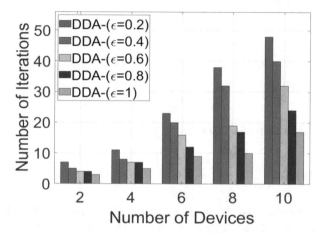

Fig. 4.11 Convergence of SCSR

of devices. We observe that the number of iterations significantly decreases as the ϵ value increases. Here ϵ controls how likely a player would change its strategy. The lower value is, the more likely a player is going to change its strategy in the game, which often requires more iterations for the algorithm to reach the convergence. The curves also show a linear trend as the number of devices increases.

Figure 4.12 shows the execution time of SCSR. The execution time includes the running time of the SCSR algorithm as well as the communication delay between the edge servers and the edge devices. We observe the execution time of SCSR grows almost linearly as the number of edge devices increases. The above results again demonstrate the suitability of using HeteroEdge for delay-sensitive SEC applications. We note that the execution time of the SCSR scheme might still become a non-trivial overhead when the number of edge devices in the system becomes very large. A possible solution to such a scalability problem is to increase the number of local edge servers and run HeteroEdge in the cluster of edge devices coordinated by the same local edge server. This solution is practical in real-world applications thanks to the increasingly popular hierarchical structure of edge computing systems [10].

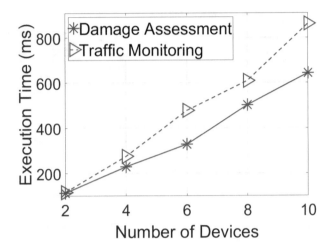

Fig. 4.12 Execution overhead of SCSR

4.4 Discussion

This chapter presents the HeteroEdge framework to address three fundamental challenges in taming the heterogeneity issue in SEC systems. We have implemented our framework on a real-world edge computing testbed including Nvidia Jetson TK1, TX2, Raspberry Pi3 boards, and personal computers. The evaluation results demonstrate that HeteroEdge achieves significant performance gains compared to state-of-the-art baselines.

Our work has some limitations that deserve further investigation. First, HeteroEdge entails security concerns. In particular, we assume that edge devices are not malicious and they follow the game protocol honestly (e.g., they will not quit abruptly or intentionally delay the execution). However, this assumption may not hold in scenarios where malicious devices do exist: (1) they may intentionally generate fake results; (2) they delay the task execution arbitrarily, making it miss its deadline. The first issue can be addressed by combining HeteroEdge with the verifiable computing techniques where the system maintains verifiable results by requiring a "proof" of the correct execution of tasks [5]. The second issue can be mitigated by adding an extra function in HeteroEdge to keep track of the normal behaviors of edge devices and actively block the identified lazy devices.

Moreover, HeteroEdge is a soft real-time task allocation scheme that minimizes the delay of the system instead of providing the hard deadline guarantee. This is due to several factors. First, the worst-case estimation of the task execution time is not precise due to the complicated computing and communication environment in SEC systems. Second, the convergence time of the Nash Equilibrium solution is also dynamic and hard to be predicted precisely. In the future, we plan to explore more sophisticated execution time prediction schemes (e.g., static program analysis [7] and narrow spectrum benchmarking [18]) and schedule schemes in HeteroEdge.

References

1. D. Bautista, J. Sahuquillo, H. Hassan, S. Petit, J. Duato, A simple power-aware scheduling for multicore systems when running real-time applications, in *IEEE International Symposium on Parallel and Distributed Processing, 2008 (IPDPS 2008)* (IEEE, 2008), pp. 1–7

2. J. Cao, L. Xu, R. Abdallah, W. Shi, Edgeos_h: a home operating system for internet of everything, in *2017 IEEE 37th International Conference on Distributed Computing Systems (ICDCS)* (IEEE, 2017), pp. 1756–1764

3. M. Curtin, Write once, run anywhere: why it matters. *Technical Article* (1998). http://java.sun.com/features/1998/01/wo

4. W. Gao, Opportunistic peer-to-peer mobile cloud computing at the tactical edge, in *2014 IEEE Military Communications Conference (MILCOM)* (IEEE, 2014), pp. 1614–1620

5. R. Gennaro, C. Gentry, B. Parno, Non-interactive verifiable computing: Outsourcing computation to untrusted workers, in *Annual Cryptology Conference* (Springer, Berlin, 2010), pp. 465–482.

6. K. Habak, M. Ammar, K.A. Harras, E. Zegura, Femto clouds: leveraging mobile devices to provide cloud service at the edge, in *2015 IEEE 8th International Conference on Cloud Computing (CLOUD)* (IEEE, 2015), pp. 9–16

7. R. Heckmann, C. Ferdinand, Worst-case execution time prediction by static program analysis, in *In 18th International Parallel and Distributed Processing Symposium (IPDPS 2004)* (IEEE Computer Society, 2004), pp. 26–30

8. S. Irnich, G. Desaulniers, Shortest path problems with resource constraints, in *Column Generation* (Springer, Berlin, 2005), pp. 33–65

9. A. Kerr, G. Diamos, S. Yalamanchili, Modeling gpu-cpu workloads and systems, in *Proceedings of the 3rd Workshop on General-Purpose Computation on Graphics Processing Units* (ACM, 2010), pp. 31–42

10. A. Kiani, N. Ansari, Toward hierarchical mobile edge computing: An auction-based profit maximization approach. IEEE Internet Things J. **4**(6), 2082–2091 (2017)

11. X. Li, D. Caragea, H. Zhang, M. Imran, Localizing and quantifying damage in social media images, in *2018 IEEE/ACM International Conference on Advances in Social Networks Analysis and Mining (ASONAM)* (IEEE, 2018)

12. M.J. Litzkow, M. Livny, M.W. Mutka, Condor-a hunter of idle workstations, in *8th International Conference on Distributed Computing Systems, 1988* (IEEE, 1988), pp. 104–111

13. Y. Liu, C. Xu, Y. Zhan, Z. Liu, J. Guan, H. Zhang, Incentive mechanism for computation offloading using edge computing: a stackelberg game approach. Comput. Netw. **129**, 399–409 (2017)

14. L. Ma, S. Yi, Q. Li, Efficient service handoff across edge servers via docker container migration, in *Proceedings of the Second ACM/IEEE Symposium on Edge Computing* (ACM, 2017), p. 11

15. A. Matsui, Best response dynamics and socially stable strategies. J. Econ. Theory **57**(2), 343–362 (1992)

16. D. Merkel, Docker: lightweight linux containers for consistent development and deployment. Linux J. **2014**(239), 2 (2014)

17. P.N. Panagopoulou, P.G. Spirakis, Efficient convergence to pure nash equilibria in weighted network congestion games, in *International Workshop on Experimental and Efficient Algorithms* (Springer, Berlin, 2005), pp. 203–215

18. R.H. Saavedra-Barrera, *CPU Performance Evaluation and Execution Time Prediction Using Narrow Spectrum Benchmarking*. Ph.D Thesis, University of California, Berkeley, 1992

19. Z. Sanaei, S. Abolfazli, A. Gani, R. Buyya, Heterogeneity in mobile cloud computing: taxonomy and open challenges. IEEE Commun. Surv. Tutorials **16**(1), 369–392 (2014)

20. M. Satyanarayanan, P. Bahl, R. Caceres, N. Davies, The case for vm-based cloudlets in mobile computing. IEEE Pervasive Comput. **8**(4) (2009)

21. C. Shen, M. Srivastava, Exploring hardware heterogeneity to improve pervasive context inferences. Computer **50**(6), 19–26 (2017)
22. D.Y. Zhang, Y. Ma, Y. Zhang, S. Lin, X.S. Hu, D. Wang, A real-time and non-cooperative task allocation framework for social sensing applications in edge computing systems, in *2018 IEEE Real-Time and Embedded Technology and Applications Symposium (RTAS)* (IEEE, 2018), pp. 316–326
23. D.Y. Zhang, Y. Ma, C. Zheng, Y. Zhang, X.S. Hu, D. Wang, Cooperative-competitive task allocation in edge computing for delay-sensitive social sensing, in *2018 IEEE/ACM Symposium on Edge Computing (SEC)* (IEEE, 2018), pp. 243–259
24. D.Y. Zhang, T. Rashid, X. Li, N. Vance, D. Wang, Heteroedge: Taming the heterogeneity of edge computing system in social sensing, in *Proceedings of the International Conference on Internet of Things Design and Implementation (IoTDI)* (ACM, 2019), pp. 37–48. https://doi.org/10.1145/3302505.3310067
25. C. Zheng, D. Thain, Integrating containers into workflows: A case study using makeflow, work queue, and docker, in *Proceedings of the 8th International Workshop on Virtualization Technologies in Distributed Computing* (ACM, 2015), pp. 31–38

Chapter 5
Real-Time AI in Social Edge

Abstract In previous chapters, we have presented several edge computing frameworks that address the rationality and heterogeneity challenges in the SEC paradigm. In this chapter, we shift our focus to real-time AI in the social edge that investigates the challenge of building time-sensitive AI models in SEC. In particular, we focus on a widely adopted AI model—deep neural networks (DNN), and review a novel optimal batching algorithm called EdgeBatch that can fully utilize the data parallelization feature of DNN to significantly expedite the execution time of DNN-based AI models at the edge. EdgeBatch represents a line of research that addresses the emerging challenges at the intersection of real-time and AI communities.

5.1 The Real-Time Social Edge

Intelligent applications in SEC are enabled by the recent development of deep neural networks, which have made breakthroughs in various application domains such as natural language understanding, computer vision, and virtual reality. Pushing intelligence to the edge devices is a major challenge because DNNs were originally designed for advanced hardware (e.g., GPU clusters) and are not suitable for resource-constrained edge devices deployed at the edge of the network [3, 16, 34, 48]. Moreover, running DNN algorithms often incurs a high energy cost, which may rapidly drain the batteries of edge devices [27]. To address this challenge, many software and hardware-based approaches have been developed. Mainstream techniques include (1) neural network compression that reduces the size and computational complexity of the DNNs [12], (2) dedicated equipment with on-board hardware such as AI Chips and powerful GPUs that are specialized for DNN tasks (e.g., AWS DeepLens [2]), and (3) innovative software accelerators that increase the energy efficiency and speed for DNN execution (e.g., DeepX [15]).

A key knowledge gap of the above solutions lies in the fact that existing approaches focus on facilitating DNNs on a *single edge device* and ignore the opportunities to optimize the performance of DNNs collectively in a social edge environment that consists of a diverse set of heterogeneous edge devices connected via network. In contrast, EdgeBatch develops a novel resource management approach where edge devices can offload deep learning tasks to each other and finish them collaboratively. For example, consider a social edge application where drivers use their edge devices (e.g., smartphones, dashcams, unmanned aerial vehicles (UAVs)) to collaboratively detect the plate number of a suspect's vehicle using deep neural network object detection algorithms [41]. In our solution, lower-edge devices (e.g., a dashboard camera) can offload complex object detection tasks to high-edge devices (e.g., a UAV with a GPU on board). Such collaboration in social edge allows edge devices to fully explore the available computing power at the edge to execute DNN tasks.

A few recent efforts have been made to facilitate the collaboration of privately owned edge devices through innovative task allocation [11, 40] and incentive design [13, 44]. However, they only focus on CPU-intensive tasks and ignore the unique execution model of GPU-intensive DNN tasks. The GPU execution model features *data parallelism*, which allows multiple DNN tasks to be processed together (referred to as "batching") and reduces the average execution time for each task [8].

In this section, we focus on a novel *optimal task batching* problem in social edge computing, where the goal is to identify the optimal batch size (i.e., the number of tasks to be processed in parallel) when the DNN tasks are processed on the GPUs of edge devices. While batching problems have been studied extensively in traditional real-time systems [20, 32], the optimal batching of DNN tasks in social edge raises several new technical challenges.

The first challenge lies in the complex tradeoff of delay and energy that is directly affected by the task batching strategy. In a single node scenario, batching can significantly save the processing time of DNN tasks through parallel computing but causes extra power consumption. Such tradeoff is more complex in a distributed social edge where the delay includes not only the processing time of the DNN tasks, but also the unpredictable task waiting time as well as data offloading overhead. We illustrate this tradeoff through an example in Fig. 5.1. Batching Strategy 1 (top) uses a batch size of 2 tasks, and Batching Strategy 2 (bottom) uses a batch size of 6 tasks. We first discuss the tradeoff between delay and batch size. We observe that a larger batch size will reduce the average processing time of a task but increase the total task waiting time (e.g., in Strategy 2, task A will have to wait until task F arrives before being processed). In contrast, a smaller batch size will lead to less waiting time but yield a higher execution time for each task due to the underutilization of the GPU [8]. A similar tradeoff is observed on the energy aspect as well. For example, a larger batch size would lead to a longer idle period where GPU is in a low-power state. However, the processing power of GPU will become higher due to its increased utilization caused by the larger batch of data being processed [35]. It becomes more difficult to analyze the above tradeoffs in the social edge where the edge devices are often heterogeneous in terms of processing capabilities and energy profile [44, 45]. It is therefore a challenging task to identify the optimal batch size that can achieve a desirable balance between the delay and energy requirements of DNN applications at the social edge.

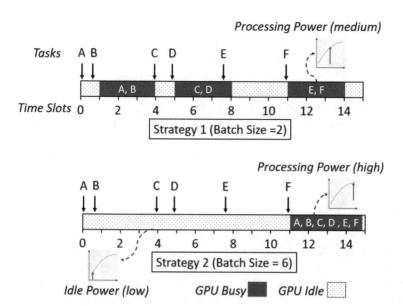

Fig. 5.1 Delay and energy tradeoff of varying batch sizes

The second challenge lies in the uncertainty of the task arrival time at the social edge. Existing work in task batching either assumes the task release time or task period is known *a priori* [32] or assumes the task arrival time follows a certain distribution or pattern [33]. In contrast, our model assumes the task release time is unpredictable and the tasks can arrive at an edge device at random times, thus making the task batching problem significantly more challenging. The rationale behind our assumption is twofold: (1) the DNN tasks are released whenever new sensing measurements are collected, which is unknown in many social edge applications; and (2) the networking environment (e.g., the queue size, available bandwidth, router status, signal strength) is dynamically changing and the data transmission time cannot be precisely estimated at the social edge. Consider the plate detection application where drivers can take a picture of a car at any moment. When the image processing tasks are offloaded over the network, the transmission time depends on the signal strength and the network traffic, both of which are hard to predict.

The third challenge lies in the fact that both edge devices and the application server lack the global knowledge of the system status. In a distributed system like social edge, locally optimal task batching decisions may not necessarily be globally optimal. Consider a social edge scenario that incorporates heterogeneous edge devices. These edge devices can have very different architectures, energy profiles, and computing capabilities. In principle, it is ideal to allocate more tasks to devices that have abundant GPU resources (e.g., a nearby UAV that is not actively using its GPU) so that the devices can efficiently perform task batching without an excessive waiting time. However, such a control mechanism requires the global knowledge of system information (e.g., the hardware specifications, the GPU utilization, the remaining battery of each device) and the centralized control of all devices in the system. Unfortunately, the edge devices in social edge are often owned by individuals who may not be willing to share the status information of their devices with the application or other users due to various concerns (e.g., privacy, energy, bandwidth) [43]. Therefore, an edge device in social edge has full information about its own status but limited information about others. This asymmetric information trait of the social edge makes the optimal task batching decisions over heterogeneous edge devices a challenging task to accomplish.

5.2   A Real-Time Optimal Edge Batching System: EdgeBatch

In this section, we present a new collaborative social edge framework called EdgeBatch to jointly address the above challenges [46]. In particular, to address the first two challenges, EdgeBatch develops a new task batching solution that can identify the optimal batch size for GPU-intensive DNN tasks to optimize the tradeoff between the end-to-end delay of tasks and the energy consumption for edge devices. To address the third challenge, EdgeBatch develops a novel supply chain based task offloading scheme that can effectively moderate the collaboration among edge devices in real-time to facilitate the batching decision process without requiring the private status information of the edge devices. To the best of our knowledge, EdgeBatch is the first DNN task batching solution with uncertain task arrival time and information asymmetry for collaborative social edge applications. We implemented a system prototype of EdgeBatch on a real-world collaborative edge testbed that consists of Nvidia Jetson TX2, TX1 and TK1 boards, and Raspberry Pis. EdgeBatch was evaluated using a real-world DNN application: *Crowd Plate Detection*. We compared EdgeBatch with the state-of-the-art baselines in real-time and edge computing systems. The results show that our scheme achieves a significant performance gain in terms of both end-to-end delay and energy savings.

5.2.1   Problem Definition

Figure 5.2 illustrates an example of a DNN application of social edge called *crowd plate detection*, where a set of private vehicles collaboratively track down suspects of AMBER alerts [41]. In this application, edge devices (e.g., vehicles equipped with dash cameras and smart devices owned by citizens) form a city-wide video surveillance network that tracks moving vehicles using the automatic license plate recognition (ALPR) technique [7].

In a social edge application, the edge devices not only collect sensor data but also perform deep learning tasks to process the data at the edge. In the plate detection

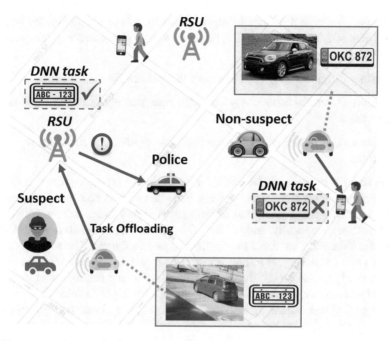

Fig. 5.2 An example of crowd plate detection application

example, the smartphones can not only capture images of the suspect's car, but also perform deep learning algorithms to detect the plate number in the captured images.

In addition to the edge devices, a set of edge servers (e.g., cloudlets, smart routers, or gateways) are deployed by the application to provide additional data storage and computation power in locations of proximity to the edge devices. In the above plate detection application, the application deploys Roadside Units (RSUs) on streets of interest as edge servers to coordinate the nearby edge devices (e.g., the vehicles currently located on the street). These edge servers provide local data processing capabilities to reduce the end-to-end latency and offer a generic communication interface between heterogeneous edge devices in the system [25, 27]. We refer to the sensing and computational resources at the edge (i.e., edge devices and edge servers) as *edge nodes* $EN = \{E_1, E_2, \ldots, E_N\}$, where N is total number of edge nodes in the system.

A key enabling technology in collaborative social edge is *task offloading*, where an edge device can choose to offload the data processing tasks to any device/server in the collaborative social edge. Due to the dynamic nature of the social edge system (e.g., the status of the computing nodes, the task pool, and the network environment can change over time), the task offloading strategies also need to be dynamic. In our model, we define the social edge application as a time-slotted system with a total of T time slots. We use $t \in [1, T]$ to denote the t-th time slot.

We then leverage the terms in supply chain models in economics [6] to define three types of edge nodes *supplier*, *manufacturer*, and *consumer* in the context of task offloading.

Definition (Supplier ($\mathcal{S}$)) The edge node that collects the sensing data.   □

Definition (Manufacturer ($\mathcal{M}$)) The edge node that performs the DNN tasks to process the data.   □

Definition (Consumer ($\mathcal{C}$)) The edge node that receives the final results from the DNN tasks.   □

We use $E_i \in \mathcal{S}$, $E_i \in \mathcal{M}$ and $E_i \in \mathcal{C}$ to denote an edge node is a supplier, manufacturer, or consumer, respectively. Note that a given node can be of multiple types. For example, a node that is both supplier and manufacturer collects and processes the data locally, and we use $E_i \in \mathcal{S}$ & $E_i \in \mathcal{M}$ to represent such a situation. Take the plate detection application as an example. The suppliers are the vehicles that use dashcams to take images of car plates. The manufacturers are the edge nodes (e.g., the RSUs) that process the images, and the consumer can be the device owned by the response team (e.g., the tablet in a police vehicle).

The goal of task offloading is to identify an optimal *dynamic supply chain graph* of the system as defined below.

Definition (Dynamic Supply Chain Graph ($\mathbf{G}_{\mathrm{edge}}^t$)) A directed 3-partite graph $\mathbf{G}_{\mathrm{edge}}^t = (\mathbf{V}_S^t, \mathbf{V}_M^t, \mathbf{V}_C^t, \mathbf{L}_{SM}^t, \mathbf{L}_{MC}^t,)$ where vertex $V_i^t \in \mathbf{V}_S^t, \mathbf{V}_M^t, \mathbf{V}_C^t$, represents that the edge node E_i is a supplier, manufacturer, or consumer, respectively at time slot t. Link $E_i \in \mathcal{S} \rightarrow E_j \in \mathcal{M} \in \mathbf{L}_{SM}^t$ signifies that supplier E_i collects the data and offloads the DNN tasks to manufacturer E_j at time slot t. Link $E_i \in \mathcal{M} \rightarrow E_j \in \mathcal{C} \in \mathbf{L}_{MC}^t$ signifies that manufacturer E_i sends the final results to the consumer E_j at time slot t.   □

For example, a supply chain of $E_a \rightarrow E_b \rightarrow E_c$ represents that E_a first collects the data, then asks E_b to process the data, which then sends the final result to E_c. Similarly, a supply chain $E_a \rightarrow E_a \rightarrow E_b$ denotes that node E_a collects the image data and runs the DNN task on-board, and then sends the final result to node E_c. The superscript t for the supply chain graph $\mathbf{G}_{\mathrm{edge}}^t$ and links (e.g., $\mathbf{L}_{SM}^t$) refers to the fact that the supply chain is dynamically changing, depending on the availability of edge devices, the status of the nodes, as well as the workloads in the system. We discuss in detail on how such dynamic supply chains are formed in Sect. 5.2.2.2.

This work focuses on a representative category of deep learning applications at the edge: deep neural network based image analysis [14]. We define a *task* that converts the captured image data to the final analysis results by running a Convolutional Neural Network (CNN), a widely used neural network algorithm for image analysis [14]. A CNN task is commonly processed using deep learning frameworks (e.g., Tensorflow, Caffe) that run on a GPU.

The key research problem we study in EdgeBatch is task batching. We assume that the above CNN tasks can be run on a GPU in parallel. The number of tasks that are executing simultaneously on GPU is referred to as the task batch size of an edge node:

Definition (Task Batching Size $|\mathbf{B_{m,i}}|$) The number of CNN tasks to be processed simultaneously on the GPU of an edge node E_i at the m-th batch. Assuming the social edge application is finite, each edge node E_i processes the tasks in a total of $M(i)$ batches $B_{1,i}, B_{2,i}, \ldots B_{M(i),i}$. The size (i.e., number of tasks to be processed) of a batch $B_{m,i}$ is denoted as $|B_{m,i}|$.   □

In a social edge application, edge devices collect sensing data from the physical world (i.e., collect and report an image from the camera). A collected image triggers a corresponding CNN task to process it. We assume that the application generates a set of $K(t)$ tasks at the time slot t, $TK^t = \{\tau_1^t, \tau_2^t, \ldots \tau_{K(t)}^t\}$. Each task is associated with a 3-tuple $\tau_k^t = (\Gamma_k^{t(R)}, \Gamma_k^{t(A)}, \Delta)$. Here $\Gamma_k^{t(R)}$ is the task release time which is the time slot when the image has been collected. $\Gamma_k^{t(A)}$ is the task arrival time which is the time slot when the image reaches a manufacturer. If the manufacturer is the same node as the supplier, we set $\Gamma_k^{t(A)} = \Gamma_k^{t(R)}$. Δ is the deadline requirement that captures the user desired Quality of Service (QoS). In this work, we assume all tasks are homogeneous (i.e., same priority level, input type, and algorithm to execute) and set all tasks to have the same deadline. This task model is quite common in image detection applications using deep learning techniques [18, 24].

Note that in an SEC application scenario, each task can be accomplished by either one or more devices. The extra communication delay will be incurred whenever a device offloads its data to another. Formally, an extra communication task will be generated to perform data offloading for every supply chain link, i.e., $E_i \in \mathcal{S} \to E_j \in \mathcal{M} \in \mathbf{L}_{SM}^t$ when $i \neq j$, and $E_i \in \mathcal{M} \to E_j \in \mathcal{C} \in \mathbf{L}_{MC}^t$ when $i \neq j$. In the scenario where the supplier is also the manufacturer (i.e., the image data is processed on the same node), or the manufacturer happens to be the consumer, no additional communication task is generated for data offloading.

Energy consumption is a major concern for battery-constrained edge devices. In EdgeBatch, the energy consumption of an edge node E_i is derived as: $e_i = \int_1^T (P_{comp,i}^t + P_{trans,i}^t) \, dt, 1 \leq i \leq N, 1 \leq t \leq T$, where $P_{comp,i}^t$ is the power consumption for computation and $P_{trans,i}^t$ is power for data transmission via wireless network for edge node E_i at time slot t. Note that P_{comp}^t can be highly dynamic and the relationship between power consumption and the workload can be non-linear and time-varying [39]. Therefore, we do not assume the application is able to precisely estimate the energy consumption on each edge node in the system. Instead, we assume each edge node can measure the power consumption on its own (e.g., through the built-in energy modules) and do not share such information with the application.

The QoS of the application is defined as the end-to-end delay (E2E delay) of each task:

Definition (End-to-end Delay of A Task ($\mathcal{D}_k^t$)) The total amount of time taken for a task to transform a unit of sensor measurement (i.e., an image) to be processed and sent to the consumer node. It includes the total computation time of the CNN to process the image in task τ_k^t, the overhead of the EdgeBatch modules, and the total communication overhead for additional data offloading process in τ_k^t.   □

Based on the definitions and models discussed above, we formally define the objective of EdgeBatch as follows. Our goal is to develop an optimal task batching scheme to minimize the total energy consumption of the edge nodes and the end-to-end (E2E) delay of the application simultaneously. Therefore, we formulate our problem as a multi-objective optimization problem that targets at finding the optimal task batching sizes $|B_{i,m}|$, $1 \leq i \leq N$, $1 \leq m \leq M(i)$ for each edge node that can:

$$\text{minimize: } e_i, \forall 1 \leq i \leq N$$

$$\text{minimize: } \sum_{t=1}^{T} \sum_{k=1}^{K(t)} \mathcal{D}_k^t, \forall 1 \leq k \leq K, 1 \leq t \leq T \tag{5.1}$$

$$\text{given: } \mathbf{G}_{\text{edge}}^t, 1 \leq t \leq T$$

5.2.2   The EdgeBatch Framework

In this section, we introduce our EdgeBatch framework to solve the problem formulated in the previous section. EdgeBatch consists of two sub-modules (Fig. 5.3): (1) a local Stochastic Optimal Task Batching (SOTB) module that identifies the optimal batch size of CNN tasks to fully utilize the data parallelization of GPU resources on edge nodes; (2) a global Optimal Contracting with Asymmetric Information (OCAI) module that manages the supply chains of the edge nodes to further utilize the idle GPU resources at the edge. The two modules work interactively to minimize the energy and delay of the system. Note that the task batching problem with even a single objective (e.g., makespan minimization) has been proven to be NP-Hard in the strong sense [4, 23]. Therefore, we break down our problem in Eq. (5.1) into two sub-problems (i.e., optimal batching solved by SOTB and the task offloading solved by OCAI) to make the problem tractable. The detailed discussion of the optimality of each sub-module is presented at the end of the following subsections.

5.2.2.1   Stochastic Optimal Task Batching Module (SOTB)

The SOTB module is designed to decide the optimal task batch size in real-time to explore a desired tradeoff between the delay of tasks and the energy consumption of the edge devices. In a collaborative social edge computing scenario, a manufacturer node cannot precisely predict when a supplier would offload the sensing data to it. For example, a manufacturer has received 3 images from suppliers after the last processing batch. The manufacturer, without knowing the arrival time of the next

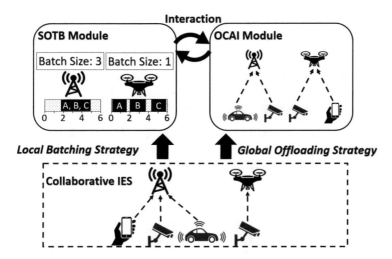

Fig. 5.3 Overview of the EdgeBatch framework

image, needs to decide whether to wait for the 4th image or process the 3 images immediately to avoid excessive waiting time. This problem shares the same intuition as the *bus waiting problem* in transportation planning, where a driver needs to decide how long a bus needs to wait at a bus stop to balance (1) the average waiting time of the arriving passengers, and (2) the chance of delayed arrival to the destination caused by the wait [37]. However, our problem is much more complex than the bus waiting problem because we do not assume prior distribution of the task arrival time and we need to consider the energy tradeoff caused by batching in the system.

We first formally define the mathematical model and key terms used in the SOTB module. For an edge node $E_i \in EN$, we assume it processes its tasks in a total of M batches, $\{B_1, B_2, \ldots, B_M\}$ where B_m denotes the m-th batch, $1 \leq m \leq M$. For ease of notation, we ignore the index for the edge node (i.e., the subscript i) in this subsection. Each batch B_m is associated with a 3-tuple: $B_m = (|B_m|, \Gamma_m^s, \Gamma_m^e)$, where $|B_m|$ is the batch size defined in Sect. 5.2.1. Γ_m^s and Γ_m^e are the batch start and end time respectively. For example, $\Gamma_m^s = t_1$ and $\Gamma_m^e = t_2$ denote the B_m starts at time slot t_1 and ends at time slot t_2.

We further define two cost functions that are associated with the batch size below.

Definition (Batch Delay Cost Function f($\cdot$)) The average processing delay for a specific batch size. In particular, $f(|B_m|)$ denotes the average processing delay of B_m.   □

Definition (Batch Power Cost Function g($\cdot$)) The average computation power consumption for a specific batch size. In particular, $g(|B_m|)$ is the average power consumption of B_m.   □

We assume the two cost functions are non-linear and are known only by the edge node itself but unknown to other nodes/servers. Therefore, each edge device needs to compute $f(\cdot)$ and $g(\cdot)$ based on its unique computing power and energy profile. We elaborate the profiling of these cost functions for different types of edge nodes. The batch size also affects the *batch holding time* defined below:

Definition (Batch Holding Time H_m) The time the edge node needs to wait till processes the next batch B_m. It is formally calculated as: $H_m = \Gamma_m^s - \Gamma_{m-1}^e$, where a larger batch size would result in a longer holding time.   □

We further assume that each edge node has a *capacity* Θ which is defined as the maximum number of images that can be processed by the GPU on the device. When the edge node reaches its capacity, adding more images will not reduce the average task processing delay.

To model the tradeoff between delay and energy, we define two loss functions: *delay loss* and *energy loss*.

Definition (Delay Loss $W_m^{(D)}$) The total delay for all tasks if performing batching B_m, including both processing delay and waiting delay.   □

Definition (Energy Loss $W_m^{(E)}$) The total energy costs of tasks if performing batching B_m, including the energy cost during both GPU idle and execution slots.

□

The delay loss $W_m^{(D)}$ depends on three factors: (1) the delay of the tasks that were left behind from the previous batch $\mathcal{L}_1$; (2) the processing time of the current batch $\mathcal{L}_2$; and (3) the total waiting time of the tasks arrived between the previous batch and the current batch $\mathcal{L}_3$. We have:

$$W_m^{(D)} = \mathcal{L}_1 + \mathcal{L}_2 + \mathcal{L}_3 \tag{5.2}$$

$\mathcal{L}_1$ can be derived as the number of left-over images from last batch times the batch holding time of the current batch B_m. Formally, we have

$$\mathcal{L}_1 = H_m \cdot L_{m-1} \tag{5.3}$$

where L_{m-1} denotes the left-over images from the last batch to be processed at B_m. It is recursively defined as follows:

$$
\begin{aligned}
L_{m-1} = \max[&(\Gamma_{m-1}^s - \Gamma_{m-1}^e) \cdot R_{\Gamma_{m-1}^s, \Gamma_{m-1}^e} \\
&+ L_{m-2} - \Theta, 0]
\end{aligned}
\tag{5.4}
$$

where $R_{\Gamma_{m-1}^s, \Gamma_{m-1}^e}$ is the average task arrival rate in $[\Gamma_{m-1}^s, \Gamma_{m-1}^e]$.

$\mathcal{L}_2$ is derived as the batch delay cost $f(\cdot)$ multiplied by the number of images to be processed. Formally, we calculate $\mathcal{L}_2$ as:

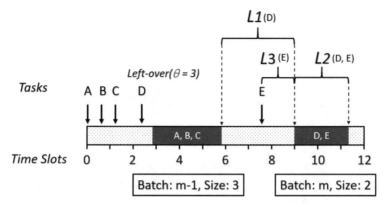

Fig. 5.4 An example break down of delay costs for EdgeBatch

$$\mathcal{L}_2 = f(|B_m|) \cdot |B_m|$$
$$= \left(\sum_{I \in B_m} f^1(I) + f^2(|B_m|) \right) \cdot |B_m| \qquad (5.5)$$

where $I \in B_m$ denotes an image I in the batch B_m. $f^1(I)$ is the preprocessing (e.g., encoding and resizing of the image) time of an image, which must be done before the CNN algorithm runs on the GPU [14]. $f^2(|B_m|)$ is the actual execution time (parallelizable) on GPU given the batch size.

$\mathcal{L}_3$ is derived as the total amount of waiting time for images that arrive between the start of B_{m-1} and the end of B_m. Formally, we derive $\mathcal{L}_3$ as:

$$\mathcal{L}_3 = \sum_{I \in A_m} (\Gamma_m^s - \Gamma_I) \qquad (5.6)$$

where A_m denotes the set of the images that arrive between the $(m-1)$-th and the m-th batch, and Γ_I, $\Gamma_{m-1}^e \leq \Gamma_I \leq \Gamma_m^e$ denotes the arrival time of an image I. Note that in this definition, $\mathcal{L}_3$ explicitly considers the communication delay of transmitting the images in A_m.

We illustrate an example of delay cost breakdown in Fig. 5.4. In this example, the previous batch B_{m-1} has a left-over Task D which cannot be processed by the GPU. Therefore, it suffers both holding delay ($\mathcal{L}_1$) and processing delay $\mathcal{L}_2$. Task E arrives between the two batches and suffers from waiting for B_m to start ($\mathcal{L}_3$), and processing delay ($\mathcal{L}_2$).

Next, we derive $W_m^{(E)}$ of the batch B_m as follows:

$$W_m^{(E)} = \sum_{\Gamma_{m-1}^e}^{\Gamma_m^s} g(0) \cdot H_m + \sum_{\Gamma_m^s}^{\Gamma_m^s + f(|B_m|)} g(|B_m|) \cdot \mathcal{L}_2 \qquad (5.7)$$

where $g(0)$ is the idle-time power consumption where the edge node is merely holding for the next batching without processing any tasks.

Using the loss functions $W_m^{(D)}$ and $W_m^{(E)}$, we can define the task batching problem as a constrained optimization problem:

$$\underset{B_1, B_2, \ldots, B_M}{\arg\min} \;\; W_m^{(D)} + \lambda \cdot W_m^{(E)}, 1 \leq m \leq M$$
$$s.t., |B_m| \leq \Theta$$
(5.8)

where λ is a weighting factor that balances the importance of delay and energy. λ is often defined by the application to reflect its emphasis on delay minimization (lower λ value) or energy savings.

In our problem, we need to predict the batching size in real-time and cannot observe the task arrivals in the future. Therefore, variables such as the future arriving tasks A_m and task holding time H_m are unknown. To address this challenge, we design an integrated offline-online regret minimization framework to dynamically decide the optimal batch size. In particular, we start with an initial batch size. After the batch has been processed, we "look back" to see if another batch size would be better (referred to as "regret") in terms of the combined loss function defined in Eq. (5.8) through an offline evaluation phase. Based on the regret, we adjust our batch size in the future so the regret can be minimized using an online learning phase. We elaborate on the two phases below.

Offline Evaluation Phase the offline phase leverages the historical data to evaluate the mistakes (regret) that the current batching strategies have made. In particular, we derive the regret function $\mathcal{R}$ as:

$$\mathcal{R}_{|B_{m-1}|} = \sum_{m'=1}^{m-1} \tilde{W}_{m'}^{(D)} + \lambda \cdot \tilde{W}_{m'}^{(E)} - W_{m'}^{(D)} - \lambda \cdot W_{m'}^{(E)}$$
(5.9)

where $W_{m'}^{(D)}$ and $W_{m'}^{(E)}$ denote the delay and energy loss if *optimal* task batching strategies $\tilde{\Gamma}_1^s, \tilde{\Gamma}_2^s, \ldots, \tilde{\Gamma}_M^s$ were picked. The optimal strategies are derived by solving Eq. (5.8) using a genetic algorithm [37]. $\tilde{W}_{m'}^{(D)}$ and $\tilde{W}_{m'}^{(E)}$ denote the delay and energy loss associated with the *actual* task batching strategies we had made in the past.

Online Learning Phase after deriving the regret, we design an online learning phase to guide the next batching strategy to be as close to the optimal solution as possible. Formally, we assume a set of available actions $\mathcal{A}$ to be taken for the next batch. Here, the actions are defined as the available batch sizes i.e., $\mathcal{A} = \{1, 2, \ldots, \Theta\}$. We use a weight vector $\mathcal{W} = \{w_1, w_2, \ldots, w_\Theta\}$ to represent the probabilistic distribution for the action set, where $w_i (1 \leq i \leq \Theta)$ is the probability of choosing batch size as i as the next strategy. The weight vector follows the constraint $\sum_{w \in \mathcal{W}} = 1$.

Given the above definitions, we derive an accumulated regret as:

$$\mathcal{R} = \sum_{i=1}^{\Theta} (w_i \cdot \mathcal{R}_i) \tag{5.10}$$

The accumulative regret represents the extra cost compared to the cost achieved by the optimal batching size. The goal of the online learning phase is to dynamically update $\mathcal{W}$ so that the overall regret $\mathcal{R}$ can be minimized. We develop an online regret minimization scheme by extending the PROD algorithm [10]. We present our algorithm in Algorithm 2. The above regret minimization algorithm allows the regret to be bounded by $O(\sqrt{\ln \Theta \cdot T})$. We refer to the proof in [10].

The offline evaluation phase is performed periodically due to its computational complexity. We refer to each period as a *control period* and the beginning of each period as a *control point*. The online learning phase is performed after each batch processing is finished.

5.2.2.2   Optimal Contracting with Asymmetric Information

The SOTB module above locally optimizes the tradeoff between delay and energy cost on a single node. This module alone is insufficient because global control of the system is necessary to provide the optimized QoS for the application. Consider a scenario where a manufacturer node receives too many tasks from its suppliers. The manufacturer node can be overloaded and fails to meet the QoS requirements of the application as well as encounters high energy consumption. On the other hand, a manufacturer node that receives too few tasks would fail to fully leverage the idle GPU resource on the node. We found global control mechanisms that dynamically adjust the task offloading (i.e., the supply chains) of edge nodes are crucial in

---

Algorithm 2 Online Regret Minimization

1: **Input:** weight vector $\mathcal{W} = \{w_1, w_2, \ldots, w_\Theta\}$, learning parameter η, current batch index m
2: **Output:** updated weight vector $\mathcal{W}' = \{w'_1, w'_2, \ldots, w'_\Theta\}$
3: **for** $t \in [0, T]$ **do**
4:     **if** t is a control point **then**
5:         **for** $i \in [1, \Theta]$ **do**
6:             Normalize $p_i = \frac{\eta \cdot w_i}{\sum_{i=1}^{\Theta} (\eta \cdot w_i)}$
7:         **end for**
8:         Update $\mathcal{R}_{B|m-1|} = \mathcal{R}_{B|m-1|} \cdot p_i$
9:         **for** $i \in [1, \Theta]$ **do**
10:             $w'_i = (w_i \cdot (1 + \eta \cdot R_i))^{\frac{\eta}{\eta-1}}$
11:         **end for**
12:     **end if**
13: **end for**
14: Return $\mathcal{W}'$

---

addressing this issue. A key challenge of designing such a global control scheme lies in the information asymmetry where no party in the system is allowed to have full information of all edge nodes. To this end, we design a decentralized Optimal Contracting model with Asymmetric Information (OCAI) scheme that allows edge nodes to negotiate and build supply chains autonomously without revealing their private information. In particular, the OCAI consists of two interactive processes: (1) a manufacturer node first evaluates its operation status and decides whether to take more tasks from the application and at what quantity through a *resource listing process*; (2) the suppliers observe the requested tasks from the manufacturers and decide which manufacturer to offload the task through a *bidding process*.

Resource Listing Process The resource listing process evaluates the utilization of an edge node (whether it is overwhelmed by too many tasks or it is underutilized) and decides how many more tasks the edge node will take. This is a challenging decision problem because the operational status (e.g., GPU usage, CPU usage, memory) is quite dynamic and hard to predict in the social edge. For example, a smartphone owned by a user can be idle when the user is charging the phone but very busy when the user is using the phone apps. Therefore, it is difficult for an edge node to decide whether it will be capable of taking more tasks in the future.

Luckily, we found the problem can be nicely mapped to an inventory model in economics [6]. In particular, the inventory model studies the problem of whether an inventory should be refilled and at what quantity if so given unpredictable demands. We map our problem as follows: the total number of tasks that an edge node processes is the "inventory size", denoted as V. The number of tasks that the edge node can finish per time slot is the "demand", denoted as D. The goal is to define a threshold R, and a refill size Q, so that every time the inventory size drops below the threshold R, a new order of Q tasks should be issued to satisfy future demands in the system.

We solve this problem by extending the classical (Q, R) reordering model [26] that can jointly derive the optimal Q and R values. Assuming the edge node needs to reorder Q tasks, the associated cost $C(Q)$ is derived as:

$$C(Q) = \lambda_h \cdot (R + \frac{Q}{2}) + \frac{\lambda_k \cdot D}{Q} + \lambda_p \cdot \frac{n(R) \cdot D}{Q} \qquad (5.11)$$

where parameter λ_h is the holding cost per task, which represents the average delay cost of each task that has not been processed, including the newly added Q tasks and the remaining R tasks. Parameter λ_k is the fixed cost for each order, which is the execution delay of the (Q, R) model. Intuitively, the smaller the Q is, the more likely the edge node will need to refill again in the near future, causing extra execution delay. Parameter λ_p is the cost per idle task if the inventory cannot satisfy demand (i.e., the edge node is not fully utilized). $n(R) = \int_R^\infty (x - R) \, dx$ is the expected idle tasks per time slot.

Taking partial derivatives of the Eq. (5.11) with regard to Q and R, we get:

$$\frac{\partial C(Q)}{\partial Q} = \frac{\lambda_h}{2} - \frac{\lambda_k \cdot D}{Q^2} - \frac{\lambda_p \cdot D \cdot n(R)}{Q^2}$$

$$\frac{\partial C(Q)}{\partial R} = \lambda_h - \frac{\lambda_p \cdot D \cdot (1 - F(R))}{Q} \tag{5.12}$$

where $F(R) = \int_R^\infty x \, dx$, denoting the probabilistic distribution of R. By making the partial derivatives as 0, we can derive the close-form solution as:

$$Q = \sqrt{\frac{2D \cdot (\lambda_k + \lambda_p \cdot n(R))}{\lambda_h}}, \quad F(R) = \frac{1 - Q \cdot \lambda_h}{\lambda_p \cdot D} \tag{5.13}$$

The optimal Q and R in the above form can be found using the iterative algorithm in [26].

Note that the resource listing process is performed on all edge nodes that can process CNN tasks (i.e., the ones with GPUs). This design allows suppliers with idle GPU resources to serve as manufacturers as well. After deriving Q and R, we develop a new bidding algorithm that allows the suppliers to pick the best manufacturer for task offloading.

Bidding Process The bidding process allows the supplier and manufacturer to identify the optimal offloading strategy using a game-theoretic framework. In particular, the manufacturer lists a bid of Q every time its inventory is less than R, meaning it can take Q more tasks from the suppliers. The suppliers will then compete with each other to bid for the Q tasks. Note that we assume the manufacturers will have no information about the supplier's status during bidding.

We design a game-theoretic bidding scheme that allows each supplier to selfishly pick the task that maximizes its own utility while taking into account the other suppliers' offloading strategies. We first define a delay and energy-aware *utility* function for a supplier E_i to offload the task to E_j as $U_{i,j}$, which is calculated as:

$$U_{i,j} = -\frac{(\pi_{\text{energy}} + \lambda \cdot \pi_{\text{delay}}) \cdot Q_j}{\mathcal{N}_j} \tag{5.14}$$

where π_{energy} and π_{delay} denote the transmission energy and transmission (i.e., data offloading) delay for device E_i to send a task to E_j, respectively. Q_j denotes the number of tasks posted by E_j, and $\mathcal{N}_j$ is the *congestion rate* representing the number of suppliers that are competing for E_j's tasks. The intuition of the above utility function is as follows. The cost term $\pi_{\text{energy}} + \lambda \cdot \pi_{\text{delay}}$ guides the suppliers to pick the nearby manufacturers that can minimize the communication delay and transmission energy. The factor $\frac{Q_j}{\mathcal{N}_j}$ further takes into account the decisions from competing suppliers and reduces the chance of picking a manufacturer whose requested tasks have already been claimed by many other suppliers.

Based on the utility function, each supplier will pick the offloading strategy that gives the highest utility until an ϵ-Nash Equilibrium [19] is reached. We say an ϵ-Nash Equilibrium is reached if any of the supplier nodes cannot further increase utility by ϵ by unilaterally changing its strategy from $U_{i,j}$ to $U'_{i,j}$, i.e., $U_{i,j} \geq U'_{i,j} + \epsilon$. The challenge for this step is that no suppliers can estimate the decision of others (due to the information asymmetric), making it difficult for them to make the best responses. Therefore, we design a decentralized Nash Equilibrium solution based on a fictitious play negotiation scheme [45]. This scheme only requires the estimation of the congestion rate $\mathcal{N}_j$ of each task. We summarize our algorithm in Algorithm 3.

Algorithm 3 Bidding Scheme

1: **Input:** A set of suppliers $S = \{S_1, S_2, \ldots, S_I\}$; task listings $Q = \{Q_1, Q_2, \ldots, Q_J\}$, decay factor $\mu \in (0, 1]$
2: **Output:** offloading strategy for each supplier $Z = \{z_1, z_2, \ldots z_I\}$.
3: **Initialize:** convergence flag $converge \leftarrow False$
4: **while** $converge \neq True$ **do**
5:     **for** $S_i \in S$ **do**
6:         S_i finds manufacturer $z_i = j'$ based on minimizing Eq. (5.14)
7:         S_i sends z_i to the edge server, receives convergence flag
8:         Server updates $\mathcal{N}_{j'}$ +=1
9:         S_i receives congestion rates $\mathcal{N}_j$, $\forall 1 \leq j \leq J$
10:       S_i predicts $\mathcal{N}_j \leftarrow \mu \cdot \mathcal{N}_j + (1 - \mu) \cdot \mathcal{N}_j$, $\forall 1 \leq j \leq J$
11:     **end for**
12: **end while**
13: Return Z

We further clarify and discuss the optimality of the OCAI algorithm. First of all, we found a globally optimal solution to our problem is both intractable (proven to be NP-Hard in [5, 29, 43]) and impractical due to the lack of global device information in social edge (i.e., the information asymmetry challenge discussed in the introduction). For example, a globally optimal solution would require the edge nodes to be fully cooperative and constantly share and synchronize their current status with the server. Given the complete status information of all edge devices in the system, a central controller (e.g., the edge server) will then be able to derive the globally optimal task offloading strategy of the system. However, such an information-sharing requirement of the global optimal solution not only violates the assumption that a social edge is composed mainly of privately owned edge devices, but also causes an excessive communication burden in the system.

Therefore, we divide the optimization problem into two sub-tasks: the resource listing process and the bidding process. For the resource listing process, the (Q, R) model we adopt identifies the *optimal* reorder threshold and order size [6] in the stochastic inventory reorder problem. We find an exact match from our problem to the stochastic inventory reorder problem. Consequently, the derived Q, R values in Eq. (5.13) are optimal as well. For the bidding process, the game theoretic approach targets at finding a *locally optimal* strategy for each edge node by reaching the Nash Equilibrium where each edge node cannot further maximize its own utilities.

We understand that such a local optimal strategy is not necessarily the optimal outcome of all edge nodes (i.e., the sum of utilities of all edge nodes). However, it is impractical to find such a global/Pareto optimal solution in a decentralized game theory problem where each edge node is not allowed to have access to other node's utility function (which would leak the device's private node status and require constant synchronization of all nodes' statuses) [50].

5.3 Real-World Case Studies

We evaluate the EdgeBatch framework using a real-world application—*Crowd Plate Detection (CPD)*. In particular, we use the CNN algorithm developed in [17]: a pre-trained ImageNet model VGG-16. The VGG-16 model is a state-of-the-art deep CNN with 16 layers for image recognition tasks. We use the automatic license plate recognition (ALPR) dataset [22] to emulate the collected images from edge devices.

We choose the following baselines from recent literature. We observe that there exists no baseline that jointly addresses the task batching and task offloading issues in collaborative edge systems. Therefore, we first picked a few representative baselines for task batching schemes.

- **No Batching (NB)**: the images are processed one by one by the GPU on edge nodes.
- **Fixed Size Batching (FS)**: a heuristic batching scheme where the batching is performed whenever the number of arrived images reaches α_1.
- **Fixed Period (FP)**: a heuristic task batching scheme where the batching is performed periodically with a period of α_2.
- **Bus Waiting (BW)**: a dynamic task batching scheme used in solving the optimal bus waiting time [9].
- **Online Learning (OL)**: an online learning-based batching algorithm that dynamically adjusts the batch holding time using an online feedback control mechanism [28].

We also choose a few state-of-the-art baselines that manage the task offloading of the edge computing systems for a fair comparison with our scheme.

- **BGTA**: a bottom-up task offloading scheme that allows manufacturers to selfishly compete for tasks to maximize utilities [43].
- **TDA**: a top-down task offloading scheme that uses Mixed Integer Linear Programming (MILP) to minimize the deadline miss rate of tasks [21].
- **CoGTA**: a recent task offloading scheme that allows edge nodes to trade tasks using a negotiation scheme that satisfies the delay and energy requirements of the application [44].

Note that both BGTA and TDA baselines do not allow edge devices to offload tasks to each other. Instead, they let edge devices offload tasks to edge servers (i.e., the TX2 board). We combine the task batching and offloading baselines as follows:

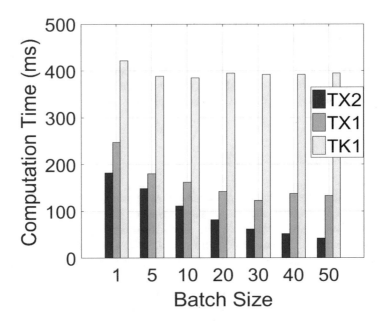

Fig. 5.5 Batch size vs computation time

we first run the task offloading scheme to dynamically organize the task flows of the collaborative edge system. We then run the task batching scheme to identify the optimal batch size for each edge node that has received offloaded tasks.

We have an initial bootstrapping phase to tune the parameters in the systems of the above schemes. We run the experiment for 100 time slots and find the parameters that give the minimum delay and energy costs (based on Eq. (5.8) in Sect. 5.2.2). In particular, we set $\alpha_1 = 4$, $\alpha_2 = 200$ ms for FS and FP baselines, respectively. We set the duration for a time slot as 100 ms and the control period for the SOTB and OCAI algorithms in EdgeBatch as 5 s.

Task Batching Profiling We first profile the computation time and energy cost functions $f(\cdot)$ and $g(\cdot)$ (defined in Sect. 5.2.2) with a varying batching size. We observe that, in general, increasing the batching size would reduce the average computation time of the images because of data parallelization (Fig. 5.5). The average delay slightly increases for TX1 and TK1 when the batch size exceeds 20 and 40, respectively. This is because the large batch sizes overload the GPUs on the two nodes and eventually delay the tasks. The above observations reiterate the potential benefit of leveraging a large batch size to improve the delay of the tasks. We also found that devices with higher-end GPUs (i.e., TX1 and TX2) have significantly more improvement than the device with lower-end GPUs (i.e., TK1). This observation highlights the importance of considering the heterogeneity of the edge nodes in the design of an optimal task batching strategy.

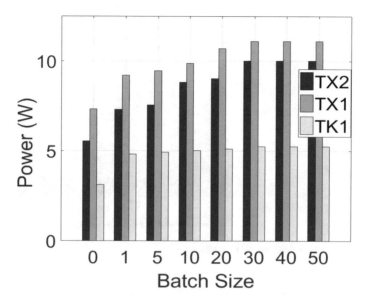

Fig. 5.6 Batch size vs power

We also observe that increasing the batch size would increase the power consumption of an edge node (Fig. 5.6). The power consumption increase is also observed to be more significant on the devices with higher-end GPUs (i.e., TX1 and TX2). The goal of EdgeBatch is to identify the optimal batching strategy that best optimizes the above delay-energy tradeoff (i.e., Eq. (5.8) in Sect. 5.2.2).

End-to-End Delay In the next set of experiments, we evaluate the end-to-end (E2E) delay of all the compared schemes. We run the experiment 100 times to generate the results and each run consists of 1000 time slots. Figure 5.7 summarizes the E2E delays of all the combinations of baselines and EdgeBatch. We show both the average delay and the one standard deviation of the results. We observe that the EdgeBatch scheme has the least E2E delay and the smallest standard deviation compared to the baselines. Compared to the best-performing baseline (CoGTA+OL), EdgeBatch achieved 31.1% decrease in E2E delay. We attribute such a performance gain to (1) the task batching module (SOTB) that fully utilizes the data parallelization of the GPUs to save the average processing time of the CNN tasks; and (2) our task offloading algorithm (OCAI) that finds the optimal supply chains that allow the edge nodes to search for the most efficient way to collaboratively finish CNN tasks. We also observe that the schemes without batching have significantly longer E2E delays compared to schemes that adopt task batching. This again highlights the importance of task batching for DNN applications at the edge.

An important concern regarding the EdgeBatch scheme is the communication overhead of the data offloading tasks in the supply chains. We found in Fig. 5.7 that

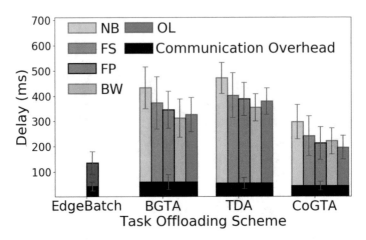

Fig. 5.7 Average E2E delay for all schemes

the data offloading overhead for all compared schemes is relatively small compared to the overall E2E delay of the tasks. We also observe that the BGTA and TDA schemes have higher communication overheads than our scheme and CoGTA.

To further evaluate the effect of the communication tasks for data offloading, we compare EdgeBatch with all the task offloading baselines by gradually increasing the number of tasks per time slot. The results are shown in Fig. 5.8. We found that the BGTA and TDA schemes consistently have significantly higher communication overheads than our scheme and CoGTA. This is due to the fact that both BGTA and TDA offload all tasks that an edge node cannot finish to the edge server, which becomes the bottleneck for the data offloading requests. In contrast, both EdgeBatch and CoGTA achieve a much lower overhead because they are able to distribute the data offloading tasks by performing peer offloading (i.e., edge devices can offload DNN tasks to each other). While EdgeBatch has a similar data offloading overhead as CoGTA, it is superior because its optimized batching strategy allows the social edge system to perform DNN tasks much faster (as shown later in Figs. 5.9 and 5.10).

We further evaluate the E2E delay with respect to the task frequency (i.e., number of tasks per time slot) in Fig. 5.9. We compare EdgeBatch against the best-performing task offloading scheme (i.e., CoGTA) coupled with different task batching schemes. We observe that EdgeBatch significantly outperforms all baselines in various task frequency settings. This shows that EdgeBatch is more robust than the baselines when the workload in the system changes. We attribute this performance gain to the adaptive design of the SOTB scheme that can adjust the batching size in real-time with uncertain arrival rate of the tasks.

We also evaluate the deadline hit rate (DHR) of the application under different deadline requirements of the system. The DHR is defined as the ratio of the CNN tasks that have finished within the deadline. We fix the task frequency as 6 tasks per time slot and gradually relax the deadline requirement. The results are

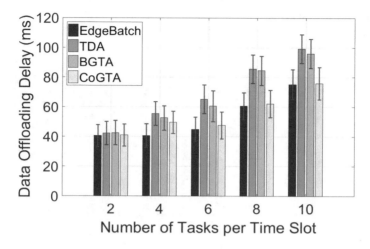

Fig. 5.8 Average data offloading overhead for all schemes

Fig. 5.9 E2E delay in CPD

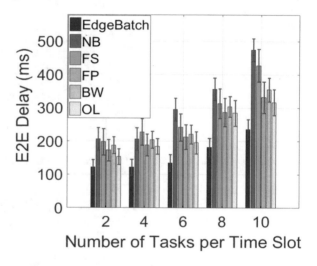

presented in Fig. 5.10. We observe that EdgeBatch significantly improves the DHR compared to all schemes and is the first one that reaches 100% DHR as the deadline increases. This result further showcases that EdgeBatch can better satisfy the real-time requirements of the application.

Energy Consumption In the next set of experiments, we focus on the energy consumption of edge nodes. As mentioned in Sect. 5.2.2, the energy consumption is normalized to reflect the proportion of battery that is consumed by a scheme to accomplish all tasks [45]. The results of the average normalized energy consumption on edge nodes are shown in Table 5.1. We can observe that EdgeBatch consumes significantly less energy as compared to all other baselines except TDA. TDA consumes the least amount of energy because it tends to push all the tasks from

Fig. 5.10 Deadline hit rate in CPD

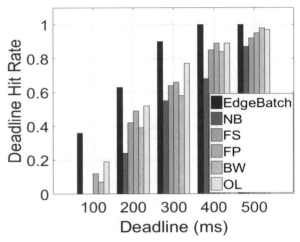

Table 5.1 Normalized energy consumption comparison

	TX2	TX1	TK1	Pi3	Overall
EdgeBatch	0.802	0.781	0.753	0.633	8.470
BGTA + NB	0.893	0.875	0.879	0.675	9.344
BGTA + FS	0.874	0.865	0.855	0.675	9.238
BGTA + FP	0.852	0.866	0.847	0.675	9.180
BGTA + BW	0.887	0.858	0.840	0.675	9.221
BGTA + OL	0.824	0.827	0.829	0.675	9.011
TDA + NB	0.923	0.903	0.803	0.553	8.576
TDA + FS	0.885	0.864	0.755	0.553	8.326
TDA + FP	0.857	0.841	0.724	0.553	8.162
TDA + BW	0.862	0.852	0.748	0.553	8.242
TDA + OL	0.833	0.839	0.719	0.553	8.100
CoGTA + NB	0.906	0.880	0.843	0.682	9.350
CoGTA + FS	0.875	0.853	0.851	0.682	9.251
CoGTA + FP	0.837	0.832	0.819	0.682	9.068
CoGTA + BW	0.842	0.866	0.830	0.682	9.168
CoGTA + OL	0.822	0.817	0.828	0.682	9.026

"Overall" is the sum of normalized energy consumption of all edge nodes

the suppliers to the edge server (i.e., the TX2 boards). In other words, the TDA scheme underutilizes the diverse resources on the edge devices and pushes all extra computation burden to the server nodes. Such a task offloading strategy gives TDA scheme the largest amount of delay as shown in Figs. 5.7 and 5.8.

5.4 Discussion

This chapter presents the EdgeBatch framework to support DNN applications in Intelligent Social Edge Systems. We develop a novel task batching scheme for GPU-enabled IoT devices that significantly accelerates CNN-based image detection tasks at the edge. We also design a new task offloading scheme by extending the supply chain and game theory models to coordinate the collaboration among edge nodes such that the QoS of the application is optimized. We implemented the EdgeBatch framework on a real-world heterogeneous edge computing testbed and evaluate it through a real-world DNN application. The results demonstrate that EdgeBatch achieves significant performance gains compared to state-of-the-art baselines in terms of reduced delay and improved energy efficiency.

There are important areas where EdgeBatch can be extended further. First, the dynamic feature of IoT network may affect the distributed sensor and processing nodes setup (e.g., the availability of some edge nodes may be intermittent due to the mobility issue). EdgeBatch can be readily extended to handle this issue by leveraging two core designs in the system. First, the OCAI module of EdgeBatch is designed to generate dynamic supply chain graphs through a game-theoretic process. In this process, each edge node evaluates the dynamic communication overhead, available computing resources, and energy consumption, and self-organizes into a dynamic supply chain that minimizes the communication delay and energy cost. In this design, if an edge node becomes unavailable (e.g., has a poor network connection or travels to a distant area), it is unlikely to be selected as a manufacturer due to the excessive communication cost. The second core design to address dynamics is the SOTB module, which assumes no prior knowledge of the task arrival time and is agnostic about the network delay variations caused by mobility. We note such a stochastic design of the SOTB batching model is also robust against the dynamics of mobile devices. One particular issue we did not consider in our model is the task reassignment where a mobile device becomes unavailable and has tasks unfinished. This can be addressed by extending the OCAI module in our system to further incorporate task-reassignment and adaptive workload management strategies (such as FemtoCloud [11], DPA [31]) where unfinished tasks could be immediately migrated to other backup devices. We leave these extensions for future work.

Second, we assume a simplified task model in the EdgeBatch system where the tasks are homogeneous and pipelined. While such a simplification is common in resource management of many edge computing systems [27], in real-world scenarios, a task can be composed of multiple subtasks with heterogeneous inputs (e.g., images, texts, videos, sensor readings, etc.) where the subtasks may also have complex dependencies [44]. A potential solution to handle heterogeneous tasks is to leverage heterogeneous supply chain models where the manufacturers with diversified facilities process different types of materials from the suppliers [30]. We plan to further improve EdgeBatch by considering the runtime scheduling of heterogeneous DNN tasks using frameworks such as SOSPCS [36], and incorporating more complex task modeling techniques such as MakeFlow [1] and DCSS [38] that regulate the system workflow to impose the relevant task dependencies.

Finally, EdgeBatch focuses on a particular type of deep learning task, namely CNN-based image detection. While this type of task enables many killer applications in edge computing (e.g., disaster response [42], abnormal event detection [47], and traffic alert systems [43]), we plan to further test EdgeBatch on a more diversified set of DNN techniques and application scenarios. For example, the recurrent neural networks (e.g., RNN, LSTM, GRU) and neural encoding techniques (e.g., autoencoders and network embedding) are also commonly used in IES applications (e.g., voice recognition and urban sensing [49]). We expect EdgeBatch to be able to accelerate these DNN algorithms as well since the task batching scheme in EdgeBatch explores the fundamental tradeoff between delay and energy, which is common to DNN algorithms that run on GPU-enabled IoT devices.

References

1. M. Albrecht, P. Donnelly, P. Bui, D. Thain, Makeflow: a portable abstraction for data intensive computing on clusters, clouds, and grids, in *Proceedings of the 1st ACM SIGMOD Workshop on Scalable Workflow Execution Engines and Technologies* (ACM, 2012), p. 1
2. Aws Deeplens, https://aws.amazon.com/deeplens/. Accessed 23 Apr 2019
3. S. Bateni, C. Liu, Apnet: approximation-aware real-time neural network, in *2018 IEEE Real-Time Systems Symposium (RTSS)* (IEEE, 2018), pp. 67–79
4. A. Bellanger, A. Janiak, M.Y. Kovalyov, A. Oulamara, Scheduling an unbounded batching machine with job processing time compatibilities. Discret. Appl. Math. **160**(1–2), 15–23 (2012)
5. J. Chen, L.K. John, Efficient program scheduling for heterogeneous multi-core processors, in *Proceedings of the 46th Annual Design Automation Conference* (ACM, 2009), pp. 927–930
6. C.J. Corbett, Stochastic inventory systems in a supply chain with asymmetric information: cycle stocks, safety stocks, and consignment stock. Oper. Res. **49**(4), 487–500 (2001)
7. S. Du, M. Ibrahim, M. Shehata, W. Badawy, Automatic license plate recognition (alpr): a state-of-the-art review. IEEE Trans. Circuits Syst. Video Technol. **23**(2), 311–325 (2012)
8. D. Franklin, Nvidia jetson tx2 delivers twice the intelligence to the edge. NVIDIA Accelerated Computing—Parallel Forall (2017)
9. L. Fu, X. Yang, Design and implementation of bus–holding control strategies with real-time information. Transp. Res. Rec. **1791**(1), 6–12 (2002)
10. P. Gaillard, G. Stoltz, T. Van Erven, A second-order bound with excess losses. in *Conference on Learning Theory* (2014), pp. 176–196
11. K. Habak, M. Ammar, K.A. Harras, E. Zegura, Femto clouds: leveraging mobile devices to provide cloud service at the edge. in *2015 IEEE 8th International Conference on Cloud Computing (CLOUD)* (IEEE, 2015), pp. 9–16
12. S. Han, H. Mao, W.J. Dally, *Deep Compression: Compressing Deep Neural Networks with Pruning, Trained Quantization and Huffman Coding*, ed. by Y. Bengio, Y. LeCun. In 2016 International Conference on Learning Representations (ICLR) 2016, San Juan, Puerto Rico, May 2–4, 2016, Conference Track Proceedings. http://arxiv.org/abs/1510.00149 (2016)
13. Y. Huang, X. Song, F. Ye, Y. Yang, X. Li, Fair caching algorithms for peer data sharing in pervasive edge computing environments, in *2017 IEEE 37th International Conference on Distributed Computing Systems (ICDCS)* (IEEE, 2017), pp. 605–614

14. A. Krizhevsky, I. Sutskever, G.E. Hinton, Imagenet classification with deep convolutional neural networks, in *Advances in Neural Information Processing Systems* (2012), pp. 1097–1105

15. N.D. Lane, S. Bhattacharya, P. Georgiev, C. Forlivesi, L. Jiao, L. Qendro, F. Kawsar, Deepx: a software accelerator for low-power deep learning inference on mobile devices, in *Proceedings of the 15th International Conference on Information Processing in Sensor Networks* (IEEE Press, 2016), p. 23

16. H. Li, K. Ota, M. Dong, Learning iot in edge: deep learning for the internet of things with edge computing. IEEE Netw. **32**(1), 96–101 (2018)

17. H. Li, P. Wang, C. Shen, Toward end-to-end car license plate detection and recognition with deep neural networks. IEEE Trans. Intell. Transp. Syst. **20**(3), 1126–1136 (2018)

18. X. Li, D. Caragea, H. Zhang, M. Imran, Localizing and quantifying damage in social media images, in *2018 IEEE/ACM International Conference on Advances in Social Networks Analysis and Mining (ASONAM)* (IEEE, 2018)

19. I. Milchtaich, Congestion games with player-specific payoff functions. Games Econ. Behav. **13**(1), 111–124 (1996)

20. G. Neubig, Y. Goldberg, C. Dyer, On-the-fly operation batching in dynamic computation graphs, in *Advances in Neural Information Processing Systems* (2017), pp. 3971–3981

21. Z. Ning, P. Dong, X. Kong, F. Xia, A cooperative partial computation offloading scheme for mobile edge computing enabled internet of things. IEEE Internet Things J. **6**(3), 4804–4814 (2018)

22. Number Plate Datasets, https://platerecognizer.com/number-plate-datasets/. Accessed 23 Apr 2019

23. A. Oulamara, G. Finke, A.K. Kuiteing, Flowshop scheduling problem with a batching machine and task compatibilities. Comput. Oper. Res. **36**(2), 391–401 (2009)

24. J. Redmon, S. Divvala, R. Girshick, A. Farhadi, You only look once: unified, real-time object detection, in *Proceedings of the IEEE Conference on Computer Vision and Pattern Recognition* (2016), pp. 779–788

25. M. Satyanarayanan, The emergence of edge computing. Computer **50**(1), 30–39 (2017)

26. D.A. Schrady, A deterministic inventory model for reparable items. Naval Res. Logist. Q. **14**(3), 391–398 (1967)

27. W. Shi, J. Cao, Q. Zhang, Y. Li, L. Xu, Edge computing: vision and challenges. IEEE Internet Things J. **3**(5), 637–646 (2016)

28. S. Sorin, Exponential weight algorithm in continuous time. Math. Program. **116**(1–2), 513–528 (2009)

29. K.W. Tindell, A. Burns, A.J. Wellings, Allocating hard real-time tasks: an np-hard problem made easy. Real-Time Syst. **4**(2), 145–165 (1992)

30. M.-L. Tseng, Green supply chain management with linguistic preferences and incomplete information. Appl. Soft Comput. **11**(8), 4894–4903 (2011)

31. N. Vance, D.Y. Zhang, Y. Zhang, D. Wang, Towards optimal incentive-driven verification in social sensing based smart city applications, in *2019 IEEE 21st International Conference on High Performance Computing and Communications; IEEE 17th International Conference on Smart City; IEEE 5th International Conference on Data Science and Systems (HPCC/SmartCity/DSS)* (IEEE, 2019), pp. 2700–2707

32. D. Wang, T. Abdelzaher, B. Priyantha, J. Liu, F. Zhao, Energy-optimal batching periods for asynchronous multistage data processing on sensor nodes: foundations and an mplatform case study. Real-Time Syst. **48**(2), 135–165 (2012)

33. D. Wang, T. Abdelzaher, L. Kaplan, C.C. Aggarwal, Recursive fact-finding: A streaming approach to truth estimation in crowdsourcing applications, in *2013 IEEE 33rd International Conference on Distributed Computing Systems* (IEEE, 2013), pp. 530–539

34. D. Wang, T. Abdelzaher, L. Kaplan, Surrogate mobile sensing. IEEE Commun. Mag. **52**(8), 36–41 (2014)

35. Y. Wang, B. Li, R. Luo, Y. Chen, N. Xu, H. Yang, Energy efficient neural networks for big data analytics, in *Proceedings of the conference on Design, Automation & Test in Europe* (European Design and Automation Association, 2014), p. 345

36. Y. Xiao, S. Nazarian, P. Bogdan, Self-optimizing and self-programming computing systems: a combined compiler, complex networks, and machine learning approach. IEEE Trans. Very Large Scale Integr. VLSI Syst. **27**(6), 1416–1427 (2019)
37. Y. Xuan, J. Argote, C.F. Daganzo, Dynamic bus holding strategies for schedule reliability: optimal linear control and performance analysis. Transp. Res. B Methodol. **45**(10), 1831–1845 (2011)
38. Y. Xue, J. Li, S. Nazarian, P. Bogdan, Fundamental challenges toward making the iot a reachable reality: A model-centric investigation. ACM Trans. Des. Autom. Electron. Syst. **22**(3), 53 (2017)
39. C. You, K. Huang, H. Chae, B.-H. Kim, Energy-efficient resource allocation for mobile-edge computation offloading. IEEE Trans. Wirel. Commun. **16**(3), 1397–1411 (2017)
40. D.Y. Zhang, D. Wang, Heterogeneous social sensing edge computing system for deep learning based disaster response: demo abstract, in *Proceedings of the International Conference on Internet of Things Design and Implementation* (ACM, 2019), pp. 269–270
41. Q. Zhang, X. Zhang, Q. Zhang, W. Shi, H. Zhong, Firework: big data sharing and processing in collaborative edge environment, in *2016 Fourth IEEE Workshop on Hot Topics in Web Systems and Technologies (HotWeb)* (IEEE, 2016), pp. 20–25
42. D.Y. Zhang, D. Wang, N. Vance, Y. Zhang, S. Mike, On scalable and robust truth discovery in big data social media sensing applications. IEEE Trans. Big Data **5**, 195–208 (2018)
43. D.Y. Zhang, Y. Ma, Y. Zhang, S. Lin, X.S. Hu, D. Wang, A real-time and non-cooperative task allocation framework for social sensing applications in edge computing systems, in *2018 IEEE Real-Time and Embedded Technology and Applications Symposium (RTAS)* (IEEE, 2018), pp. 316–326
44. D.Y. Zhang, Y. Ma, C. Zheng, Y. Zhang, X.S. Hu, D. Wang, Cooperative-competitive task allocation in edge computing for delay-sensitive social sensing, in *2018 IEEE/ACM Symposium on Edge Computing (SEC)* (IEEE, 2018), pp. 243–259
45. D.Y. Zhang, T. Rashid, X. Li, N. Vance, D. Wang, Heteroedge: taming the heterogeneity of edge computing system in social sensing, in *Proceedings of the International Conference on Internet of Things Design and Implementation (IoTDI)* (ACM, 2019), pp. 37–48. https://doi.org/10.1145/3302505.3310067.
46. D.Y. Zhang, N. Vance, Y. Zhang, M.T. Rashid, D. Wang, Edgebatch: towards ai-empowered optimal task batching in intelligent edge systems, in *2019 IEEE Real-Time Systems Symposium (RTSS)* (IEEE, 2019), pp. 366–379
47. Y. Zhang, H. Wang, D.Y. Zhang, D. Wang, Deeprisk: a deep transfer learning approach to migratable traffic risk estimation in intelligent transportation using social sensing, in *2019 15th International Conference on Distributed Computing in Sensor Systems (DCOSS)* (IEEE, 2019), pp. 123–130
48. G. Zhong, A. Dubey, C. Tan, T. Mitra, Synergy: an hw/sw framework for high throughput cnns on embedded heterogeneous soc. ACM Trans. Embed. Comput. Syst. **18**(2), 13 (2019)
49. W. Zhou, Z. Shao, C. Diao, Q. Cheng, High-resolution remote-sensing imagery retrieval using sparse features by auto-encoder. Remote Sens. Lett. **6**(10), 775–783 (2015)
50. V.I. Zhukovskiy, K.N. Kudryavtsev, Pareto-optimal nash equilibrium: sufficient conditions and existence in mixed strategies. Autom. Remote Control **77**(8), 1500–1510 (2016)

Chapter 6
Human-AI Interaction

Abstract Artificial Intelligence (AI) has been widely adopted in many important application domains such as speech recognition, computer vision, autonomous driving, and AI for social good. While AI algorithms often significantly reduce the detection time and labor cost in such applications, their performance sometimes falls short of the desired accuracy and is considered to be less reliable than domain experts. To exacerbate the problem, the black-box nature of the AI algorithms also makes them difficult to troubleshoot the system when their performance is unsatisfactory. The SEC paradigm brings about the opportunity to incorporate human intelligence from the crowd into AI algorithms at the edge. In this chapter, we introduce two human-AI frameworks—CrowdLearn and interactive Disaster Scene Assessment (iDSA), that utilize the crowd intelligence to troubleshoot and significantly improve the accuracy of the AI-based disaster damage assessment (DDA) models in SEC applications.

6.1 Interactive Human-Machine Edge Intelligence

We highlight the importance of combining human and machine intelligence via the lens of a unique SEC application of AI-based disaster response. Disaster response is a critical application to ensure immediate resolution to emergent and hazardous events [35, 41, 44, 46]. A critical step in disaster response is to perform damage assessment (e.g., determine the severity of the damages caused by a disaster based on imagery data). Traditionally, the damage assessment models were built on remote sensing data (e.g., satellite images). For example, Facebook recently proposed an AI framework to identify the areas that were severely affected by a disaster using convolutional neural networks (CNNs) on satellite imagery [8]. In a more recent work, Nguyan et al. developed a deep CNN model with domain-specific fine-tuning (referred to as VGG16) to effectively detect the level of damage from social media images [21]. Li et al. further extends the VGG16 model to accurately locate the damage area by combining CNN and Grad-CAM to generate a damage heatmap of a given image [19].

D. Wang, D. Y. Zhang, *Social Edge Computing*,
https://doi.org/10.1007/978-3-031-26936-3_6

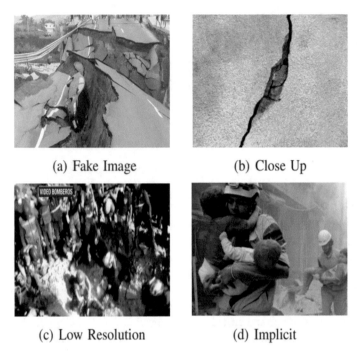

(a) Fake Image   (b) Close Up

(c) Low Resolution   (d) Implicit

Fig. 6.1 Example failures of AI algorithm in DDA. Image (**a**) is a fake image showing a car falling from a huge cleavage of a road. Image (**b**) is a close-up of a crack on a road. The AI algorithms mistakenly return a false detection result of "severe damage" for both images. Image (**c**) shows a disaster scene image with low resolution. Image (**d**) shows kids were injured and taken away from a damaged area. The AI algorithms mistakenly return false detection result of "no damage" for both images

While AI algorithms can significantly reduce the labor cost and improve the detection efficiency in DDA applications, they are prone to various failure scenarios (see Fig. 6.1). For example, the AI algorithms mistakenly report severe damage for the images in Fig. 6.1a, b, and report no damage for images in Fig. 6.1c, d (please refer to the detailed discussions under Fig. 6.1).

One main reason for the above failure scenarios is that the AI-based DDA algorithms can only capture the low-level features of the images (e.g., color, layout, shapes) but fail to "understand" the high-level context of the images (e.g., the story behind the image). Such failure may lead to severe consequences (e.g., the rescue team may be sent to the wrong places while places where people's lives are at stake are not responded). In contrast, human intelligence (HI) is often more accurate in such failure scenarios [49]. For example, humans can reliably assess the damage severity by identifying fake or irrelevant images and observing the actual events happening in the images.

Black-Box AI Challenge The first challenge in combining HI and AI lies in the black-box nature of AI algorithms. In particular, the lack of interpretability of the results from AI algorithms makes it extremely hard to diagnose the failure scenarios such as performance deficiency—why the AI model fails? Is this due to the lack of training data or the model itself? Such questions make it hard for the crowd to effectively improve the black-box AI model. The interpretability issue was initially identified in [22, 23] where accountable AI solutions were proposed to leverage humans as annotators to troubleshoot and correct the outputs of AI algorithms. However, these solutions simply use humans to verify the results of AI and ignore the issue where human annotators can be both slow and expensive. There also exist some human-AI systems that use crowdsourcing platforms to obtain labels or features to retrain the model [2, 18]. However, these systems do not address the problem where the AI algorithms themselves are problematic in which no matter how many training samples are added, the AI performance will not increase. Given the black-box nature of AI, the research question we address here is: *how do we accurately identify the failure scenarios of AI that can be effectively addressed by the crowd?*

Black-Box Crowdsourcing Platform Challenge The second unique challenge lies in the black-box nature of the crowdsourcing platform, which is characterized by two unique features. First, the requester (e.g., the DDA application that queries the platform) often cannot directly select and manage the workers in the crowdsourcing platform. In fact, the requester can only submit tasks and define the incentives for each task. The lack of control makes the incentive design for the crowdsourcing platform very difficult since we cannot cherry-pick the highly reliable and responsive workers to complete the tasks. For this reason, the current incentive design solutions that assume the full control of the crowd workers cannot be applied to our problem [6, 20, 31, 39, 48]. Second, the time and quality of the responses from the crowd workers are highly dynamic and unpredictable, and their relationships to incentives are not trivial to model. Existing solutions often assume that more incentives will lead to less response time and high response quality [18, 30]. However, we found the quality of the responses from the crowd workers is diversified and does not simply depend on the level of incentives provided in our experiments (e.g., the quality can be high even with low incentives provided). Similarly, we observe the response delay from the crowd is not simply proportional to the incentive level. With these unique features, the research question to tackle here is: *how to effectively incentivize the crowd to provide reliable and timely responses to improve AI performance?*

6.2   A Crowd-AI Hybrid System: CrowdLearn

We present a CrowdLearn framework that leverages human feedback from the crowdsourcing platform to troubleshoot, calibrate and boost the AI performance in DDA applications [52].

In particular, CrowdLearn address the black-box challenges of AI and the crowdsourcing platform by developing four new schemes: (1) a query set selection (QSS) scheme to find the best strategy to query the crowdsourcing platform for feedback; (2) a new incentive policy design (IPD) scheme to incentivize the crowd to provide a timely and accurate response to the query; (3) a crowd quality control (CQC) scheme that refines the responses from the crowd and provides trustworthy feedback to the AI algorithms; (4) a machine intelligence calibration (MIC) scheme that incorporates the feedback from the crowd to improve the AI algorithms by alleviating various failure scenarios of AI. The four components are integrated into a holistic closed-loop system that allows the AI and crowd to effectively interact with each other and eventually achieve boosted performance for the DDA application. The CrowdLearn framework was evaluated using Amazon Mechanical Turk (MTurk) and a real-world DDA application. We compared CrowdLearn with the state-of-the-art baselines in both AI-only algorithms and human-AI frameworks. The results show that our scheme achieves significant performance gain in terms of classification accuracy in disaster damage assessment with reasonably low response time and costs.

6.2.1   Problem Definition

In this subsection, we first introduce the AI and crowd models respectively, and then formally define our problem.

AI-Based Disaster Damage Assessment Model   We first introduce the AI-based Disaster Damage Assessment (DDA) model. In a DDA application, images posted from social media related to a disaster event are dynamically crawled and classified based on the levels of damage reported in the image. Figure 6.2 shows an example of different levels of damage from images in a DDA application. The damage assessment provides the critical information for emergency responses (e.g., sending out the rescue teams, allocating resources). The DDA application is constantly running, and the images of the disaster are periodically crawled and analyzed. We refer to the updating period as a *sensing cycle*.

We assume a DDA application has a total of T sensing cycles. The input data samples to the DDA algorithm is a set of N images, denoted as $I_1^t, I_2^t, \ldots, I_N^t$, where I_i^t denotes the ith input image at the tth sensing cycle. Each image I_i^t is associated with a ground truth label O_i^t and an estimated label (i.e., classification result) from the AI algorithm $\tilde{O}_i^t$.

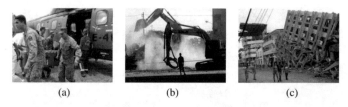

(a)   (b)   (c)

Fig. 6.2 Example output labels of DDA. (**a**) No damage. (**b**) Moderate damage. (**c**) Severe damage

As discussed in the introduction, we make a few observations about the deep learning based DDA algorithms below.

1. *Black-box:* the DDA algorithms are black-box deep neural network models and the classification results in general lack interpretability.
2. *Failure accountability:* the AI-based DDA algorithms can fail (i.e., providing wrong classification labels for images) and the failure scenarios cannot be easily diagnosed without human scrutiny [23].

The above observations are critical in the design of the CrowdLearn scheme. To alleviate the performance deficiency of the AI algorithms, we meld AI and crowd intelligence into a holistic system by leveraging the crowdsourcing platform. We elaborate the crowdsourcing platform model below.

Crowdsourcing Platform Model   Crowdsourcing platforms are well known for their cost efficiency and the massive amount of freelance workers [5]. We first define the key terms used in our crowdsourcing platform.

Definition (Crowd Query (q_x^t)) A set of questions assigned to the crowdsourcing platform.   □

Definition (Query Response (r_x^t)) The corresponding answers provided to the crowd query q_x^t.   □

An example query is shown in Fig. 6.3. We assume a set of $X(t)$ queries are sent at each sensing cycle t to the crowdsourcing platform $\mathcal{Q}(t) = \{q_1^t, q_2^t, \ldots, q_X^t(t)\}$ where q_x^t denotes the xth query submitted to the crowd at the tth sensing cycle. Each query q_x^t is associated with an incentive provided by the application, denoted as b_x^t. We assume the application has a total budget of B for the crowdsourcing platform.

The responses to the queries are denoted as $\mathcal{R}(t) = \{r_1^t, r_2^t, \ldots, r_X^t(t)\}$ where r_x^t denotes the answer to q_x^t. For each query, two items are solicited from the crowd: the *label of the image* and *a set of questions*. The questions collect the contextual information observed by humans that cannot be easily extracted by AI. For example, we ask humans whether the image is fake and what is actually happening in that image (e.g., car damage or bridge falling down). Such contextual information cannot be easily captured by AI but is crucial in determining the damage severity. We leverage the contextual information to decide the actual label of the image (more

Fig. 6.3 An example of crowd query on MTurk

details in Sect. 6.2.2.3). Each response is associated with a response delay denoted as d_x^t. We also make a few observations about the crowdsourcing platform:

1. *Black-box:* the crowdsourcing platform is a black-box where the requester cannot directly control or pick the workers for the queries.
2. *Unreliable Workers:* the crowd workers are not perfectly reliable and can provide responses based on their own biases and personal opinions.
3. *Non-trivial incentive-delay-quality Relationship:* the relationship between incentives and the delay and quality of the response from the crowd cannot be simply modeled as linear relationships (e.g., the quality is proportional to the incentives and the delay is inversely proportional to the incentives). Instead, such relationships can be complex, dynamic and context-dependent.

Given the above definitions and assumptions, the goal of our CrowdLearn system can be formulated as a constrained multi-objective optimization problem. In particular, CrowdLearn targets at maximizing the classification accuracy of the AI-based DDA algorithms, while minimizing the average delay from the crowd for a given budget on the crowdsourcing platform. The accuracy maximization objective ensures that the crowd can help AI assess the damage severity with high accuracy in the absence of domain experts. The delay minimization objective ensures that the crowd provides feedback to AI in a timely manner. The resource constraints make sure the CrowdLearn framework does not incur unexpected excessive costs to the DDA application. Formally we have:

$$\text{max:} \quad Pr(O_i^t = \tilde{O}_i^t | \mathcal{R}(t), B), \forall 1 \leq i \leq N, 1 \leq t \leq T$$

$$\text{min:} \quad \frac{\sum_{x=1}^{X} d_x^t}{X}, \forall 1 \leq x \leq X(t), 1 \leq t \leq T \tag{6.1}$$

$$\text{s.t.:} \quad \sum_{t=1}^{T} \sum_{x=1}^{X(t)} b_x^t \leq B, 1 \leq x \leq X(t), 1 \leq t \leq T$$

6.2.2   The CrowdLearn Framework

An overview of the CrowdLearn framework is shown in Fig. 6.4. The CrowdLearn is designed as a crowd-AI hybrid system that consists of four main modules: (1) a Query Set Selection (QSS) scheme that identifies failure instances in AI algorithms and sends queries to the crowd; (2) an Incentive Policy Design (IPD) scheme that takes the query set from QSS and assigns effective incentives for the queries to achieve the desired response delay; (3) a Crowd Quality Control (CQC) scheme that derives truthful answers from the crowd response; (4) a Machine Intelligence Calibration (MIC) scheme that incorporates query answers from CQC to improve the accuracy of the AI algorithms. We present them in detail below.

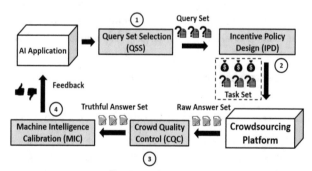

System workflow - ① QSS selects a set of data samples to query the crowd. ② IPD takes in the query set and generates a monetary incentive for each query. The query set with incentives is submitted to the crowdsourcing platform as a set of tasks. ③ The workers take the tasks and provide answers to the queries. CQC takes the answers from the crowd and provides quality control to generate truthful answers. ④ MIC compares the crowd answers with the results of the AI algorithms and improve their accuracy.

Fig. 6.4 System architecture of CrowdLearn

6.2.2.1 Query Set Selection (QSS)

The design of QSS is motivated by two common failure scenarios of AI algorithms:
(1) the lack of sufficient training data, and (2) the innate problem of the AI algorithm
itself (e.g, oversimplified assumptions, inappropriate models). In CrowdLearn, we
address the first failure scenario by actively asking the crowd to provide more
reliable labels (e.g., the damage severity of specific images in DDA application) and
use the labels to retrain the model. With more training samples that are judiciously
selected by QSS, the performance of AI is expected to improve. We address the
second failure scenario by directly offloading the inference tasks to the crowd—
i.e., asking the crowd to take over the AI algorithm. In both cases, we need to first
identify the subset of data samples to be labeled from the crowdsourcing platform.
Note that it is often impractical to send all data samples for the crowd to label due to
budget and time constraints [18, 50]. The QSS module is designed to find the subset
of data samples to query the crowd that can effectively address the failure scenarios
of AI algorithms.

To identify the query subset, the key strategy is to identify the data samples that
the AI algorithm is uncertain about—i.e., cannot confidently decide the label of
the sample. Take DDA as an example. If the AI algorithm cannot distinguish which
damage level best describes the image, then it is better to send the image to the crowd
for labeling. Based on this intuition, we first design a Query by Committee (QBC)
based active learning (AL) scheme to derive the uncertainty of the AL algorithms.
In the QBC scheme, a set of relevant AI algorithms vote which new data sample
needs to be queried from the crowd. Such a technique has been proven to be robust
by removing the bias of a single classifier [29]. We define a few key terms for our
QBC-based model.

Definition (Committee) A committee is set of AI algorithms for our DDA
application.   □

Definition (Expert) An expert is an AI algorithm selected into the committee.   □

In the DDA application, we choose a diverse set of M representative DDA
algorithms $AI_1, AI_2, \ldots, AI_M$ that all take images as inputs. At a given sensing
cycle, each expert (e.g., a deep neural network DDA algorithm) independently labels
all the unseen data samples. The output of each expert is defined as an "expert vote".

Definition (Expert Vote) An expert vote is the output of the AI algorithm, which
is a probabilistic distribution of all possible class labels estimated by the algorithm.
                                                                                 □

We use $\mathcal{V}(AI_{m,i}^t)$ to denote the vote of AI_m at a given data sample I_i^t by AI_m.
For each algorithm AI_m, we define an expert weight w_m^t as follows.

Definition (Expert Weight (w_m^t)) The level of trustworthiness of the algorithm
in determining the final label of the data sample. The higher the weight, the more
trustworthy the algorithm's classification result is.   □

In CrowdLearn, the expert weights are dynamically adjusted based on the feedback from the crowd. We discuss the adjustment process in Sect. 6.2.2.4. Given the expert weights and votes of the experts, the committee decides the final label of the data sample (referred to as "committee vote"), which is the weighted sum of the label distributions of all committee members. Formally, we calculate the committee vote ρ for sample I_i^t as:

$$\rho_i^t = \sum_{m=1}^{M} w_m^t \times \mathcal{V}(AI_{m,i}^t) \tag{6.2}$$

The label distribution is further normalized with a sum of 1 to emulate an aggregated probabilistic distribution of the inference results. To quantify the uncertainty of AI algorithms in a committee, we define a new metric *Committee Entropy*.

Definition (Committee Entropy ($\mathcal{H}$)) The committee's overall uncertainty of labeling a data sample. □

We derive $\mathcal{H}_i^t$ as the entropy of the normalized ρ_i^t.

$$\mathcal{H}_i^t = -\sum_{\rho \in \rho_i^t} Pr(\rho) \times \log Pr(\rho) \tag{6.3}$$

Given the committee entropy of each data sample, the intuitive query set selection strategy is to pick data samples with the highest committee entropy. However, such a strategy would fail when all classifiers confidently report the same wrong result. For example, in the DDA application, if all classifiers fail to capture fake images and report the fake images as "severe damage" with high confidence, the QSS will never pick the fake images for the crowd to check. Therefore, the QSS scheme also has to occasionally include the data samples with low committee entropy in the query set. This turns out to be an exploitation-exploration problem in reinforcement learning. We adopt an ϵ-*greedy* strategy [33] in our QSS scheme to solve this problem. We summarize the detailed procedure of the QSS scheme in Algorithm 4.

6.2.2.2 Incentive Policy Design (IPD)

It is critical to provide timely and high-quality responses from the crowd in the DDA application. Therefore, CrowdLearn will decide how to incentivize the crowd after QSS selects a query set. We found the design of an incentive policy is a non-trivial problem due to two canonical challenges: (1) modeling the relationship between the incentives and the quality and delay of the crowd response is a non-trivial problem for the black-box crowdsourcing platform; (2) the quality and delay are context-dependent (e.g., the response delay has different characteristics at different times of the day). To address the above challenges, we design a new reinforcement

---

Algorithm 4 QSS scheme

1: **Input -** Size of query set Y, Images $I_1^t, I_2^t, \ldots, I_N^t$
2: **Initialize**: $Committee = AI_1, AI_2, \ldots, AI_M$, $votes = newArray[M]$, $CommitteeEntropy$
   = null, $output = newArray[Y]$
3: **for** $1 \leq t \leq T$ **do**
4:    **for** $1 \leq i \leq N$ **do**
5:       **for** $1 \leq m \leq M$ **do**
6:          $votes[m] \leftarrow \mathcal{V}(AI_{m,i}^t)$
7:       **end for**
8:       calculate $CommitteeEntropy$ using Eqs. (6.2) and (6.3).
9:    **end for**
10:   build sorted list s_list based on $CommitteeEntropy$ (high to low)
11:   **for** $1 \leq t \leq Y$ **do**
12:      $output.append(s\_list.pop())$ w.p. $(1 - \epsilon)$
13:      $output.append(s\_list[rand(1, sizeof(s\_list))])$ w.p. ϵ
14:   **end for**
15: **end for**
16: **return** $output$

---

learning based Incentive Policy Design (IPD) scheme to incentivize the black-box crowdsourcing platform for timely responses to the queries from the crowd.

Characterizing the Influence of Incentive on Response Delay and Quality We first perform a pilot study to understand the effect of changing the level of incentives w.r.t. response delay and quality on our crowdsourcing platform MTurk. For the pilot study, we chose 7 incentive levels (1 cent, 2 cents, 4 cents, 6 cents, 8 cents, 10 cents, and 20 cents) and four different temporal contexts (morning, afternoon, evening, and midnight). At each (incentive level, temporal context) combination, we assign a total of 100 HITs (Human Intelligence Tasks) to the MTurk platform: we issue a total of 20 queries, and each query is allowed to be answered by 5 workers. In the existing literature, the response time of human workers is often assumed to be proportional to the incentives provided [18, 22, 47]: the higher the incentive per task, the faster a crowd worker will provide a response. While this assumption is intuitive, our pilot study shows it may not always hold on MTurk. Figure 6.5 shows the response time of the crowd across different temporal contexts and incentive levels. We observe that the response time does seem to decrease as the incentive increases in the morning and afternoon. However, we also observe that most incentive levels (except for the lowest and highest) have very similar response times during evening and midnight. We attribute this observation to the fact that MTurk workers are often more active at night (e.g., after work) so that a query can always find a set of workers who are willing to take HITs. However, during the daytime, workers are less active and appear to be more "selective" in taking HITs. Such dynamics indicate the importance of considering the temporal contexts in the design of the incentive scheme for CrowdLearn.

We also study the quality of the annotated labels from the crowd with respect to the incentives provided. The results are shown in Fig. 6.6. We observe that while

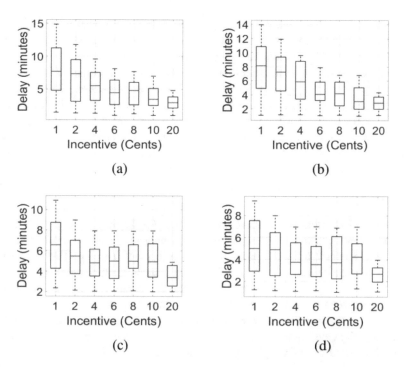

Fig. 6.5 Crowd response time vs. incentives on MTurk. (a) Morning. (b) Afternoon. (c) Evening. (d) Midnight

Fig. 6.6 Label quality vs. incentives on MTurk

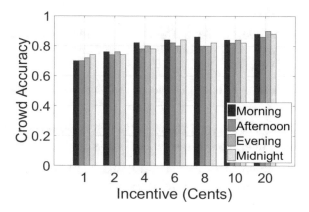

very low incentives (e.g., 1 and 2 cents per HIT) generate relatively low label quality, increasing the incentives does not always significantly increase the quality. By performing Wilcoxon Test [12] (a statistical hypothesis test commonly used to compare two related samples), we found no statistical significance (significant if $p \leq 0.05$) when the incentive level increases from 2 to 4 ($p = 0.12$), from 4 to 6 ($p = 0.45$), from 6 to 8 ($p=0.77$), and from 8 to 10 ($p=0.25$). We attribute the above observation to the fact that the image labeling tasks for the workers are relatively intuitive—workers often do not need to exert much effort/expertise to accurately label the images notwithstanding the incentives.

The above results offer us the following design principles for the IPD module: (1) the context information must be incorporated into the policy design; (2) the dynamic response delay must be explicitly considered; (3) it may not be wise to increase the incentives merely for improved annotation quality. With the above principles, we design a reinforcement learning based framework that targets at minimizing the response delay of the crowd workers. Note that we do not intend to use an incentive mechanism to control the response quality considering the third design principle. Instead, we design another module to perform the crowd quality control in Sect. 6.2.2.3.

Constrained Contextual Multi-Armed Bandit for Incentive Policy We found that the incentive design problem can be nicely mapped to a constrained contextual multi-armed bandit (CCMB) problem in reinforcement learning. The key reason for choosing the contextual bandit is that it can incorporate the *context information* into the incentive policy design (e.g., the contextual bandit can design fine-grained policy assignments under different temporal contexts). Also, the reinforcement learning framework allows CCMB to dynamically adapt to the uncertain black-box crowdsourcing environments and derive the optimal incentive policy. We formally define the key terms in CCMB and its mapping to IPD below.

Definition (Uncertain Environment) The uncertain environment in IPD refers to the black-box crowdsourcing platform that has the non-trivial incentive-delay tradeoff.   □

Definition (Context) The context in IPD refers to the temporal context for the crowdsourcing platform. We choose four contexts—morning, afternoon, evening, and midnight.   □

Definition (Action) The action in IPD refers to the choice of incentive levels for a query.   □

Definition (Payoff) The payoff in IPD refers to the additive inverse of the average delay of the query answers. The less delay, the higher payoff.   □

Definition (Action Cost and Resource Budget) The action cost is the incentive set for each query. The resource budget is the total cost of using the crowdsourcing platform.   □

We formally define our CCMB model below. We consider a CCMB with a context set $\mathcal{X} = \{1, 2, \ldots, Z\}$ and an action set $\mathcal{A} = \{1, 2, \ldots, K\}$. An example context set is $\mathcal{X} = \{morning, afternoon, night, midnight\}$ and an example action set is $\mathcal{A} = \{1, 2, 4, 6, 8, 10, 20\}$ where each entry in $\mathcal{A}$ denotes the amount of money (in cents). We assume the crowdsourcing platform is associated with a specific context and each action $k \in \mathcal{A}$ generates a non-negative payoff p_k^t with cost c_k at each sensing cycle. We assume the conditional expectation $e[p_k^t | \mathcal{X}^t = z]$

is unknown to the application. We use C^t to denote all the costs incurred at the tth cycle. We assume the context $\mathcal{X}^t$ is observable at the beginning of a cycle. However, the payoff of the action taken by the agent is only revealed at the end of the cycle (i.e., you do not know the delay until the responses are submitted by the crowd).

The goal of CCMB is to derive an optimal incentive policy that decides to perform which action in which context to maximize the payoffs while keeping the total action cost within the resource budget. The CCMB problem is a decision making process that maps the historical observations $\{\mathcal{X}^1, \mathcal{A}^1, \mathcal{P}^1; \mathcal{X}^2, \mathcal{A}^2, \mathcal{P}^2; \ldots; \mathcal{X}^{t-1}, \mathcal{A}^{t-1}, \mathcal{P}^{t-1}\}$ and the current context $\mathcal{X}^t$ to an action $\mathcal{A}^t \in \mathcal{A}$. The objective of the CCMB problem is to maximize the expected total payoff for a given resource budget constraint as follows:

$$
\begin{aligned}
&\underset{\mathcal{A}^t}{\operatorname{argmax}} \sum_{t=1}^{T} P^t, 1 \le t \le T \text{ (payoff maximization)} \\
&\text{s.t.: } \sum_{t=1}^{T} C^t \le B, 1 \le t \le T \text{ (budget constraint)}
\end{aligned}
\tag{6.4}
$$

This objective function can be solved using the adaptive linear programming approach in [43]. The detailed discussion of the training process of IPD is discussed in Sect. 6.3.

6.2.2.3   Crowd Quality Control (CQC)

A key challenge of the crowdsourcing platform is that the quality of the answers varies and some workers can provide wrong answers due to their limited knowledge or subjective opinions. In fact, our pilot studies show the average labeling accuracy of the crowd workers is not perfect (i.e., around 80% in Fig. 6.6). Several existing solutions are developed to address this issue. For example, majority voting is a common technique (**Voting**) where the aggregated result is simply the one returned by the majority of the workers. This approach is known to be suboptimal when workers have different reliability [36, 37, 51]. More principled approaches such as truth discovery (**TD-EM**) [35] is able to jointly derive the truthful label of the queries as well as the reliability of the workers. However, this technique does not work well when the number of responses per worker is low [45]. Another commonly used technique is worker quality filtering (**Filtering**) [18], which blacklists the workers with a record of poor labeling quality. However, this approach may fail when the workers are new to the platform and do not have sufficient labeling history. There also exist some expertise-aware worker assignment schemes [13, 38, 42, 47] that directly assign queries to workers with high quality. However, they assume the application has full control of the worker pool [16], which does not apply to the black-box crowdsourcing platform we study.

Table 6.1 Aggregated label accuracy. Bold values indicate the best performance achieved by CQC scheme compared to the baselines

	Morning	Afternoon	Evening	Midnight	Overall
CQC	**0.93**	**0.92**	**0.94**	**0.94**	**0.9350**
Voting	0.82	0.83	0.85	0.87	0.8425
TD-EM	0.86	0.85	0.85	0.89	0.8625
Filtering	0.84	0.86	0.88	0.90	0.8775

In light of the knowledge gap of existing crowd quality control schemes, we devise a new idea: we not only ask the crowd to provide direct labels of data samples, but also provide their evidence. The evidence is captured by a set of questionnaires (Fig. 6.3). For example, in the DDA application, we ask the workers to answer "Is the image photoshopped (i.e., fake image)?" or "Does this image show a damage of road?" Note that we use the format of a fixed-form questionnaire rather than free-form input (e.g., ask the worker to describe the image) to eliminate the challenge of parsing natural language. The questionnaire collected a set of extra features that can help derive the truthful labels of the images.

Given the labels and features provided by the workers, we train a supervised classifier that takes both the labels and the questionnaire answers of a query as inputs and outputs the truthful label of the image. We choose the state-of-the-art gradient boosting model (XGBoost) [4] as our classifier. The combination of labels and questionnaire answers allows CQC to achieve at least 5.75% higher accuracy than existing approaches (shown in Table 6.1). The accurate truthful labels generated by CQC module provide us with a good basis to evaluate and calibrate the AI algorithms. We elaborate the details of the calibration process next.

6.2.2.4   Machine Intelligence Calibration (MIC)

The MIC module is designed to calibrate and improve the AI algorithms based on the labels provided by the crowd workers. The MIC module includes three complementary calibration strategies that are performed simultaneously right after the execution of CQC module within each sensing cycle.

Dynamic Expert Weights Update Strategy Recall that a set of AI algorithms form a committee in QSS module to collectively decide the classification result of a data sample and each algorithm is assigned an expert weight. The expert weight is crucial in determining the performance of the AI algorithms. We design a dynamic expert score update strategy that can learn the performance of each expert in the committee as the feedback is collected from the crowd. This strategy builds a feedback control process using the crowd feedback as the control signal. In particular, for each AI algorithm AI_m, we compute a loss function based on the discrepancy of its classification result and the truthful label from the crowd as:

$$\mathcal{L}_m^t = \sum^{i \in \mathcal{Q}^t} 1 - \delta(KL^{sym}(\mathcal{D}(AI_{m,i}^t), \mathcal{D}(TL_i^t)) \tag{6.5}$$

where $\mathcal{Q}^t$ denotes the set of images chosen by QSS for MTurks at the tth sensing cycle. $\mathcal{D}(TL_i^t)$ is the probabilistic distribution of the labels obtained from CQC module. $KL^{sym}(\mathcal{D}(AI_{m,i}^t), \mathcal{D}(TL_i^t))$ is the symmetric KL-Divergence between the two label distributions. δ is a normalization process to map the divergence to a [0, 1] scale. Intuitively, the more different that the output from the AI algorithm is from the truthful label from the crowd, the higher the loss is. Given the loss function, we dynamically update the expert weights of the AI algorithms at each sensing cycle using a classical exponential weight update rule [3]. The updated weights reflect the reliability of each expert at the current sensing cycle. We use the updated weights to derive the final labels of the input images as discussed in Sect. 6.2.2.1.

Model Retraining and Crowd Offloading Strategies The model retraining strategy is to address the failure case of AI algorithms that is caused by insufficient training samples. Similar to existing hybrid AI-human frameworks [18], we use the truthful labels provided by the crowdsourcing platform to retrain the AI models for the next sensing cycle. The crowd offloading strategy is implemented to tackle the cases where the AI algorithms may have innate flaws (e.g., failure to handle fake images in DDA applications). In this strategy, the truthful labels derived from the CQC is used to directly replace the classification labels of the query set from QSS in the current sensing cycle. The query set contains two categories of images that AI potentially fails: (1) the images that the AI algorithms in the committee do not agree with each other on their labels (captured by the committee entropy); and (2) the images that the AI algorithms happen to make the same wrong decision (captured by the ϵ-greedy strategy). By replacing both categories of images with human labels, the crowd offloading strategy not only prevents AI from giving uncertain classification labels but also addresses the failure case when AI algorithms make a common mistake.

6.3   Real-World Case Studies of CrowdLearn

In this section, we present an extensive evaluation of our CrowdLearn scheme. We first discuss the evaluation setup and baselines for comparison. We then present the evaluation results using a real-world deep learning-based damage assessment (DDA) application in the aftermath of a disaster event. The results show that CrowdLearn achieves significant performance gains in terms of classification accuracy and crowd delay compared to the state-of-the-art baselines.

We choose the following state-of-the-art DDA schemes and hybrid human-AI solutions as our baselines. For the QSS module in CrowdLearn, we use VGG16, BoVW, and DDM as the committee.

- **VGG16**: a DDA scheme that uses deep Convolutional Neural Networks (CNN) [21].
- **BoVW**: a DDA scheme that uses handcrafted features (e.g., scale-invariant feature transform, histogram of oriented gradients) to train a neural network classifier [1].
- **DDM**: a DDA scheme that combines CNN and Gradient-weighted Class Activation Mapping (Grad-CAM) to produce a damage heatmap of a given image, which is used to derive the damage severity [19].
- **Ensemble**: an aggregation of the above algorithms (VGG16, BoVW, DDM) using a boosting technique [26].
- **Hybrid-Para**: a human-AI hybrid system where humans and AI independently label the images and their results are integrated using a complexity index [15].
- **Hybrid-AL**: a crowdsourcing-based active learning framework for AI algorithms where the annotated labels collected from MTurk are used to re-train the AI algorithm for performance improvement [18].

We use a total of 960 social media images with golden ground truth labels about the Ecuador Earthquake in 2016 from Instagram and Twitter [21]. In our experiments, the dataset is split into a *training set* and a *test set*. The training set is used to (1) perform the pilot study to characterize the black-box MTurk platform; (2) train the reinforcement learning based IPD module as described in Sect. 6.2.2.2; and (3) train the AI-based DDA algorithms. The training set contains a total of 560 images and the test set has a total of 400 images that emulates unseen data dynamically generated during each sensing cycle.

We run the application over 40 sensing cycles during 4 different temporal contexts (i.e., morning, afternoon, evening, midnight)—10 cycles for each temporal context. Each sensing cycle lasts 10 min and has a set of 10 images from the test set. The input and output to CrowdLearn and all baseline schemes are the same: each scheme takes an image as input and output severity level of the image (including *severe*, *moderate*, and *no damage*). Note that Hybrid-Para, Hybrid-AL, and CrowdLearn are different from other baselines in the sense that they all leverage humans from MTurk. To that end, we allow the three hybrid schemes to query the same amount of images to MTurk (i.e., 5 images per sensing cycle).

Classification Accuracy In the first set of experiments, we focus on the overall performance of all schemes in terms of classification accuracy, which is evaluated using the classic metrics for multi-class classification: *Accuracy, Precision, Recall* and *F1 Score*. Similar to [19, 21], these scores are *macro-averaged* since the dataset has balanced class labels.

The results are reported in Table 6.2. We observe that CrowdLearn consistently outperforms other baselines. In particular, CrowdLearn achieved 5.3% improvement on the F1 Score compared to the best-performing baseline (i.e., Hybrid—AL). The reason is that CrowdLearn can effectively integrate human intelligence into the DDA algorithm. In particular, the MIC module leverages human intelligence to improve the results by fine-tuning the expert weights of candidate AI algorithms

Table 6.2 Classification accuracy for all schemes. Bold values indicate the best performance achieved by CrowdLearn scheme compared to the baselines

Algorithms	Accuracy	Precision	Recall	F1
CrowdLearn	**0.877**	**0.904**	**0.885**	**0.894**
VGG16	0.770	0.845	0.744	0.791
BoVW	0.670	0.707	0.744	0.725
DDM	0.807	0.891	0.765	0.823
Ensemble	0.815	0.892	0.778	0.831
Hybrid-Para	0.797	0.849	0.795	0.821
Hybrid-AL	0.823	0.883	0.803	0.841

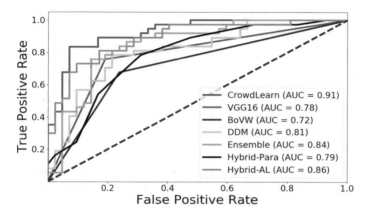

Fig. 6.7 Macro-average ROC curves for all schemes

to outperform the AI-only schemes. Compared to other hybrid human-AI systems, CrowdLearn actively troubleshoots and eventually fixes the failure scenarios of AI algorithms. In contrast, Hybrid-Para only takes the crowd as a source of annotations and does not directly interact with the AI algorithm. Hybrid-AL only leverages crowd annotations for retraining and cannot address the innate failure mode of the AI algorithm. We further plot the ROC curves of all schemes in Fig. 6.7. We observe that CrowdLearn continues to outperform other baselines when we tune the classification thresholds.

Delay Analysis Next, we evaluate the delay of all compared schemes in terms of (1) execution time, and (2) delay of query answered by the crowdsourcing platform. In a practical setting, the complete life cycle of the DDA application should include both of these delays. The experiment is conducted on a PC with Nvidia RTX 2070 GPU and Intel i7-8700K 6-core CPU and 16G of RAM. The average delay of algorithm execution time and crowd delay of all schemes are listed in Table 6.3. We observe that the execution delay of CrowdLearn is higher than AI-only schemes (i.e., VGG16, BoVW and DDM) because CrowdLearn incorporates all three AI-only algorithms as its committee and runs extra modules to generate incentives and perform quality control to the crowd. We also observe that response delay from the crowdsourcing platform is the major contributor to the overall delay of human-

Table 6.3 Average delay (in seconds) per sensing cycle. Bold values indicate the best performance achieved by CrowdLearn scheme compared to the baselines

Algorithms	Algorithm Delay	Crowd Delay
CrowdLearn	**55.62**	**342.77**
VGG16	47.83	N/A
BoVW	37.55	N/A
DDM	52.57	N/A
Ensemble	85.82	N/A
Hybrid-Para	94.28	588.75
Hybrid-AL	53.54	527.61

AI hybrid systems including CrowdLearn. This observation further demonstrates the importance of designing an effective incentive policy to minimize the response delay from the crowd and provide a timely response to the application. The results show that the CrowdLearn scheme significantly reduces the crowd delay by 35% compared to Hybrid-Para and Hybrid-AL that both adopt a fixed incentive policy. We attribute such a performance gain to our novel IPD module that leverages a context-aware reinforcement learning scheme to dynamically identify the optimal incentive strategy to reduce the response delay from the crowd.

To further examine the crowd response delay, we show the delay across different temporal contexts. In addition to the fixed incentive policy adopted by Hybrid-Para and Hybrid-AL, we also compare another heuristic baseline where the incentives are randomly assigned. For the fixed incentive strategy, we use the maximum incentive for each query (i.e., the total budget divided by the number of queries). The results are shown in Fig. 6.8. We observe that the IPD module in CrowdLearn achieves the lowest delay with the least variations across different contexts compared to both fixed and random incentive mechanisms. This is because CrowdLearn can adjust its incentives based on how responsive the crowd is. For example, if the crowd is less responsive (e.g., in the morning), CrowdLearn would provide higher incentives to stimulate timely responses. On the other hand, CrowdLearn would decrease the incentives when the crowd is very proactive (e.g., in the evening). The results show that CrowdLearn is robust against the change of contexts and provides consistently faster responses from the crowd than alternative strategies.

Impact of Human Intelligence A key parameter in our problem setting is the size of the query set (i.e., the amount of images that are sent to the MTurk for query). We tune the size of the query set from 0% of the images at each sensing cycle (AI only) to 100% (crowd only) to examine its effect on the classification performance. We only compare CrowdLearn with hybrid human-AI baselines that include the crowd component and the best-performing AI-only baseline (i.e., Ensemble) as a reference point. The results are shown in Fig. 6.9. We observe that the performance gain of CrowdLearn compared to the baselines increases as we increase the size of the query set, which demonstrates the benefit of incorporating human intelligence into the AI algorithms. Interestingly, we note that the performance of other hybrid human-AI systems (i.e., Hybrid-AL and Hybrid-Para) is rather stable even with the increase in the number of queries to the crowd. We attribute this observation to the

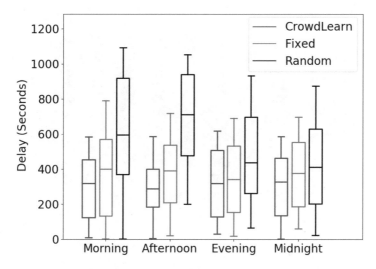

Fig. 6.8 Crowd delay at different temporal contexts

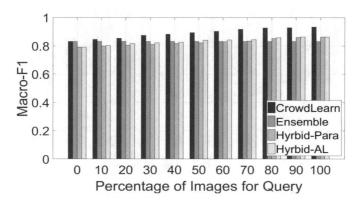

Fig. 6.9 Size of query set vs. classification performance

fact that these baselines did not really fix the innate problem of AI as we discussed in the classification accuracy section.

We also observe that the performance of CrowdLearn degrades to Ensemble when there is no HI (i.e., 0% query set). However, our scheme still outperforms Hybrid-Para and Hybrid-AL when there is no AI (i.e., 100% query set). This is because the CQC component in CrowdLearn can provide much more accurate human annotations than the two baselines that simply use majority voting for quality control.

Impact of Budget In our last set of experiments, we study the impact of the resource budget on the classification accuracy and delay of CrowdLearn. We tune the total budget from 2 USD (1 cent per task on average) to 40 USD (20 cents per task on average). The classification accuracy and delay are reported in

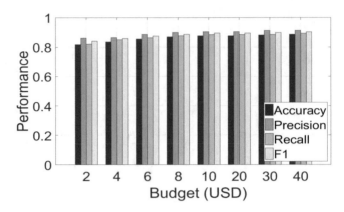

Fig. 6.10   Budget vs. F1

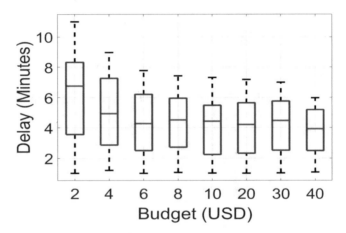

Fig. 6.11   Budget vs. delay

Figs. 6.10 and 6.11 respectively. We observe that the classification performance of CrowdLearn is worse with low incentives as compared to higher ones. However, the performance becomes stable as long as a reasonable budget is provided (e.g., above 6 USD or 3 cents per task on average). For example, the F1 score only increases by 0.18 from the budget of 8 USD to the budget of 40 USD. We observe a similar impact of budget on the crowd response delay. The above results show that the CQC scheme and IPD schemes in CrowdLearn are robust to the changes in the budget and can consistently perform well with reasonable budgets.

6.4 Incorporating Human Visual Attention

The design of CrowdLearn neglects an important advantage of human—"the visual attention" [53]. In particular, we found one key element that directly contributes to the failure of DDA algorithms is the inaccurate "visual attention" in these algorithms. The visual attention refers to the region of an image that the AI algorithm focuses on to identify the damage level of the scene. We show examples of visual attention (illustrated as a heatmap) of three representative DDA algorithms in Fig. 6.12. We also plot the ground truth annotation of human attention (marked in the red region) in the figure. Ideally, the visual attention of a DDA scheme should focus on the damaged regions that are the same/similar as those captured by human perception. However, all three DDA schemes in Fig. 6.12 fail to perform such tasks to different extents. In contrast, human attention is often much superior and more reliable than the neural attention mechanism in identifying regions of interest in images [17]. For example, in Fig. 6.12, humans can easily identify the damage areas correctly.

A possible approach to improve the visual attention of DDA algorithms is to introduce neural attention mechanisms [40] that can emulate the human's visual perception by learning from the labeled data. However, such an approach has several limitations in DDA applications: (1) the lack of dedicated training data for disaster events (which is often caused by expensive labeling costs); (2) the innate algorithm bias caused by the design and structure of the neural network [17, 52]; (3) the noisy nature of the social media images that are taken with diverse camera angles, backgrounds, and resolutions. To address these limitations, we develop a new human-AI DDA system called interactive Disaster Scene Assessment (iDSA). A key novelty of iDSA is to leverage human knowledge to interact with the DDA algorithms to troubleshoot and adjust the attention region of images, which in turn will improve the accuracy of the DDA results. We use crowdsourcing platforms (e.g., Amazon Mechanical Turk (MTurk)) to obtain human knowledge because they are known for their cost efficiency and the massive amount of freelance workers [5]. However, designing such a human-AI interactive system brings some critical technical challenges.

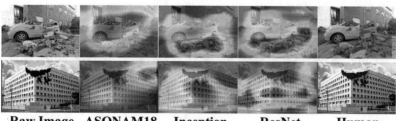

Raw Image   ASONAM18   Inception   ResNet   Human

Fig. 6.12 Visual attention of various DDA schemes

The key challenge lies in the difficulty of understanding and fixing the inaccurate visual attention of AI-based DDA models. We observe that existing attention solutions can be easily misled by a diverse set of objects and the noisy background of disaster scenes. Since these AI-based attention mechanisms are often trained in a black-box fashion, their failure scenarios are hard to explain [40]—is it due to the lack of training data? Or, is it due to the wrong design of the attention mechanism? These questions make it non-trivial to leverage the crowd to effectively improve the AI's attention. Current solutions on human-AI systems improve AI primarily by obtaining new ground truth labels and retraining the model [15, 18]. However, such approaches treat an AI model as a black-box and do not intend to understand and troubleshoot its internal attention mechanism. Unfortunately, we found no existing work has been done to leverage the crowd intelligence to troubleshoot and improve AI attention of DDA applications.

To address the first challenge, iDSA develops a new CNN model which designs a novel interactive attention mechanism to allow crowd workers to intervene and adjust the internal visual attention of the DDA model. To our knowledge, iDSA is the first solution to leverage human knowledge from crowdsourcing to directly adjust the internal attention mechanism of AI algorithms in DDA applications.

6.4.1 The iDSA Framework

iDSA is designed as a crowd-AI hybrid system (Fig. 6.13) that consists of four main modules: (1) a Crowd Task Generation (CTG) module; (2) a Budget Constrained Adaptive Incentive (BCAI) module; (3) an Interactive Attention Convolutional Neural Network (IACNN) module; (4) a Social Media Image Normalization (SMIN) module. We present them in detail below.

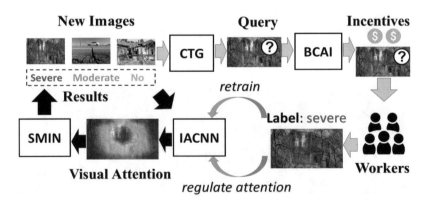

Fig. 6.13 iDSA overview

Fig. 6.14 Example query in CTG on MTurk

6.4.1.1 Crowd Task Generation to Acquire Human Perception

The Crowd Task Generation (CTG) module is designed to generate a set of crowd queries to acquire human knowledge to improve the AI-based DDA algorithms. An example query is illustrated in Fig. 6.14. It consists of two parts. The first part is the ground truth annotation where we directly ask the crowd to label their assessment of the damage. The mapping from the annotation score to the class label is discussed in detail in Sect. 6.5. The ground truth annotation allows the AI algorithm to obtain more training data on the fly. The second part of the query is attention annotation where we ask participants to draw the region in the image that they focus on when they assess the damage. The attention annotation allows the AI model to troubleshoot and improve its internal attention mechanism for better performance (discussed in the next subsection). Due to the budget constraint, it is impractical to send all data samples (i.e., images) for the crowd to label [18]. In CTG, we selectively choose images to query the crowd based on two criteria: (1) *uncertainty*: the images that cannot be confidently identified by the DDA algorithms should be prioritized in the queries; (2) *diversity*: keeping the annotated data samples diverse will help avoid the repetitive crowd annotations on similar images.

We design a Query by Committee (QBC) based active learning (AL) [29] scheme to derive the uncertainty of the DDA algorithms. In particular, we choose a diverse set of M state-of-the-art DDA algorithms $AI_1, AI_2, \ldots, AI_M$ (referred to as a "committee"). The committee introduces robustness by removing the bias of a single DDA scheme. At a given sensing cycle, each algorithm independently labels all the unseen data samples. We use $Y_{m,i}^t$ to denote the output of AI_m for a given data sample X_i^t. For each algorithm AI_m, we define a weight—w_m^t, representing the authority of the algorithm. We discuss the weight assignment in the IACNN module. The committee decides the classification result of X_i^t as:

$$Y_i^t = \sum_{m=1}^{M} w_m^t \times Y_{m,i}^t \tag{6.6}$$

Y_i^t is normalized by $\sum_{y \in Y_i^t} y = 1$ where y denotes the probability of a class label in the final output Y_i^t. Then we calculate an entropy score $\mathcal{H}_i^t$ for each DDA algorithm as:

$$\mathcal{H}_i^t = - \sum_{y \in Y_i^t} Pr(y) \times \log Pr(y) \tag{6.7}$$

We note that highly ranked images in terms of entropy score can be of high similarity (e.g., images all related to road damages, or images look alike). This is not ideal based on the diversity criterion. Therefore, we design a redundancy filtering algorithm to regulate the diversity of the crowd queries. With a total of K^t queries for the crowd under a given budget, we first assign a pool of K^t candidate images with the highest entropy scores. Then we iteratively remove images from the pool that are significantly similar to others, until all images in the pool have a similarity score lower than a predefined threshold. When removing an image, a new image with the next highest entropy is added to the pool. The similarity scores are calculated using the deep auto encoding technique in [9].

6.4.1.2   Budget Constrained Adaptive Incentive Policy

After the queries are generated, we design a Budget Constrained Adaptive Incentive (BCAI) module to incentivize the crowdsourcing platform for timely responses to the queries from the crowd. We found that the incentive design problem can be nicely mapped to a constrained multi-armed bandit (CMB) problem in reinforcement learning. The key reason for choosing the bandit solution is that it allows the CMB to dynamically adapt to uncertain crowdsourcing environments and derive the optimized incentive policy.

We consider a CMB with an action set $\mathcal{A}^t = \{1, 2, ..., Z\}$ at each sensing cycle t, where each entry in $\mathcal{A}$ denotes the amount of money (in cents). We assume each action $z \in \mathcal{A}^t$ generates a non-negative payoff p_z^t (representing the inverse of the crowd response delay) with cost c_z^t at each sensing cycle. The payoff is only revealed at the end of the cycle (i.e., delay is unknown until the responses are submitted by the crowd). We use C^t to denote the costs from all actions taken at sensing cycle t. The objective of CMB is to derive an optimal incentive policy to maximize the payoffs while keeping the total action cost within the resource budget. The objective is formulated as:

$$\underset{\mathcal{A}^t}{\text{argmax}} \sum_{t=1}^{T} P^t, 1 \leq t \leq T \text{ (payoff maximization)}$$

$$\text{s.t.:} \sum_{t=1}^{T} \mathcal{C}^t \leq B, 1 \leq t \leq T \text{ (budget constraint)}$$

(6.8)

This objective function can be solved using the classical Epsilon-first policies approach in [34].

6.4.1.3 Interactive Attention Convolutional Neural Network

Next, we present the Interactive Attention Convolutional Neural Network (IACNN) that leverages an interactive attention design to identify damage areas in disaster scenes. An overview of IACNN is shown in Fig. 6.15. The IACNN employs the deep convolutional neural network, which has been a popular and effective tool for the image classification task [7]. Our CNN model contains 5 convolutional blocks (with 16 convolutional layers and 5 pooling layers) as shown in Fig. 6.15. We initialize our model with the pre-trained VGG19 model for all convolutional blocks, and fine-tune it using disaster-related images. The existing DDA algorithms lack an explicit attention mechanism to pinpoint the damaged area in the image. To address this issue, our IACNN model develops two attention mechanisms. The first one is a trainable gated attention mechanism that is an internal component of the CNN model. We employ the gated attention approach from [27], where three separate attention blocks (connected to the last three pooling layers) are aggregated and connected to the final output layer. Compared to existing single attention block approaches such as Residual Attention Network [40], the gated attention allows the CNN to capture the attention of images in different resolutions and is more robust against the low resolution and noisy image inputs. However, this internal attention alone is not enough to accurately capture the damage region given the limited amount of training data [17]. Therefore, we design the second interactive external attention mechanism to further enhance the attention of IACNN.

The intuition of the interactive attention is to develop an ensemble of visual attention from a set of DDA algorithms to decrease the bias of the attention of each individual algorithm. The attention annotations from the crowd are leveraged to derive the weight of each algorithm in the ensemble. In particular, we design an attention ensemble approach by employing the class activation map (CAM) [28] technique. CAM is a visualization technique that can identify the important regions (i.e., pixels) that contribute significantly to the final classification results. Following [19], we use the last convolutional layer to derive CAM. Assuming the dimension of the last convolutional layer of ICNN is $U \times V \times L$ (e.g, $14 \times 14 \times 512$ in the proposed CNN), we calculate the CAM score $s_{u,v}$ for each image region (u, v) as:

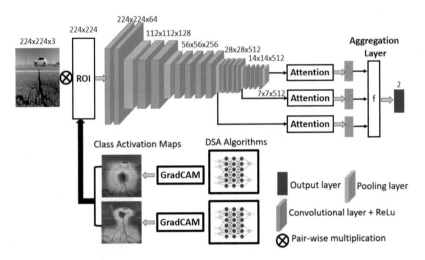

Fig. 6.15 IACNN overview

$$s_{u,v} = \sum_{l \in L} \left(\lambda_l \times f_l(u, v) \right)$$

$$\lambda_l = \frac{1}{U \times V} \sum_{u \in U, v \in V} \frac{\partial Y}{\partial f_l(u, v)} \tag{6.9}$$

where λ_l is a gradient-based weight parameter for the last convolutional layer, and $f_l(u, v)$ represents the value at image location (u, v) in the l-th feature vector. λ_k is derived as the sum of the gradients of output Y with respect to $f_l(u, v)$.

To ensemble the CAMs from each DDA algorithm, we can either (1) find the union of the CAMs; (2) find the intersection of the CAMs; or (3) find the weighted sum of the CAMs. In this work, we pragmatically pick the last approach because it gives the best empirical performance. The weights of each CAM is determined based on how similar it is as compared to the ground truth attention region provided by the crowd workers. We calculate the weight of each DDA algorithm as:

$$w_m^t \propto \sum_{i=1}^{N} IOU_i^t; \quad \sum_{m=1}^{m} w_m^t = 1, \forall 1 \leq t \leq T \tag{6.10}$$

where IOU is the Intersection-Over-Union metric, which is frequently used to evaluate image segmentation and object detection schemes [11]. The IOU metric is defined as $IOU = \frac{Area\ of\ Overlap}{Area\ of\ Union}$. The "Area of Overlap" and "Area of Union" are computed with respect to a ground truth visual attention, where the damaged area is manually marked by annotators. IOU takes values in [0,1] where 1 represents a complete overlap with the ground truth annotation. Here, we use IOU_i^t to denote the IOU for input X_i^t.

After combing the CAMs of DDA algorithms, we generate a binary map called Region of Interest (ROI) [10]. This binary map is used as a preprocessing layer to the input of IACNN to first filter out the irrelevant regions of image and focus only on the potentially important areas (i.e., damages). The binary map is calculated as:

$$ROI_{u,v} = \begin{cases} 1, & \sum_{m=1}^{M} w_m^t \times s_{u,v,m} > \Theta \\ 0, & \sum_{m=1}^{M} w_m^t \times s_{u,v,m} \leq \Theta \end{cases} \tag{6.11}$$

where $ROI_{u,v}$ is the ROI score of the region (u, v) of the image. $s_{u,v,m}$ is the CAM at region (u, v) from AI_m. Θ is a threshold parameter. We set the Θ to be a relatively small value, so it provides rough filtering of non-important regions based on the CAMs. Then the more fine-grained attention is captured by the trainable gated attention described above.

6.4.1.4 Social Media Image Normalization

Finally, we develop a Social Media Image Normalization (SMIN) module to handle the noisy input of social media images and generate the final classification output. Note that in the IACNN module, we only output two classes—"damage" and "no damage". The reason we chose two classes for IACNN is that the boundary between damage severity levels such as "moderate" and "severe" is unclear to the AI algorithms and they often output the wrong results. Therefore, we adopt the approach from [8] where the damage severity is derived as the percentage of damage regions (e.g., captured by the CAM) in the image. However, the social media images can be taken with diverse camera angles where the absolute size of the damage region cannot always reflect the damage severity levels (Figs. 6.16 and 6.17). To address this issue, we designed a normalized damage score as $\sum_{u \in U, v \in V} \left(\frac{s_{u,v}}{U \times V} \right) * \delta$, where δ is a weighting factor denoting the level of "zoom in" of an image. To calculate δ, we first identify the anchor objects in the images (e.g., cars, bridges, and road signs) using the YOLO V3 object detection tool [24]. We then compare the actual size of the anchor objects (based on prior knowledge) with the size of the objects in the image. We observed such normalization significantly improves the classification results as discussed in Sect. 6.5.

Fig. 6.16 Classified as severe (✗)

Fig. 6.17 Classified as moderate (✓)

6.5 Real-World Case Studies of iDSA

In this section, we conduct extensive experiments on real-world datasets to answer the following questions:

- **Q1:** Can iDSA achieve a better classification accuracy than the state-of-the-art DDA algorithms?
- **Q2:** Can the interactive attention in iDSA accurately capture the damaged area of a social media image?

- **Q3:** Can iDSA achieve a high crowd responsiveness for DDA applications given a limited budget?
- **Q4:** How does each component of iDSA contribute to its overall performance?

We use a dataset [21] that consists of a total of 21,384 social media images related to two disaster events—the 2016 Ecuador Earthquake (2,280 images) and the 2015 Nepal Earthquake (19,104 images). The dataset contains ground truth labels of damage severity levels. We further collect the ground truth of the exact damaged areas in the image that were labeled by multiple human annotators via the LabelMe tool [25]. We use Amazon MTurk, one of the largest crowdsourcing platforms, to acquire human intelligence for iDSA. In particular, we choose 3 workers to assess the damage severity level of each queried image using the scale from 0 to 5 (see Fig. 6.14). We then use the following rubrics to decide the class label of the image: the aggregated score (from three workers) > 10: severe damage; the aggregated score ≤ 1: no damage; otherwise: moderate damage. For the attention annotation, we treat a pixel in the image as part of the visual attention if it appears in the annotation from at least two workers. For each crowd response, we assign 6 incentive levels (2, 4, 6, 8, 10, and 20 cents) decided by the BCAI module.

In our experiments, the dataset is split into a *training set* and a *test set*. The training set contains all 19,104 images from Nepal Earthquake, and the test set includes all images from the Ecuador Earthquake. The choice of data from different events for training and test sets is to emulate the real-world DDA scenarios where the training data is often acquired from the disasters that happened in the past. All compared schemes were run on a server with Intel Xeon E5-2637 v4 3.50GHz CPU and 4 NVIDIA GTX 1080Ti GPUs.

Baselines   We choose a few AI-only algorithms as our DDA baselines, including **ASONAM18** [19], **Inception** [32], **ResNet** [14], and **VGGATT** [40]. We further consider 3 state-of-the-art human-AI hybrid baselines.

- **DirectEnsemble**: it directly ensembles the outputs of the above AI-only schemes [52].
- **Hybrid-Para**: a human-AI hybrid system where the labels from humans and AI algorithms are integrated using a complexity index [15].
- **Hybrid-AL**: an active learning framework where the annotated labels collected from humans are used to re-train the AI algorithms [18].

For a fair comparison, we let all AI-only algorithms randomly query the same amount of images as the human-AI schemes from the crowd. The obtained labels are used as ground truth to retrain the DDA algorithm of the baseline.

Classification Effectiveness (Q1)   In the first set of experiments, we focus on the overall performance of all schemes in terms of classification effectiveness, which is evaluated using the classic metrics for multi-class classification: *Accuracy, Precision, Recall* and *F1 Score*. Similar to [19, 21], these scores are *macro-averaged* since our dataset has balanced class labels.

Table 6.4 Classification accuracy for all schemes.Bold values indicate the best performance achieved by iDSA scheme compared to the baselines

Algorithms	Accuracy	Precision	Recall	F1
iDSA	**0.869**	**0.881**	**0.853**	**0.867**
ASONAM18	0.808	0.819	0.79	0.804
Inception	0.755	0.75	0.765	0.757
ResNet	0.812	0.819	0.8	0.809
VGGATT	0.799	0.803	0.791	0.797
DirectEnsemble	0.817	0.828	0.799	0.813
Hybrid-Para	0.814	0.826	0.797	0.811
Hybrid-AL	0.821	0.828	0.809	0.818
Gain(%)	5.8	6.4	5.4	6.0

The results are reported in Table 6.4. We observe iDSA consistently outperforms all baselines. Compared to AI-only schemes, iDSA is able to achieve a 7.8% higher F1 score than the best-performing baseline (i.e., ResNet). The reason is that the iDSA can effectively incorporate human intelligence into the DDA algorithm. iDSA is also superior to the human-AI hybrid baselines. For example, iDSA achieved a 6% improvement on F1 score compared to the best-performing human-AI baseline (i.e., Hybrid-AL). This is because none of the hybrid baselines addresses the innate issue of inaccurate attention of the CNN models they use. For example, DirectEnsemble simply aggregates the results of all AI-only algorithms without touching the internal model of these algorithms. In contrast, iDSA directly interacts with the internal attention mechanism of AI and leverages human intelligence to troubleshoot, calibrate, and eventually improve the attention of AI. We further evaluate all schemes by tuning the size of training data (in terms of percentage of the whole training set as shown in Fig. 6.18) as well as the number of images that we use to query the crowd (from 5 to 25% of the testing set as shown in Fig. 6.19). We observe iDSA outperforms the baselines with different sizes of training data and different amounts of knowledge from the crowd.

Attention Accuracy (Q2) We further investigate whether iDSA can outperform baselines in terms of correctly attending to the damaged areas in the images. We use the IOU metric mentioned above. Considering the accuracy of the attention is directly affected by the number of answers collected from the crowd, we tuned the percentage of images that we send out to query the MTurk from 5 to 25%. The results are presented in Table 6.5. We skip DirectEnsemble and Hybrid-Para in the table because tuning the number of crowd queries will not affect their attention since they do not retrain their models. We observe that iDSA continues to outperform all baselines. The improved accuracy in both attention (Table 6.5) and classification (Table 6.4) also validates our hypothesis that improving the attention detection accuracy of DDA algorithms will eventually boost the classification performance of DDA applications.

Crowd Responsiveness (Q3) We then evaluate the delay of all human-AI hybrid schemes in terms of (1) execution time, and (2) delay of query answered by the

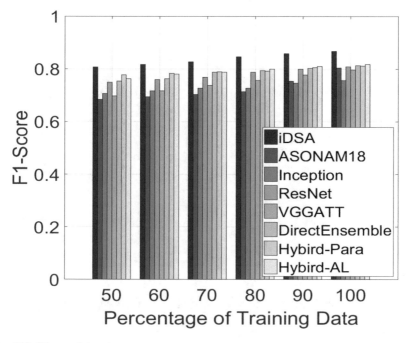

Fig. 6.18 F1 vs. training size

Table 6.5 IOU for all schemes w.r.t % of images. Bold values indicate the best performance achieved by iDSA scheme compared to the baselines

Algorithms	5% (Images)	10%	15%	20%	25%
iDSA	**0.549**	**0.558**	**0.570**	**0.582**	**0.598**
ASONAM18	0.389	0.392	0.397	0.401	0.405
Inception	0.316	0.322	0.335	0.337	0.341
ResNet	0.451	0.461	0.479	0.490	0.496
VGGATT	0.322	0.329	0.339	0.352	0.358
Hybrid-AL	0.462	0.469	0.474	0.482	0.499
Gain(%)	18.8	19.5	20.2	20.4	19.8

crowdsourcing platform. The results are shown in Table 6.6. We observe that the response delay from the crowdsourcing platform is the major contributor to the overall delay of human-AI hybrid systems including iDSA. This observation further demonstrates the importance of designing an effective incentive policy to minimize the delay from the crowd and provide timely responses to the DDA applications. The results show that iDSA scheme significantly reduces the crowd delay by 16.8, 27.3, and 18.9% compared to DirectEnsemble, Hybrid-Para, and Hybrid-AL, respectively, which all adopt a fixed incentive policy. We attribute such a performance gain to our adaptive incentive module that leverages a multi-arm bandit scheme to dynamically identify the optimal incentive strategy to reduce the response delay from the crowd.

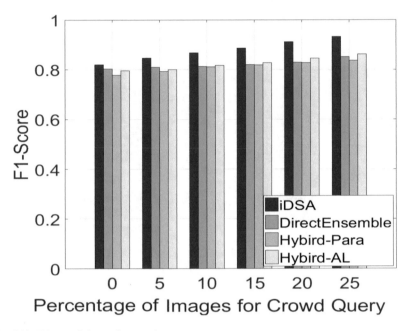

Fig. 6.19 F1 vs. training and query sizes

Table 6.6 Average delay (in seconds) per sensing cycle. Bold values indicate the best performance achieved by iDSA scheme compared to the baselines

Algorithms	Algorithm Delay	Crowd Delay	Total Delay
iDSA	**66.98**	**427.81**	**494.79**
DirectEnsemble	55.62	513.24	568.86
Hybrid-Para	94.28	588.75	683.03
Hybrid-AL	53.54	527.61	581.15

Ablation Study (Q4) Finally, we perform a comprehensive *ablation study* to examine the effect of each component of iDSA. In particular, we present the classification results (Table 6.7) by removing each of the four modules of iDSA. We found that, by adding the interactive attention design, iDSA is able to increase its F1 score by 5.2%. The incentive module contributes to 2.8% increase in F1 score, which highlights the importance of minimizing the response delay from the crowd. We also found the crowd task generation is indeed helpful—yielding 3.5% higher F1 score. The normalization module helps iDSA to achieve 6.25% performance again by making iDSA more robust against noisy social media images.

Table 6.7 Ablation study of iDSA. Bold values indicate the best performance achieved by iDSA scheme compared to the baselines

Algorithms	Accuracy	Precision	Recall	F1
iDSA	**0.869**	**0.881**	**0.853**	**0.867**
iDSA w/o CTG	0.839	0.842	0.835	0.838
iDSA w/o IACNN	0.826	0.831	0.818	0.824
iDSA w/o SMIN	0.821	0.842	0.791	0.816
iDSA w/o BCAI	0.843	0.849	0.835	0.842

6.6 Discussion

In this chapter, we present two crowd-AI interactive learning frameworks, CrowdLearn and iDSA, that utilize the crowd intelligence to troubleshoot and significantly improve the accuracy of the AI-based application. We evaluate CrowdLearn and iDSA using a representative application scenario—disaster damage assessment (DDA). The discussed solutions are able to fully leverage the advantage of humans in localizing the damage region of disaster scenes to improve the visual attention of existing AI models for DSA. Novel dynamic incentive designs were further introduced to optimize the responsiveness and quality of the responses provided by the crowd. Our evaluation results on a real-world case study on Amazon Mechanical Turk have demonstrated that the discussed frameworks can provide timely and more accurate assessments of natural disaster events than the state-of-the-art AI-only and human-AI integrated systems.

References

1. A. Bosch, A. Zisserman, X. Munoz, Image classification using random forests and ferns, in *IEEE 11th International Conference on Computer Vision (ICCV 2007)* (IEEE, Piscataway, 2007), pp. 1–8
2. S. Branson, C. Wah, F. Schroff, B. Babenko, P. Welinder, P. Perona, S. Belongie, Visual recognition with humans in the loop, in *European Conference on Computer Vision*, pp. 438–451 (Springer, Berlin, 2010)
3. N. Cesa-Bianchi, G. Lugosi, *Prediction, Learning, and Games* (Cambridge University Press, Cambridge, 2006)
4. T. Chen, C. Guestrin, XGBoost: a scalable tree boosting system, in *Proceedings of the 22nd ACM Sigkdd International Conference on Knowledge Discovery and Data Mining* (ACM, New York, 2016), pp. 785–794
5. X. Chen, E. Santos-Neto, M. Ripeanu, Crowdsourcing for on-street smart parking, in *Proceedings of the Second ACM International Symposium on Design and Analysis of Intelligent Vehicular Networks and Applications* (ACM, New York, 2012), pp. 1–8
6. W. Dai, Y. Wang, Q. Jin, J. Ma, Geo-QTI: a quality aware truthful incentive mechanism for cyber–physical enabled geographic crowdsensing. Future Gen. Comput. Syst. **79**, 447–459 (2018)
7. J. Deng, W. Dong, R. Socher, L.-J. Li, K. Li, L. Fei-Fei, Imagenet: A large-scale hierarchical image database, in *IEEE Conference on Computer Vision and Pattern Recognition (CVPR 2009)* (IEEE, Piscataway, 2009), pp. 248–255

8. J. Doshi, S. Basu, G. Pang, From satellite imagery to disaster insights (2018). arXiv:1812.07033
9. A. Dosovitskiy, T. Brox, Generating images with perceptual similarity metrics based on deep networks, in *Advances in Neural Information Processing Systems* (2016), pp. 658–666
10. S. Eppel, Setting an attention region for convolutional neural networks using region selective features, for recognition of materials within glass vessels (2017). arXiv:1708.08711
11. M. Everingham, L. Van Gool, C.K. Williams, J. Winn, A. Zisserman, The pascal visual object classes (VOC) challenge. Int. J. Comput. Vis. **88**(2), 303–338 (2010)
12. E.A. Gehan, A generalized wilcoxon test for comparing arbitrarily singly-censored samples. Biometrika **52**(1–2), 203–224 (1965)
13. C. Harris, You're hired! An examination of crowdsourcing incentive models in human resource tasks, in *Proceedings of the Workshop on Crowdsourcing for Search and Data Mining (CSDM) at the Fourth ACM International Conference on Web Search and Data Mining (WSDM), Hong Kong* (2011), pp. 15–18
14. K. He, X. Zhang, S. Ren, J. Sun, Deep residual learning for image recognition, in *Proceedings of the IEEE Conference on Computer Vision and Pattern Recognition* (2016), pp. 770–778
15. J. Jarrett, I. Saleh, M.B. Blake, R. Malcolm, S. Thorpe, T. Grandison, Combining human and machine computing elements for analysis via crowdsourcing, in *2014 International Conference on Collaborative Computing: Networking, Applications and Worksharing (CollaborateCom)* (IEEE, Piscataway, 2014), pp. 312–321
16. A. Kittur, E.H. Chi, B. Suh, Crowdsourcing user studies with mechanical turk, in *Proceedings of the SIGCHI Conference on Human Factors in Computing Systems* (ACM, New York, 2008), pp. 453–456
17. Q. Lai, W. Wang, S. Khan, J. Shen, H. Sun, L. Shao, Human *vs* machine attention in neural networks: a comparative study (2019). arXiv:1906.08764
18. F. Laws, C. Scheible, H. Schütze, Active learning with amazon mechanical turk, in *Proceedings of the Conference on Empirical Methods in Natural Language Processing* (Association for Computational Linguistics, Cedarville, 2011), pp. 1546–1556
19. X. Li, D. Caragea, H. Zhang, M. Imran, Localizing and quantifying damage in social media images, in *2018 IEEE/ACM International Conference on Advances in Social Networks Analysis and Mining (ASONAM)* (IEEE, Piscataway, 2018)
20. E. Mitsopoulou, I. Boutsis, V. Kalogeraki, J.Y. Yu, A cost-aware incentive mechanism in mobile crowdsourcing systems, in *2018 19th IEEE International Conference on Mobile Data Management (MDM)* (IEEE, Piscataway, 2018), pp. 239–244
21. D.T. Nguyen, F. Ofli, M. Imran, P. Mitra, Damage assessment from social media imagery data during disasters, in *Proceedings of the 2017 IEEE/ACM International Conference on Advances in Social Networks Analysis and Mining 2017* (ACM, New York, 2017)
22. B. Nushi, E. Kamar, E. Horvitz, D. Kossmann, On human intellect and machine failures: troubleshooting integrative machine learning systems, in *Proceedings of the Thirty-First AAAI Conference on Artificial Intelligence* (2017), pp. 1017–1025
23. B. Nushi, E. Kamar, E. Horvitz, Towards accountable AI: hybrid human-machine analyses for characterizing system failure (2018). arXiv:1809.07424
24. J. Redmon, S. Divvala, R. Girshick, A. Farhadi, You only look once: unified, real-time object detection, in *Proceedings of the IEEE Conference on Computer Vision and Pattern Recognition* (2016), pp. 779–788
25. B.C. Russell, A. Torralba, K.P. Murphy, W.T. Freeman, Labelme: a database and web-based tool for image annotation. Int. J. Comput. Vis. **77**(1–3), 157–173 (2008)
26. R.E. Schapire, Y. Singer, Improved boosting algorithms using confidence-rated predictions. Mach. Learn. **37**(3), 297–336 (1999)
27. J. Schlemper, O. Oktay, L. Chen, J. Matthew, C. Knight, B. Kainz, B. Glocker, D. Rueckert, Attention-gated networks for improving ultrasound scan plane detection (2018). arXiv:1804.05338
28. R.R. Selvaraju, M. Cogswell, A. Das, R. Vedantam, D. Parikh, D. Batra, Grad-CAM: visual explanations from deep networks via gradient-based localization, in *Proceedings of the IEEE International Conference on Computer Vision* (2017), pp. 618–626

29. H.S. Seung, M. Opper, H. Sompolinsky, Query by committee, in *Proceedings of the Fifth Annual Workshop on Computational Learning Theory* (ACM, New York, 1992), pp. 287–294
30. A. Sorokin, D. Forsyth, Utility data annotation with amazon mechanical turk, in *IEEE Computer Society Conference on Computer Vision and Pattern Recognition Workshops (CVPRW'08)* (IEEE, Piscataway, 2008), pp. 1–8
31. M.A. Suryanto, E.P. Lim, A. Sun, R.H. Chiang, Quality-aware collaborative question answering: methods and evaluation, in *Proceedings of the Second ACM International Conference on Web Search and Data Mining* (ACM, New York, 2009), pp. 142–151
32. C. Szegedy, V. Vanhoucke, S. Ioffe, J. Shlens, Z. Wojna, Rethinking the inception architecture for computer vision, in *Proceedings of the IEEE Conference on Computer Vision and Pattern Recognition* (2016), pp. 2818–2826
33. M. Tokic, G. Palm, Value-difference based exploration: adaptive control between epsilon-greedy and softmax, in *Annual Conference on Artificial Intelligence* (Springer, Berlin, 2011), pp. 335–346
34. L. Tran-Thanh, A. Chapman, E.M. de Cote, A. Rogers, N.R. Jennings, Epsilon–first policies for budget–limited multi-armed bandits, in *Twenty-Fourth AAAI Conference on Artificial Intelligence* (2010)
35. D. Wang, L. Kaplan, H. Le, T. Abdelzaher, On truth discovery in social sensing: a maximum likelihood estimation approach, in *Proceedings of ACM/IEEE 11th International Information Processing in Sensor Networks (IPSN) Conference* (2012), pp. 233–244
36. D. Wang, T. Abdelzaher, L. Kaplan, C.C. Aggarwal, Recursive fact-finding: a streaming approach to truth estimation in crowdsourcing applications, in *2013 IEEE 33rd International Conference on Distributed Computing Systems* (IEEE, Piscataway, 2013), pp. 530–539
37. D. Wang, T. Abdelzaher, L. Kaplan, *Social Sensing: Building Reliable Systems on Unreliable Data.* (Morgan Kaufmann, Burlington, 2015)
38. J. Wang, J. Tang, D. Yang, E. Wang, G. Xue, Quality-aware and fine-grained incentive mechanisms for mobile crowdsensing, in *2016 IEEE 36th International Conference on Distributed Computing Systems (ICDCS)* (IEEE, Piscataway, 2016), pp. 354–363
39. Y. Wang, X. Jia, Q. Jin, J. Ma, Quacentive: a quality-aware incentive mechanism in mobile crowdsourced sensing (MCS). J. Supercomput. **72**(8), 2924–2941 (2016)
40. F. Wang, M. Jiang, C. Qian, S. Yang, C. Li, H. Zhang, X. Wang, X. Tang, Residual attention network for image classification, in *Proceedings of the IEEE Conference on Computer Vision and Pattern Recognition* (2017), pp. 3156–3164
41. D. Wang, B.K. Szymanski, T. Abdelzaher, H. Ji, L. Kaplan, The age of social sensing. Computer **52**(1), 36–45 (2019)
42. P. Welinder, P. Perona, Online crowdsourcing: rating annotators and obtaining cost-effective labels, in *2010 IEEE Computer Society Conference on Computer Vision and Pattern Recognition Workshops (CVPRW)* (IEEE, Piscataway, 2010), pp. 25–32
43. H. Wu, R. Srikant, X. Liu, C. Jiang, Algorithms with logarithmic or sublinear regret for constrained contextual bandits, in *Advances in Neural Information Processing Systems* (2015), pp. 433–441
44. D.Y. Zhang, D. Wang, Heterogeneous social sensing edge computing system for deep learning based disaster response: demo abstract, in *Proceedings of the International Conference on Internet of Things Design and Implementation* (ACM, New York, 2019), pp. 269–270
45. D.Y. Zhang, R. Han, D. Wang, C. Huang, On robust truth discovery in sparse social media sensing, in *2016 IEEE International Conference on Big Data (Big Data)* (IEEE, Piscataway, 2016), pp. 1076–1081
46. D.Y. Zhang, C. Zheng, D. Wang, D. Thain, X. Mu, G. Madey, C. Huang, Towards scalable and dynamic social sensing using a distributed computing framework, in *2017 IEEE 37th International Conference on Distributed Computing Systems (ICDCS)* (IEEE, Piscataway, 2017), pp. 966–976
47. X. Zhang, Y. Wu, L. Huang, H. Ji, G. Cao, Expertise-aware truth analysis and task allocation in mobile crowdsourcing, in *2017 IEEE 37th International Conference on Distributed Computing Systems (ICDCS)* (IEEE, Piscataway, 2017), pp. 922–932

48. D.Y. Zhang, Y. Ma, Y. Zhang, S. Lin, X.S. Hu, D. Wang, A real-time and non-cooperative task allocation framework for social sensing applications in edge computing systems, in *2018 IEEE Real-Time and Embedded Technology and Applications Symposium (RTAS)* (IEEE, Piscataway, 2018), pp. 316–326
49. D.Y. Zhang, L. Shang, B. Geng, S. Lai, K. Li, H. Zhu, M.T. Amin, D. Wang, Fauxbuster: a content-free fauxtography detector using social media comments, in *2018 IEEE International Conference on Big Data (Big Data)* (IEEE, Piscataway, 2018), pp. 891–900
50. Y. Zhang, D.Y. Zhang, N. Vance, D. Wang, Optimizing online task allocation for multi-attribute social sensing, in *2018 27th International Conference on Computer Communication and Networks (ICCCN)* (IEEE, Piscataway, 2018), pp. 1–9
51. D.Y. Zhang, D. Wang, N. Vance, Y. Zhang, S. Mike, On scalable and robust truth discovery in big data social media sensing applications. IEEE Trans. Big Data **5**, 195–208 (2019)
52. D.Y. Zhang, Y. Zhang, Q. Li, T. Plummer, D. Wang, Crowdlearn: a crowd-ai hybrid system for deep learning-based damage assessment applications, in *2019 IEEE 39th International Conference on Distributed Computing Systems (ICDCS)* (IEEE, Piscataway, 2019), pp. 1221–1232
53. D.Y. Zhang, Y. Huang, Y. Zhang, D. Wang, Crowd-assisted disaster scene assessment with human-ai interactive attention, in *Proceedings of the AAAI Conference on Artificial Intelligence* (2020), pp. 2717–2724

Chapter 7
Privacy in Social Edge

Abstract Privacy is an essential human-centric challenges to address for the success of the SEC paradigm. This is especially true for health-related applications in SEC. In this chapter, we review the work that studies the above challenge in a particular category of smart health application for SEC—Abnormal Health Detection Systems (AHDS). In particular, we present FedSens, a new federated learning framework dedicated to addressing the imbalanced data problem in AHDS applications with explicit considerations of participant privacy and device resource constraints.

7.1 Understanding Privacy in Social Edge

The wide adoption of ubiquitous sensing and mobile edge computing (MEC) has brought new opportunities for more efficient, and cost-effective healthcare for common citizens [22]. For example, we can continuously collect health data of participants by using mobile edge devices (e.g., smart wearables, or smartphones equipped with an array of increasingly advanced embedded sensors) and provide intelligent health services in real time. In this work, we focus on a particular category of smart health application—abnormal health detection systems or AHDS [1], which leverages various machine learning models to accurately infer abnormal health conditions of people, such as depression [2], stroke [10], and Asthma [6]. The early detection of these abnormal conditions is essential for timely treatments of these conditions and keeping them from evolving into more serious (e.g., life-threatening) situations [15, 23].

AHDS applications often rely on advanced machine learning models that are trained using a very large amount of health data from the participants in the application. However, such a training phase is especially challenging in AHDS due to two critical issues: (1) training with participants' health data can lead to serious privacy concerns of leaking personally identifiable information and health records of participants [20]; (2) AHDS data often exists in the form of "isolated islands", where the health data is collected from the massive amount of individual participants rather than a centralized organization. It causes excessive delay and bandwidth consumption by transferring the raw sensor data from all individuals to a central server for training [5]. The emergence of federated learning (FL) and MEC has provided a compelling paradigm for learning AHDS models using the smart devices of participants. In particular, FL carefully protects the privacy of the participants by enabling the smart edge devices to collaboratively learn a shared inference model for AHDS without sharing any private health data to the server [12, 17]. MEC on the other hand, allows AHDS to fully leverage the computation power of the edge devices to train the model *in-situ* and deliver the detection results immediately back to the participants [21].

Several initial attempts have been made to adapt federated learning to smart health applications, such as FedHealth [5] and FADL [14]. However, the discussed federated learning frameworks in those solutions fail to address a fundamental issue—*class imbalance*, where the health data of participants often contain imbalanced class labels. Take depression detection as an example. People may not constantly be under depression throughout the day, but only at certain periods, leading to much more negative classes (i.e., no depression) than positive ones (i.e., under depression). We refer to such a class imbalance as the *local class imbalance*. Moreover, we observe that not all participants are prone to depression, meaning some people can contribute more positive samples than others. Such a class imbalance between participants is referred to as the *global class imbalance*. Due to the two types of class imbalance, the sensing data collected from the participants is often imbalanced (i.e., it contains significantly more negative class labels than positive ones). Training with such an imbalanced dataset can lead to degraded model performance [7, 11]. We found addressing such a class imbalance issue introduces two unique technical challenges in developing the federated learning framework for AHDS: (1) strict privacy protection of the participants; and (2) the resource constraints on heterogeneous MEC devices in AHDS. We elaborate these challenges below.

Participant Privacy Protection The first challenge refers to the strict privacy requirements from the participants and their implication on leveraging the imbalanced class labels of the participants' health data. In AHDS, we assume that the server cannot access any private information about the participants including their raw health data as well as the class distribution of their data samples. This assumption prevents us from applying a rich set of existing solutions in machine learning (e.g., adaptive sampling [7] and oversampling [3]) to address the class imbalance issue in AHDS. The reason is that the current solutions all make an important assumption in their models: the sampling server either has access to the labels of the raw data from the participants or has the global knowledge of the class distributions of the data samples. Such an assumption, unfortunately, violates the strict privacy-preserving requirements of users in our AHDS applications. To our knowledge, addressing the class imbalance issue in a federated learning framework without knowing the class distribution of the data from participants *a priori* has not been addressed in existing literature.

Heterogeneous Resource Constraints The second challenge lies in the unique tradeoff between improving the model robustness against class imbalance and satisfying the diverse resource constraints of heterogeneous edge devices in AHDS. AHDS is comprised of privately owned edge devices such as smartphones and wristbands to collect and process the personal health data from the participants [1, 4]. Those edge devices are often of heterogeneous hardware profiles (e.g., GPU, CPU specifications) and diverse resource constraints (e.g., different battery status), which present a unique challenge to the resource allocation problem in FL. In particular, a few key parameters (e.g., global and local model update frequency) need to be carefully designed in federated learning to ensure the robustness of the model against the class imbalance issue [24]. However, the values of these parameters are affected by the heterogeneous set of resources available on edge devices. For example, a participant who has frequent abnormal health conditions (e.g., frequently under depression) can often contribute more positive samples than a participant in a normal health condition to improve the overall accuracy of FL models [7]. However, it also indicates the abnormal participant has to train the local model on her/his edge device and update the global model at a higher frequency, which will impose a higher resource requirement (e.g., energy) on the participant's device. The heterogeneity of edge devices in AHDS further complicates the above tradeoff (e.g., some devices may be more energy efficient than others, thus are more tolerable for frequent local/global updates). Several efforts have been designed to deploy federated learning on resource-constrained devices [19, 24]. However, none of these solutions studies the unique tradeoff between the robustness of the model against class imbalance and the heterogeneous resource constraints of the device.

7.2   A Privacy-Aware Framework for Distributed Edge Learning: FedSens

We present FedSens, a new edge-based federated learning framework that is robust against the class imbalance issue of AHDS applications while respecting the strict privacy requirements of participants and the heterogeneous resource constraints of their edge devices [26]. In FedSens, we design (1) a new local update scheme inspired by the curiosity-driven reinforcement learning model, and (2) an adaptive global update scheme using the online regret minimization. These two components jointly allow each edge device to decide the optimized local and global update strategy that maximizes the accuracy of the AHDS model in the presence of class imbalance. The bottom-up design of both components allows FedSens to meet device-specific optimization goals (e.g., energy savings) while strictly protecting user privacy. The FedSens system assumes the server has zero knowledge of the class distribution of data contributed by individual participants and the edge device of each participant is not aware of the class distribution of any other participants to fully preserve the privacy of users. To our knowledge, FedSens is the first solution that addresses the class imbalance issue in federated learning by explicitly considering both strict user privacy protection and resource constraints in a heterogeneous edge computing system. The discussed framework is general in addressing federated learning with class imbalanced data beyond the context of AHDS application.

We implemented a system prototype of FedSens on a real-world collaborative edge testbed that consists of Nvidia Jetson TX2, TX1, and TK1 boards. FedSens was evaluated using two real-world smart health applications: *stress detection* and *driver drowsiness monitoring*. We compared FedSens with the state-of-the-art federated learning baselines. The results show that our scheme achieves a significant performance gain in terms of both accuracy and energy consumption.

7.2.1 Problem Definition

In this section, we formulate the problem of federated learning based AHDS that is robust to class imbalance issue and respects the strict privacy requirements of participants and the heterogeneous resource constraints of their devices. We first present the system overview, assumptions and the privacy model we used, and then formally define the objectives of our problem.

We illustrate the overview of an AHDS-based FL system in Fig. 7.1. It consists of N distributed worker nodes and a server node. In our setting, we assume the worker nodes are a set of smart devices/sensors (e.g., smartphones and smartwatches) that participants use to collect health data. We refer to them as smart edge devices (edge devices for short) as they are capable of performing local computation on the collected data. Let $ED = \{E_1, E_2, \ldots, E_N\}$ denote the set of all edge devices (worker nodes) in the system. The application server can be deployed as a nearby edge server such as smart gateways, smart routers, base stations, Cloudlets, or a remote backend such as virtual machines in the cloud.

In a federated learning setting, the AHDS system targets at learning a global machine learning model $\mathcal{M}$ across all edge devices of participants without having access to each device's private health data. We assume that each edge device has private local health data D_i, $1 \leq i \leq N$. Each edge device can train a local model M_i by minimizing a loss function $\mathcal{L}_i(w_i)$ based on D_i. The loss function describes the difference between the inferred class labels with the actual class labels of the training set. Then, the global loss function on all the distributed health data for $\mathcal{M}$ can be defined as:

$$\mathcal{L}(w) = \sum_{i=1}^{N} g_i \times |D_i| \times \sum_{\xi \in D_i} \mathcal{L}_i(w_i; \xi) \tag{7.1}$$

where w_i are the weights of M_i, and w are the weights of the global model $\mathcal{M}$. ξ is a sample of the training data D_i, and $\mathcal{L}_i(w_i; D_i)$ is the training loss of each

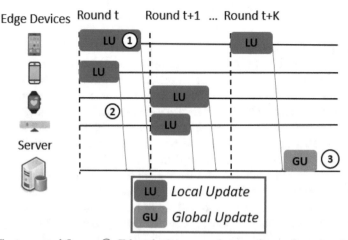

System workflow - ① Edge devices asynchronously perform local training at the beginning of each communication round; ② each edge device sends its model weight updates to the server; ③ server aggregates updates from edge devices every K communication rounds and broadcasts the global model's weights to all edge devices for model update.

Fig. 7.1 Federated learning for AHDS overview

edge device's local model. g_i is a scalar for edge device E_i that is constrained by $\sum_{i=1}^{N} g_i = 1$ that represents the importance of each edge device's local health data, often proportional to the data size. The goal of the federated learning process is to identify the optimal global weight w^* that minimizes the global loss function:

$$w^* = \arg\min \mathcal{L}(w) \tag{7.2}$$

In the federated learning framework, the above loss minimization is achieved through a distributed stochastic gradient descent process by aggregating local weight updates from edge devices over time. In particular, we assume the federated learning process is composed of a total of T communication rounds, and at each communication round $t \in [1, T]$, the parameters of the local model M_i of an edge device, denoted as w_i^t, are updated by learning from the local health data of the participant using the gradient descent method as follows:

$$w_i^t = w_i^{t-1} - \eta \times \frac{\partial \mathcal{L}^t(w_i)}{\partial w_i^t} \tag{7.3}$$

This learning process is referred to as a **local update**.

The server then aggregates the weight updates of all devices $w_1^t, w_2^t, \ldots, w_N^t$, and updates its global weights w^t via a simple weighted average function [12]. This process is referred to as a **global update**. The new global weights are then sent back to each edge device to update their local models, i.e., by setting $w_i^t = w^t, \forall 1 \leq i \leq N$.

To capture the privacy concerns of participants in AHDS, we consider the following information of a participant as private and cannot be shared with other parties: **PR1:** the raw health data from participants; **PR2:** the ground truth labels of raw data; **PR3:** the class distribution of the training data of each participant; and **PR4:** the information of each device's status. While **PR1** and **PR2** are often considered in existing federated learning schemes [12], this chapter is particularly interested in **PR3** and **PR4** which have not been well studied in existing literature. The intuition of preserving the class distribution (PR3) is that such distribution can reveal the health condition of a participant to the server or other participants. For example, if the server knows a device has more positive samples, it can guess the participant of the device is more likely to have an abnormal health condition. Similarly, the status information of a device (PR4), such as CPU usage, battery status, and location information, can also reveal the identity or residence information of a participant [8].

In this problem, we strictly prohibit any violations of the above privacy requirements, and the only information that is allowed to be sent to the server is the weight updates generated by locally trained models on each edge device. We found such strict privacy requirement makes it a very challenging task to address the class imbalance issue and meet the heterogeneous resource constraints of edge devices in a federated learning based AHDS.

In a real-world AHDS application, the system must be designed to be user-friendly and carefully satisfy the resource constraints of each edge device. In this problem, we mainly focus on the energy cost as the resource constraint as battery life is one of the most valuable resources on mobile edge devices [21]. We estimate energy consumption on each edge device as follows.

$$e_i = (Power_{\text{comp},i} + Power_{\text{trans},i}) \cdot c_i \tag{7.4}$$

where c_i is the total time incurred on edge device E_i performing federated learning. It includes local training time, delay in communicating the local model updates to the server, and receiving the global model updates from the server. $Power_{comp,i}$ is the computational power consumption for E_i, and $Power_{trans,i}$ is the power consumption for data transmission via the wireless network and is proportional to the data size been transferred.

The ultimate goal of our problem is to minimize the loss function $\mathcal{L}(w)$ of the global model while satisfying the privacy requirements of participants and the resource constraints of their edge devices. We formulate a multi-objective constrained optimization problem as follows:

$$\text{minimize } \mathcal{L}(w)$$

$$\text{minimize } e_i, \forall 1 \leq i \leq N \tag{7.5}$$

s.t.: **PR1, PR2, PR3, and PR4** are all satisfied

The above optimization problem is challenging due to potentially competing objectives of maximizing the performance of the FL model and minimizing the costs of edge devices. The problem is further complicated by the stringent privacy requirements from the participants and the imbalance of their data in the AHDS application, which leaves the system with a very limited amount of useful information for decision-making. In the next section, we present the FedSens framework to address this problem.

7.2.2   Framework Overview and Model Intuition

The original federated learning framework includes two main components: (1) the local update process, and (2) the global update process. The FedSens framework addresses the following two fundamental problems in these two components to develop an effective federated learning system dedicated to AHDS.

1. When should a device participate in the local update process?
2. When should the global update process be performed?

The FedSens framework develops two main modules (Fig. 7.2) to address the above questions: (1) a device selection module to identify the optimal local update strategy for each edge device that effectively addresses the class imbalance issue of the model while minimizing the energy cost of the edge device, and (2) an adaptive global update module to identify the optimized global update frequency that guides the above bottom-up device selection process by providing effective feedback. The two modules work cohesively to allow the edge devices to identify the best timing (i.e., communication rounds) for local updates and global updates that can maximize model accuracy while preserving the energy of edge devices.

7.2.3   Device Selection with Intrinsic-Extrinsic Deep Reinforcement Learning

We first focus on the local update strategy—which edge device should participate in the local model training at each communication round? We referred to this problem as "device selection". We observe that if an edge device has high-quality data (e.g., with balanced class labels), it should contribute more often to the local updates. However, frequent local updates will also introduce high energy cost to the edge device. Therefore, identifying the optimal device selection strategy is critical in finding the "sweet spot" in improving the model performance against class imbalance while minimizing the energy cost on the edge devices.

We found that existing solutions to the device selection problem in federated learning are often top-down, where a central controller (e.g., server) globally

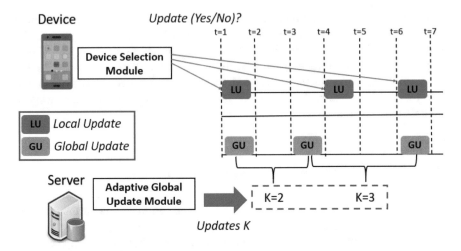

Fig. 7.2 FedSens overview

manages the selection of devices at each communication round [12, 24]. The main issue of applying the top-down design to solve our problem is the lack of private device information at the server (due to the stringent privacy requirements of participants in AHDS) to make effective decisions on device selections. For example, it is not possible for a server to optimize the resource cost on each edge device without knowing the status of the device. Similarly, the server cannot address the class imbalance issue without accessing either the raw data or the distribution of the data on each device. Therefore, FedSens is designed to be asynchronous and bottom-up where each edge device can have the discretion to decide which communication round they would like to participate without revealing any private information to the server or other devices.

The design of the bottom-up approach for device selection faces several key challenges. First, performing the local training on an edge device that has more positive samples (i.e., data collected from an abnormal condition) may help improve the accuracy of the global model at the server. However, it also indicates more energy consumption to that device. We refer to this challenge as "competing objectives" between the server and edge devices. Second, since each edge device makes the device selection decision on its own, it is a non-trivial task to ensure their collection decisions will lead to the optimal accuracy improvement of the global model. We referred to this challenge as "myopic view" of edge devices. In light of these challenges, FedSens develops a novel device selection model—the extrinsic-intrinsic deep reinforcement learning model (EIDR) that allows edge devices to collaboratively identify the optimized participation strategy for each edge device that can maximize the accuracy of the global model while minimizing the energy costs of edge devices. We present the EIDR model as follows.

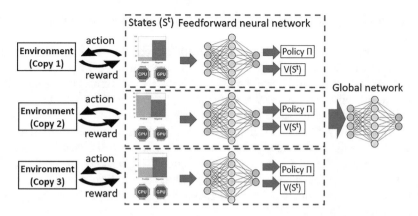

Fig. 7.3 Illustration of the EIDR model

EIDR Overview An overview of the EIDR model is presented in Fig. 7.3. In this model, each edge device identifies the device selection action that optimizes a reward function that is designed to guide the device selection to maximize model accuracy with class imbalance. In particular, we develop a deep reinforcement learning scheme that allows edge devices to learn to manage local updates directly from their experience (i.e., past actions and rewards) [16].

To introduce the EIDR model, we first define a few key terms.

Definition (Environment) The environment in EIDR refers to the current models in the federated learning framework, including both the global model and local models.   □

Definition (Agent) The agent in EIDR refers to the edge device that interacts with the environment by taking actions.   □

Definition (Action (a_i^t)) The action in EIDR refers to the choice of whether to participate in a local update or not. It is a binary variable where 1 refers to "participate" and 0 refers to "not participate". We use a_i^t to denote the action take by device E_i at round t.   □

Definition (Reward (r_i^t)) After an action is taken, the environment will provide a reward to the agent that can be used to judge how good the action taken is.   □

Definition (State (S_i^t)) A variable describing the context of the agent, such as the status and the energy profile of the device and the class distribution of the device's health data. We use S_i^t to represent the state of E_i at round t.   □

The goal of the EIDR model is to identify a *policy* (π), which is a function $a_i^t = \pi(S_i^t, R_i^t)$ that returns the best action picked by an edge device in order to maximize its reward. We will later show that FedSens employs a novel curiosity-driven design that awards improvements in model accuracy while penalizing the energy cost, which targets at addressing the "competing objective" of the bottom-up design.

We adopt the dual deep reinforcement learning neural network structure in the Asynchronous Advantage Actor Critic (A3C) algorithm [18]. In particular, each device deploys a composite neural network that takes the current state of each edge device as the input and outputs two variables: (1) the policy of the model π, and (2) the value function of the state $V(s)$. The policy function informs the edge device whether to participate in the local update or not during each communication round. The value function evaluates the benefits of being in a specific state. The policy learned by each edge device is further shared through a global network and as each agent gains more knowledge. The global network is a critical design to address the "myopic view" challenge discussed above. We will further elaborate the global network later in this subsection.

Reward and State of EIDR We observe that the policy of each edge device depends on two factors: the *reward* and the *state* of an edge device. We first introduce the reward of the EIDR model. Intuitively, the reward should be tightly related to the objectives of the FedSens: (1) maximizing the global model accuracy, and (2) minimizing energy consumption of edge devices. There is a subtle complexity in defining such a reward because the reward for the first objective (i.e., accuracy) can be provided by the server as it is aware of the performance of the global model. However, the reward for the second objective (i.e., energy) cannot be provided by the server as it cannot observe the energy cost of the edge devices. Therefore, we design a novel extrinsic-intrinsic reward mechanism where the server provides an extrinsic global reward to guide the edge device to maximize model performance, and each edge device provides an intrinsic local reward to guide the device to minimize energy cost. We first define the extrinsic reward below.

Definition (Extrinsic Reward (RE_i^t)) The extrinsic reward is the feedback provided by the environment. In this study, we define the extrinsic reward as the performance (e.g., an accuracy metric such as F1 score) of the global model.   □

Formally, we have:

$$RE_i^t = \begin{cases} F1(M') - F1(M), & t \bmod K == 0 \\ 0, & t \bmod K\,! = 0 \end{cases} \tag{7.6}$$

where $F1(M')$ is the F1 score of the global model after the local update, and $F1(M)$ is the F1 score before the update. K is the global update frequency defined at Sect. 7.2.1. $t \bmod K == 0$ means the global update happens at time t and the F1 score of the updated model is available. $t \bmod K\,! = 0$ means the model has not been updated yet, so the extrinsic feedback is not available. We can see that the choice of K is crucial in determining the "sparsity" of the extrinsic rewards. We discuss the tuning process of K in the next subsection.

Then we further define an intrinsic reward.

Definition (Intrinsic Reward (RI_i^t)) In contrast to the extrinsic reward which is global to all edge devices, the intrinsic reward is defined individually for each edge device. It is a curiosity mechanism defined by each agent to evaluate the value of an action, independent of the environment. Here, we use the local update significance (i.e., whether the training significantly updated the weights of the model) and the energy cost as the intrinsic reward.   □

The intuition of the intrinsic reward design is to address two issues. The first one is the sparsity of the extrinsic reward where the global model may not yet be updated (see Eq. 7.6). The second issue is the heterogeneity of resource constraints on edge devices (e.g., a non-energy efficient edge device may offer fewer rewards than an energy-efficient one for the local update). In our model, the intrinsic reward is affected by two factors: (1) the significance of the local model update; and (2) the energy cost of the device. This design is intuitive: an edge device should pick the local training action that contributes to the accuracy improvement of the global model significantly. It should also try to selfishly minimize the energy cost in the local training process. Formally, we define the intrinsic reward as:

$$RI_i^t = \frac{|M_i^{t'} - M_i^t|}{|M_i^t|} - \lambda \times e_i \tag{7.7}$$

where $\frac{|M_i^{t'} - M_i^t|}{|M_i^t|}$ is the significance of the model update and $M_i^{t'}$ is the updated local model if device E_i participates in the local training at round t. $|\cdot|$ denotes the Euclidean distance. e_i is the energy cost of E_i when performing local training defined in Sect. 7.2.1. λ is a model parameter that governs the importance of energy cost—the higher λ value is, the more emphasis the model will put on the objective of minimizing the energy of edge devices.

The input to our EIDR model is the state of each device, including the class distribution and the energy profile of the device. Such design allows our model to keep track of the context of the device to identify the optimal action accordingly. For example, if an edge device is in a state where it has many positive class labels and the device is energy efficient, it may be encouraged to take the action to participate in the local update frequently.

In FedSens, the state is composed of two context variables: (1) the class distribution of the private health data $\mathcal{P}(\xi_i^t)$ on an edge device; and (2) the energy profile of the device $\mathcal{E}_i$. Formally, we define:

$$S_i^t = f(\mathcal{P}(\xi_i^t), \mathcal{E}_i) \tag{7.8}$$

where $\mathcal{P}(\xi_i^t)$ is coded as the proportion of the negative samples in the training data ξ_i^t at time t. The energy profile $\mathcal{E}_i$ is the total amount of energy needed to train a local model at device E_i. We combine the above two variables using an aggregation function $f(\cdot)$ (e.g., concatenation) as the state of the device.

Global Network Design As discussed before, the bottom-up design of the device selection can suffer from the "myopic view" of edge devices where the actions taken by each device may not collectively lead to the optimal solution to the system as a whole. We develop two unique designs to address this problem. The first design is the extrinsic-intrinsic reward design where each device not only optimizes its own objective through the intrinsic reward but also contributes to the performance optimization objective of the global model through the extrinsic reward. In the second design, the EIDR model leverages a global network to further address the "myopic view" of the edge devices as shown in Fig. 7.3. The global network work allows edge devices to share the policies they learned with each other. For example, if a device is at the state of (60% positive classes, 1W per training) and learned the policy that it should participate in the local update, then it can share this policy with other devices who have not been in such a state yet.

EIDR Model Training Given the above definitions, we can derive the loss function of the EIDR model as follows:

$$\mathcal{L}1_i = \sum_{t=1}^{T} \sum_{}^{s \in S_i^t} (R_i^t - V(s))^2 \quad \text{(Value Loss)} \tag{7.9}$$

$$\mathcal{L}2_i = \sum_{}^{s \in S_i^t} -log(\pi(s)) \times (R_i^t - V(s)) - \beta \times H(\pi) \quad \text{(Policy Loss)} \tag{7.10}$$

where R_i^t is the discounted reward derived by $R_i^t = \gamma^t \times (RI_i^t + RE_i^t)$, and $R - V(s)$ is the advantage function [18] representing how much better it is to take a specific action compared to the average rewards of all the actions at a given state. H is the entropy score of the policy distribution. Given the above loss functions, the model can be trained using the gradient ascent method [18].

7.2.4 Adaptive Global Update Control

After discussing the local update process, we focus on our design of the other critical component of federated learning—the global update process. An important parameter of interest is the global update frequency—how often should each edge device pull the global model to update their local models? We observe that the global update frequency can significantly affect the device selection decisions made by the edge devices and ultimately affect the global model accuracy and energy cost of edge devices. In particular, the more often the global model is updated, the less sparse the extrinsic reward will be. This is because each device can now get immediate feedback from the server as illustrated in Eq. 7.6. Therefore, frequent global updates can lead to better device selection decisions made by each edge device. However, frequent global updates can also impose significant energy costs to the edge devices. To identify the optimized frequency of updating the global model, we design an adaptive global update control (AGUC) scheme.

We note that, to identify the optimal tradeoff described above, it is necessary to assess the energy cost of edge devices under the choice of K. However, it is not possible since the server is not allowed to probe the status of edge devices, including energy due to the stringent privacy requirements in AHDS applications. Therefore, we design another bottom-up approach to let edge devices (rather than the server) pick the value of K. In particular, we assume a set of available frequencies $\mathcal{K}$ to be taken for global update: $\mathcal{K} = \{1, 2, \ldots, Z\}$. For each edge device, we use a weight vector $\Theta_i^t = \{\theta_1, \theta_2, \ldots, \theta_K\}$ to represent the probabilistic distribution for the frequencies to be chosen at round t, where $\theta_k (1 \leq k \leq Z)$ is the probability of choosing frequency k. The weight vector follows the constraint $\sum_{\theta \in \Theta_i^t} = 1$. The AGUC scheme is built on the adaptive control framework that can dynamically adjust the weight of each frequency setting based on a feedback control signal. The control signal for each edge device is a regret function defined by:

$$\phi_i^t = \sum_{i=1}^{Z} \theta_k \times (F1_k^t(M)/e_k) \tag{7.11}$$

where e_k denotes the average energy cost incurred on the edge devices when the global update frequency is set to k. $F1_k^t(M)$ refers to the average performance (measured by F1 score) of the global model when the frequency is set to k at round t. The regret function is intuitive: if a frequency constantly causes high energy cost or low performance of the global model, then the weight of this frequency should be lowered.

Given the regret function, the goal for each edge device is to dynamically update Θ_i^t so that the regret ϕ_i^t can be minimized. We develop an online regret minimization scheme by extending the PROD algorithm [9]. We present the AGUC scheme for each edge device in Algorithm 5. After each device obtains the weight vector, the server then picks the frequency that has the highest overall weights $K = \arg\max_k \sum_{i=1}^{N} \Theta_i^t$.

7.2.5   Summary of FedSens Workflow

Finally, we summarize the FedSens framework in Algorithms 6. FedSens has dual offline-online phases, including an offline pre-training phase and an online federated learning phase.

Offline Pre-training The pre-training phase targets at bootstrapping the EIDR model. The input is the current global state vector of the environment defined in Eq. 7.8. The output is an optimal policy of the EIDR that returns the action of each edge device given the current state. The pre-training can be performed in an

---

Algorithm 5 AGUC algorithm

1: **Input:** device index i, previous weight vector $\Theta_i^{t-1} = \{\theta_1, \theta_2, ..., \theta_Z\}$, learning parameter η, current round index t
2: **Output:** updated weight vector $\Theta_i^t = \{\theta_1', \theta_2', ..., \theta_Z'\}$
3: **for** $t \in [1, T]$ **do**
4:     **for do** $k \in [1, Z]$
5:         Calculate $p_k = \frac{\eta \times \theta_k}{\sum_{k=1}^{Z}(\eta \times \theta_k)}$
6:     **end for**
7:     Update $\phi_i^t = \phi_i^{t-1} \times p_k$
8:     **for** $k \in [1, Z]$ **do**
9:         $\theta_k' = (\theta_k \times (1 + \eta \times \phi_i^t))^{\frac{\eta}{\eta-1}}$
10:    **end for**
11: **end for**
12: Return Θ_i^t

"offline mode" where each device can learn its best policy by exploring various local update decisions when they are plugged into an outlet (similar to Google's FedAVG algorithm [17]). Note the unique global network design of the EIDR model allows edge devices to share the learned parameters with other homogeneous devices in the training phase. Therefore, only a small subset of heterogeneous devices is required to train the EIDR model.

Online Federated Learning The learned policy from the offline training phase is then applied to the online federated learning phase, where the edge devices selectively participate in the local update process in FL to train an optimized global AHDS model. In this online phase, the server process (Lines 1–13) in Algorithms 6 is in charge of performing the global model updates, deciding the global update frequency, and evaluating the model performance. The client process (Lines 14–26) runs the EIDR algorithm to decide the local update strategy, and runs the AGUC algorithm to propose a global update strategy Θ_i to the server. The two processes work interactively until the training of the global model is completed. The overall workflow is summarized in Algorithm 6. The FedSens framework is implemented by leveraging the OpenAI Gym reinforcement learning library[1] and the PySyft Federated Learning library.[2]

7.3 Real-World Case Studies

In this section, we present an extensive evaluation of FedSens using data traces collected from two real-world AHDS applications—*driver drowsiness detection* and *stress detection*. The results show that FedSens achieves significant performance

---

[1] https://gym.openai.com/.

[2] https://github.com/OpenMined/PySyft.

Algorithm 6 FedSens algorithmic workflow

1: **The Server Process:**
2: At t = 0, initialize w^t
3: **for** $1 \leq t \leq T$ **do**
4:      Set t = t+1
5:      Receive w_i^t, Θ_i^t from any worker E_i
6:      Derive the global update frequency K based on received Θ_i^t
7:      **if** t mod K ==0 **then**
8:          Update w^t from every w_i^t
9:          Evaluate $F1^t(M)$ of the model from test data
10:         Broadcast w^t to edge devices
11:     **end if**
12: **end for**
13: **The Client Process:**
14: At t = 0, initialize $w_i^0 = w^0$
15: **for** $1 \leq t \leq T$ **do**
16:     Derive extrinsic and intrinsic reward via Eqs. 7.6 and 7.7 respectively
17:     action = EIDR's output policy π_i^t
18:     **if** action == True **then**
19:         Update $w_i^t = w_i^{t-1} - \eta \times \frac{\partial \mathcal{L}_i(w)}{\partial w_i}$
20:         Derive Θ_i^t via Algorithm 2.
21:         Broadcast w_i^t, Θ_i^t to server
22:     **end if**
23: **end for**

---

gains in terms of FL model accuracy and energy consumption savings compared to state-of-the-art baselines. We first introduce the two real-world AHDS applications and the publicly availabledatasets we use.

Driver Drowsiness Detection In the first case study, the wearable sensors of drivers are used to detect driver drowsiness, one of the major causes of road accidents and can lead to severe physical injuries and deaths. The early drowsiness detection system could alert the driver before a mishap happens. We use the Ford Challenge dataset[3] for this application. The dataset contains a training set of 604,329 sensor entries from 100 drivers. The sensor entries include 6 physiological measurements, 11 environmental measurements, and 11 vehicular features taken from real-world trials. It also contains a test set that contains 120,840 entries.

Stress Detection The second case study focuses on a stress detection system that actively detects if a participant is under stress based on the physiological signals monitored by non-intrusive sensors on the participant. We use the SWELL dataset,[4] which collects multi-modal health information such as body postures from a Kinect 3D sensor and heart rate (variability) and skin conductance from body sensors of 25

---

[3] www.kaggle.com/c/stayalert/data.
[4] http://cs.ru.nl/~skoldijk/SWELL-KW/Dataset.html.

participants. The training set contains a total of 369,289 entries. The test set contains 41,034 entries.

For both applications, we observe a significant class imbalance issue in the collected dataset. For the driver drowsiness detection application, only 16.2% of the dataset are positive data samples. Similarly, in the stress detection application, only 19.7% of the dataset is of positive class labels. Therefore, it makes good sense to evaluate the discussed FedSens framework on both datasets in terms of robustness against the class imbalance issue.

We present the details of the critical parameter settings for FedSens. In particular, for the pre-training phase of the EIDR, we set the key parameters for the reinforcement learning model as follows: policy learning rate = 0.0001, value learning rate = 0.001, $\gamma = 0.9$, $\lambda = 1.0$. For the FL phase, we set B = 100 (local batch size) , and $E = 1$ (local epoch number).

Baselines First, we observe that there exist no federated learning baselines that address the class imbalance issue that respects both the strict privacy requirements of the participants and the heterogeneous resource constraints of edge devices in AHDS applications. Therefore, we choose the following baselines that are representative of the state-of-the-art schemes that can be adapted and applied to federated learning based AHDS applications.

- **FedHealth**: the state-of-the-art federated learning based smart health system that leverages the classical FedAvg algorithm for distributed training of health data [5]. It considers neither the resource constraints of edge devices nor the class imbalance of participants' data.
- **Astraea**: a self-balancing federated learning framework that addresses the class imbalance issue via adaptive sampling technique to improve the classification accuracy of mobile deep learning applications [7]. However, it does not consider the resource constraints of edge devices and makes the assumption that the server has global knowledge of the class distribution of data samples of each participant.
- **BGTA**: a bottom-up scheme that allows each device to selfishly pick local training rounds to minimize the energy cost of the devices through a game-theoretic approach [25].
- **Individual SMOTE (ISMOTE)**: An over-sampling technique that balances the class labels on each individual device by generating synthetic data using the SMOTE technique [3].
- **Individual Down-sample (IDSample)**: A down-sampling technique that balances the class labels on each individual device by randomly removing data samples of the dominant class [13].

Note that we assume the strict privacy requirements (i.e., PR1–PR4) as discussed in Sect. 7.2.1 are applied to all schemes for a fair comparison. Therefore, the compared schemes are not allowed to access either the raw data or the class distribution of the raw data from participants. The only exception is *Astraea*, which does require the access to the class distribution of the participants' data.

We favor *Astraea* by letting it "cheat" to violate the PR3 in our experiment. We also compare the discussed scheme with the popular over-sampling and down-sampling techniques (i.e., ISMOTE and IDSample) that are considered as the *de facto* approaches to address the class imbalance issue in our problem.

Detection Performance   In the first set of experiments, we examine the overall performance of all compared schemes. In particular, we emulate 10 devices for each device type (TX2, TX1, and TK1) and evenly distribute the training set to each of the emulated devices. The results are reported in Figs. 7.4 and 7.5. We observe that the FedSens scheme consistently outperforms all compared baselines. Compared to the best-performing baseline IDSample, FedSens is able to boost the F1 score from 0.748 to 0.816 in the driver drowsiness detection application. In the stress detection application, FedSens is able to improve the F1 score from 0.759 to 0.808 compared to the best-performing baseline—Astraea. The reason of such performance gains is that the EIDR model in FedSens allows each edge device to make the best local update policy based on its own class distribution. Consequently, FedSens can effectively address the class imbalance issue of training data and is able to learn an unbiased model via the local training update algorithm.

We also observe that, while over-sampling and down-sampling techniques (i.e., ISMOTE and IDSample) have been shown to be effective in centralized learning schemes [13], they are not very effective in the federated learning scenarios due to the following reasons. First, the down-sampling technique will discard useful training data which will in turn degrade the system performance. In contrast, FedSens does not discard training data but instead tries to find smart ways to combine local training data that mitigate the class imbalance. Such difference can be best illustrated by a simple example. Consider a naïve scenario where there are two edge devices A and B, where A has 20 positive samples and 80 negative samples, while B has 80 positive samples and 20 negative samples. Our approach will combine the data of A and B so that the overall data is class-balanced while the down-sampling approach will discard 60 data from each device, which significantly downsizes the overall training data. Similarly, over-sampling techniques can introduce too many fake/synthetic data that may not fit well with the actual distribution of the health data of patients. In contrast, FedSens only learns from real health data and does not depend on synthetically generated datasets.

Energy Consumption of Edge Devices   In the second set of experiments, we study the energy cost of the edge devices of all compared schemes. In particular, we evaluate the energy consumption that is required for each edge device when the global model of the system is converged. Note that, we do not include the energy consumption during the pre-training phase described in Sect. 7.2.5 as they can be done offline when the edge devices are plugged into power outlets. We present the normalized average power consumption on each type of edge devices (10 for each type) in Tables 7.1 and 7.2. We observe that FedSens consumes less overall energy as compared to all baselines. Combined with the results shown in Figs. 7.4 and 7.5, we can conclude that FedSens achieves a sound accuracy—energy tradeoff: it can

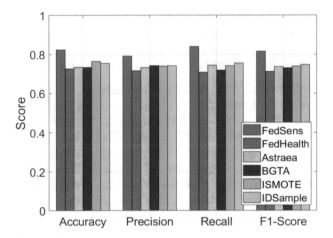

Fig. 7.4 Detection accuracy for drowsiness detection

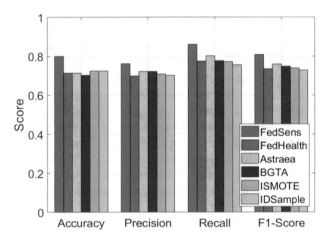

Fig. 7.5 Detection accuracy for stress detection

significantly improve the model performance of AHDS applications but at the same
time reduces the average energy consumption of the edge devices in the system.
While the ISMOTE and IDSample schemes have an apparent advantage in terms of
energy savings due to their simple implementations, FedSens is able to outperform
all other baselines in both datasets. We attribute this performance gain to the energy-
aware design of the local training assignment of FedSens where each edge device
can selfishly minimize the energy cost via the intrinsic reward design in the EIDR
scheme. We also observe that FedSens tends to push more local training to the TX2
and TX1 as they are more energy efficient (i.e., less energy cost to train the same
amount of data as compared to TK1). This will incur higher energy cost to TX1

Table 7.1 Average power of edge devices in drowsiness detection (W). Bold values indicate the best performance achieved by the FedSens scheme compared to other baselines

	TX2	TX1	TK1	Overall
FedSens	4.872	4.531	2.244	**116.47**
FedHealth	4.185	4.421	3.621	122.27
Astraea	4.309	4.177	3.432	119.18
BGTA	5.052	4.688	3.247	129.87
ISMOTE	4.372	4.621	2.490	114.83
IDSample	4.176	4.211	2.170	105.77

Table 7.2 Average power of edge devices in stress detection (W). Bold values indicate the best performance achieved by the FedSens scheme compared to other baselines

	TX2	TX1	TK1	Overall
FedSens	5.655	4.781	2.138	**125.74**
FedHealth	4.893	4.249	3.772	129.14
Astraea	5.277	4.315	3.675	132.67
BGTA	5.252	4.688	3.247	131.87
ISMOTE	5.316	4.617	2.589	125.22
IDSample	4.782	4.043	2.410	112.35

Table 7.3 Ablation study of FedSens. Bold values indicate the best performance achieved by the FedSens scheme compared to other baselines

	Driver Drowsiness Detection			Stress Detection		
	Precision	Recall	F1	Precision	Recall	F1
FedSens	**0.792**	**0.841**	**0.816**	**0.762**	**0.861**	**0.808**
w/o EIDR	0.753	0.784	0.768	0.728	0.783	0.754
w/o global net.	0.752	0.767	0.759	0.748	0.792	0.769
w/o AGUC	0.776	0.780	0.778	0.715	0.802	0.756

and TX2 boards as compared to baselines but allow the overall system to be more energy efficient.

Ablation Study Finally, we perform a comprehensive *ablation study* to examine the effect of each component of FedSens. In particular, we present the classification accuracy of FedSens by removing three important components of the system (Table 7.3). We found that, by adding the EIDR module, FedSens is able to increase its F1 score by 4.8 and 5.4% respectively for the two case studies. We also found the global network design in EIDR is indeed helpful—yielding 5.7 and 3.9% increase in F1 scores, respectively. The AGUC module also contributes to 3.6 and 5.2% in F1 score over two case studies. The above results demonstrate that the key components of FedSens construct a holistic FL scheme that best optimizes the performance of FedSens.

7.4   Discussion

This chapter presents the FedSens, a federated learning framework to perform privacy-aware training for AHDS applications with the class imbalance in mobile edge computing systems. We develop a novel curiosity-driven reinforcement learning based local update scheme as well as an adaptive global update scheme to jointly improve the model accuracy in AHDS with class imbalance. The FedSens framework was implemented on a real-world heterogeneous edge computing testbed and evaluated through two real-world case studies in AHDS. The evaluation results demonstrated that FedSens achieves significant performance gains in terms of improved model accuracy and energy efficiency compared to state-of-the-art baselines. We also envision the general framework of FedSens can be extended and applied to other SEC applications where privacy is the key concern of the applications.

References

1. M.M. Baig, H. Gholamhosseini, Smart health monitoring systems: an overview of design and modeling. J. Med. Syst. **37**(2), 9898 (2013)
2. A. Bogomolov, B. Lepri, M. Ferron, F. Pianesi, A.S. Pentland, Daily stress recognition from mobile phone data, weather conditions and individual traits, in *Proceedings of the 22nd ACM International Conference on Multimedia* (ACM, New York, 2014), pp. 477–486
3. N.V. Chawla, K.W. Bowyer, L.O. Hall, W.P. Kegelmeyer, Smote: synthetic minority over-sampling technique. J. Artif. Intell. Res. **16**, 321–357 (2002)
4. M. Chen, W. Li, Y. Hao, Y. Qian, I. Humar, Edge cognitive computing based smart healthcare system. Future Gener. Comput. Syst. **86**, 403–411 (2018)
5. Y. Chen, J. Wang, C. Yu, W. Gao, X. Qin, Fedhealth: a federated transfer learning framework for wearable healthcare (2019). arXiv:1907.09173
6. J. Dieffenderfer, H. Goodell, S. Mills, M. McKnight, S. Yao, F. Lin, E. Beppler, B. Bent, B. Lee, V. Misra, et al., Low-power wearable systems for continuous monitoring of environment and health for chronic respiratory disease. IEEE J. Biomed. Health Inform. **20**(5), 1251–1264 (2016)
7. M. Duan, Astraea: self-balancing federated learning for improving classification accuracy of mobile deep learning applications (2019). arXiv:1907.01132
8. K. Fawaz, K.G. Shin, Location privacy protection for smartphone users, in *Proceedings of the 2014 ACM SIGSAC Conference on Computer and Communications Security* (ACM, New York, 2014), pp. 239–250
9. P. Gaillard, G. Stoltz, T. Van Erven, A second-order bound with excess losses, in *Conference on Learning Theory* (2014), pp. 176–196
10. D.F. Hayes, H.S. Markus, R.D. Leslie, E.J. Topol, Personalized medicine: risk prediction, targeted therapies and mobile health technology. BMC Med. **12**(1), 37 (2014)
11. N. Japkowicz, S. Stephen, The class imbalance problem: a systematic study. Intell. Data Anal. **6**(5), 429–449 (2002)
12. J. Konečnỳ, H.B. McMahan, F.X. Yu, P. Richtárik, A.T. Suresh, D. Bacon, Federated learning: strategies for improving communication efficiency (2016). arXiv:1610.05492
13. J.L. Leevy, T.M. Khoshgoftaar, R.A. Bauder, N. Seliya, A survey on addressing high-class imbalance in big data. J. Big Data **5**(1), 42 (2018)

14. D. Liu, T. Miller, R. Sayeed, K. Mandl, FADL: federated-autonomous deep learning for distributed electronic health record (2018). arXiv:1811.11400
15. J. Lockman, R.S. Fisher, D.M. Olson, Detection of seizure-like movements using a wrist accelerometer. Epilepsy Behav. **20**(4), 638–641 (2011)
16. H. Mao, M. Alizadeh, I. Menache, S. Kandula, Resource management with deep reinforcement learning, in *Proceedings of the 15th ACM Workshop on Hot Topics in Networks* (ACM, New York, 2016), pp. 50–56
17. H.B. McMahan, E. Moore, D. Ramage, S. Hampson, et al., Communication-efficient learning of deep networks from decentralized data (2016). arXiv:1602.05629
18. V. Mnih, A.P. Badia, M. Mirza, A. Graves, T. Lillicrap, T. Harley, D. Silver, K. Kavukcuoglu, Asynchronous methods for deep reinforcement learning, in *International Conference on Machine Learning* (2016), pp. 1928–1937
19. T. Nishio, R. Yonetani, Client selection for federated learning with heterogeneous resources in mobile edge, in *ICC 2019-2019 IEEE International Conference on Communications (ICC)* (IEEE, Piscataway, 2019), pp. 1–7
20. Y. O'Connor, W. Rowan, L. Lynch, C. Heavin, Privacy by design: informed consent and internet of things for smart health. Proc. Comput. Sci. **113**, 653–658 (2017)
21. W. Shi, J. Cao, Q. Zhang, Y. Li, L. Xu, Edge computing: vision and challenges. IEEE Internet Things J. **3**(5), 637–646 (2016)
22. A. Solanas, C. Patsakis, M. Conti, I.S. Vlachos, V. Ramos, F. Falcone, O. Postolache, P.A. Pérez-Martínez, R. Di Pietro, D.N. Perrea, et al., Smart health: a context-aware health paradigm within smart cities. IEEE Commun. Mag. **52**(8), 74–81 (2014)
23. U. Varshney, Pervasive healthcare and wireless health monitoring. Mobile Netw. Appl. **12**(2–3), 113–127 (2007)
24. S. Wang, T. Tuor, T. Salonidis, K.K. Leung, C. Makaya, T. He, K. Chan, Adaptive federated learning in resource constrained edge computing systems. IEEE J. Sel. Areas Commun. **37**(6), 1205–1221 (2019)
25. D.Y. Zhang, Y. Ma, Y. Zhang, S. Lin, X.S. Hu, D. Wang, A real-time and non-cooperative task allocation framework for social sensing applications in edge computing systems, in *2018 IEEE Real-Time and Embedded Technology and Applications Symposium (RTAS)* (IEEE, Piscataway, 2018), pp. 316–326
26. D.Y. Zhang, Z. Kou, D. Wang, Fedsens: a federated learning approach for smart health sensing with class imbalance in resource constrained edge computing, in *IEEE INFOCOM 2021-IEEE Conference on Computer Communications* (IEEE, Piscataway, 2021), pp. 1–10

Chapter 8
Further Readings

Abstract This chapter provides further readings that are related to the work presented in this book. The readers are recommended to take the content of this chapter as references if they would like to explore future problems from a broader perspective. Examples of the reviewed areas in this chapter include: Social Sensing, Edge Computing, Distributed System with Heterogeneous Computing Nodes, IoT Middleware, Human-AI Systems, Active Learning, and Learning with Imbalanced Data.

8.1 Social Sensing

Social sensing has emerged as a new sensing paradigm due to the proliferation of low-cost mobile sensors and the ubiquitous Internet connectivity [2, 67, 68]. The ideas of getting people involved into the loop of the sensing process (e.g., participatory [8], opportunistic [31] and human-centric [20] sensing) have been investigated at length in projects such as MetroSense [9], SurroundSense [5], RobustSense [82], and TurnsMap [12]. A recent survey of social sensing [70] covers many sensing challenges in human context such as accommodating energy constraints of mobile sensing devices [39, 62], quantifying the quality of sensing data [65, 66, 77], understanding the physical constraints [64, 69], heterogeneous data modality [51, 52], spatio-temporal data sparsity [46, 54], mitigating data bias and ensuring model fairness [25, 79], and addressing the privacy and security concerns of the end users [40, 44]. A large set of social sensing applications are also sensitive to delay. Examples of such applications include intelligent transportation systems [71], video-based crowdsensing [73], smart urban monitoring [78], social-driven pandemic sensing [45], intelligent environment monitoring [53], and disaster and emergency response [47]. However, most of the data processing and computation tasks in social sensing are done on dedicated servers or commercial clouds [43, 66, 72]. The Social Edge Computing (SEC) complements current "backend" based social sensing solutions by exploring the rich computing capability available at the social edge devices.

D. Wang, D. Y. Zhang, *Social Edge Computing*,
https://doi.org/10.1007/978-3-031-26936-3_8

8.2   Edge Computing

A comprehensive survey of edge computing is given by Shi et al. [55]. A critical challenge in edge computing is *computation offloading* where heavy data analytic tasks are transferred to external servers from edge devices with limited memory, battery and computation power [38]. Pushing all the computation tasks to the remote servers can be rather ineffective, particularly for delay-sensitive applications [56]. Various efforts have focused on offloading computation tasks to the edge devices to reduce communication costs and application latency [29]. For example, Satyanarayanan et al. introduced an intermediate layer (i.e., "Cloudlet") located between the cloud and mobile devices to address the high latency issue between edge devices and servers [49]. Gao et al. proposed a probabilistic computational offloading framework that offloads the computation tasks to the mobile devices [16]. Kosta et al. proposed an energy-aware code offloading framework to dynamically switch between edge devices and cloud servers to improve the energy efficiency of the system [23]. Recently, Saurez et al. proposed a programming infrastructure "Foglet" to jointly address resource discovery, incremental deployment, and live task migration commensurate with application dynamism and resource availability [50]. The SEC framework is complementary to the above solutions in that we explicitly consider the *rational*, *trust sensitive*, and *heterogeneous* nature of the social edge devices and their implications in the task allocation process of the SEC systems.

8.3   Task Allocation in Real-Time Systems

Task allocation is a fundamental problem in real-time systems, and both centralized and distributed solutions have been developed [6, 11, 59, 63]. For example, Zhu et al. proposed a Mixed Integer Linear Programming based approach to minimize the end-to-end latency in hard real-time systems [83]. Su et al. developed a mixed-criticality task allocation model to maximize the number of low-criticality tasks being executed without influencing the high-criticality tasks [59]. A set of task allocation schemes have been developed to optimize hardware reliability and energy efficiency [11, 36]. Most of the above schemes adopt a centralized approach which fails in the edge computing systems where the devices might refrain from providing necessary information to accomplish the centralized task allocation [74]. Decentralized task allocation schemes have been developed to address this limitation. For example, Ahmad et al. proposed a distributed approach for scheduling tasks on multi-core processors to jointly optimize performance and energy [3]. Bertuccelli et al. proposed a decentralized task allocation protocol for a dynamic and uncertain environment [6]. However, these decentralized schemes do not explicitly consider the heterogeneity of the edge devices and task models in SEC applications. SEC develops a HeteroMask scheme to explicitly address the heterogeneity issues in the task allocation process.

8.4   Distributed System with Heterogeneous Computing Nodes

Taming heterogeneity of heterogeneous computing nodes has been identified as a critical undertaking in distributed systems. Various solutions have been developed in the past that target either resource heterogeneity or network heterogeneity. For example, the HTCondor system can harness the idle computational cycles from distributed workstations to accomplish computation tasks [35]. Habak et al. proposed FemtoCloud, which is a dynamic and self-configuring system architecture that enables privately owned mobile devices to be configured into a coordinated computing cluster [19]. More recently, Zhang et al. proposed a coordinated edge computing system that allows non-cooperative and heterogeneous edge devices to trade tasks and claim rewards [75]. However, the above schemes suffer from two major limitations: (1) they made strong assumptions that the tasks only require homogeneous computational resources (i.e., CPU and memory) which is not true in SEC where complicated social sensing tasks may require a diversified set of resources such as sensors, CPU and GPU; (2) they assume the edge devices are always compatible with the computation tasks which is again not necessarily true in SEC where the edge devices may have different runtime environments such as OS and software dependencies.

8.5   IoT Middleware

The IoT middleware targets at enabling connectivity for heterogeneous IoT devices, making communication possible among devices. Typical IoT middleware solutions include TerraSwarm [33], Xively [58], and Global Sensor Networks [1]. There exists an important knowledge gap in the above IoT middleware solutions by largely ignoring the potential of performing non-trivial computation tasks on increasingly powerful and ubiquitous edge devices owned by individuals. HeteroEdge focuses on providing reliable *computing power* over heterogeneous edge devices in IoT systems to accomplish computationally intensive tasks (e.g., deep learning-based inference, image processing) that are traditionally done in the backend/cloud. Such "computation-centric" focus is different from the focus of providing *interconnectivity* and *interoperability* from the traditional *sensing-centric* IoT middleware solutions. Our work is also significantly different from recent computing-centric IoT middleware solutions. Examples of such solutions include FemtoCloud [19], Deviceless [17], and AWS Greengrass IoT [30]. However, the current computing-centric solutions have several key limitations compared to SEC: (1) they largely ignore the fact that many computationally capable IoT devices are now owned by individuals, and there exists a significant runtime heterogeneity in those devices (different OS, software libraries); (2) they do not fully consider the heterogeneity of the computational tasks (e.g., tasks that require CPU, GPU or sensing modules) together with non-trivial task dependencies; (3) they do not fully explore the diversified configurations of hardware components (e.g., GPU, single-core CPU, multi-core CPU, sensors) of the edge devices). In fact, the solutions mentioned above primarily focus on tasks that require CPU.

8.6   Human-AI Systems and Active Learning

Humans have traditionally been an integral part of artificial intelligence systems as a means of generating labeled training data [37, 42, 48]. Such a paradigm has been proven to be effective in supervised learning tasks such as image classification [13], speech recognition [18], autonomous driving [61], social media mining [76], and virtual reality [57]. However, it also suffers from two key limitations. First, some applications (e.g., damage assessment) may require a large amount of training data to achieve reasonable performance, which could be impractical due to the labor cost [21, 34]. Second, the AI models are often black-box systems, and it is difficult to diagnose in the event of failure and unsatisfactory performance [80, 81]. To address these limitations, a few human-AI hybrid frameworks have been developed in recent years [21, 24, 27, 41]. For example, Holzinger et al. proposed the notion of interactive human-machine learning ("iML") where humans directly interact with AI by identifying useful features that could be incorporated into the AI algorithms [21]. Branson et al. invented a human-in-the-loop visual recognition system to accurately classify the objects in the picture based on the descriptions of the picture from humans [7]. Nushi et al. developed an accountable human-AI system that leverages workers on MTurk to identify the limitations of the AI algorithms [41] and provide suggestions to improve them.

Active Learning (AL) is a common technique to combine machine and human intelligence in human-AI systems [26, 32]. In an active learning framework, an AI algorithm actively asks for the labels of some instances from domain experts [60]. The major benefit of AL is that it selects a "subset" of data samples to be labeled and significantly reduces the labeling costs and improves the efficiency. For example, Ambati et al. proposed Active Crowd Translation (ACT), a new machine translation paradigm where active learning technique is applied to dynamically query the crowd for annotations of texts. The annotations are then used to train an AI model to automatically translate low-resource languages [4]. Laws et al. proposed an active learning framework using a retraining technique for supervised learning tasks—the algorithm iteratively identifies instances for the crowd to obtain the labels and retrain the model using the newly obtained labels [32]. However, these solutions could not handle scenarios where AI algorithms fail due to the flaws in their model design instead of insufficient training data. In contrast, SEC is able to diagnose the model and query the crowd to directly take over the AI algorithm in such failure scenarios.

8.7   Learning with Imbalanced Data

Class imbalance is a common issue in machine learning, especially in applications of health monitoring, fraud detection, anomaly detection, medical diagnosis. It is observed that the class imbalance can lead to significant degradation of the performance of the machine learning models [14, 22]. Many approaches have been developed to address this problem, which mainly fall into two categories: (1) over-sampling based, and (2) down-sampling based. An example of the over-sampling technique is Synthetic Minority Over-sampling Technique (SMOTE), which generates synthetic samples from the minority class so as to obtain a nearly class-balanced training set to train the classifier [10]. Similarly, the down-sampling techniques (the opposite of over-sampling) have also been developed to decrease the number of instances in a majority class to obtain a balanced training set [15, 28]. Both types of sampling techniques have been empirically shown to be effective in improving the classification performance of the model with imbalanced class labels [22]. In SEC, we assume that only the participant who owns the data knows its class distribution and will not share either the raw data or class labels with another party (server or other participants). This assumption requires a new technique to address the class imbalance issue in intelligent edge applications.

References

1. K. Aberer, M. Hauswirth, A. Salehi, *Global Sensor Networks, Technical Report LSIR-REPORT-2006-001*. (2006)
2. C.C. Aggarwal, T. Abdelzaher, Social sensing, in *Managing and Mining Sensor Data* (Springer, Berlin, 2013), pp. 237–297
3. I. Ahmad, S. Ranka, S.U. Khan, Using game theory for scheduling tasks on multi-core processors for simultaneous optimization of performance and energy, in *IEEE International Symposium on Parallel and Distributed Processing, 2008. IPDPS 2008* (IEEE, 2008), pp. 1–6
4. V. Ambati, S. Vogel, J.G. Carbonell, Active learning and crowd-sourcing for machine translation, in *Language Resources and Evaluation Conference*, vol. 1 (Citeseer, 2010), p. 2
5. M. Azizyan, I. Constandache, R.R. Choudhury, Surroundsense: mobile phone localization via ambience fingerprinting, in *Proceedings of the 15th Annual International Conference on Mobile Computing and Networking* (ACM, 2009), pp. 261–272
6. L.F. Bertuccelli, H.-L. Choi, P. Cho, J.P. How, Real-time multi-UAV task assignment in dynamic and uncertain environments. In AIAA guidance, navigation, and control conference 2009 Aug 10, p. 5776 (2009)
7. S. Branson, C. Wah, F. Schroff, B. Babenko, P. Welinder, P. Perona, S. Belongie, Visual recognition with humans in the loop, in *European Conference on Computer Vision* (Springer, 2010), pp. 438–451
8. J.A. Burke, D. Estrin, M. Hansen, A. Parker, N. Ramanathan, S. Reddy, M.B. Srivastava, Participatory sensing. In Proceedings of the International Workshop on World-Sensor-Web. 1–5.
9. A.T. Campbell, S.B. Eisenman, N.D. Lane, E. Miluzzo, R.A. Peterson, People-centric urban sensing, in *Proceedings of the 2nd Annual International Workshop on Wireless Internet, WICON '06, New York, NY, USA* (ACM, 2006)

10. N.V. Chawla, K.W. Bowyer, L.O. Hall, W.P. Kegelmeyer, Smote: synthetic minority over-sampling technique. J. Artif. Intell. Res. **16**, 321–357 (2002)

11. J.-J. Chen, C.-F. Kuo, Energy-efficient scheduling for real-time systems on dynamic voltage scaling (dvs) platforms, in *13th IEEE International Conference on Embedded and Real-Time Computing Systems and Applications, 2007. RTCSA 2007* (IEEE, 2007), pp. 28–38

12. D. Chen, K.G. Shin, Turnsmap: enhancing driving safety at intersections with mobile crowdsensing and deep learning. Proc. ACM Interact. Mob. Wearable Ubiquitous Technol. **3**(3), 78 (2019)

13. J. Deng, W. Dong, R. Socher, L.-J. Li, K. Li, L. Fei-Fei, Imagenet: a large-scale hierarchical image database, in *IEEE Conference on Computer Vision and Pattern Recognition, 2009. CVPR 2009* (IEEE, 2009), pp. 248–255

14. M. Duan, D. Liu, X. Chen, Y. Tan, J. Ren, L. Qiao, L. Liang, Astraea: self-balancing federated learning for improving classification accuracy of mobile deep learning applications. In 2019 IEEE 37th international conference on computer design (ICCD), pp. 246–254. IEEE (2019)

15. E.A. Freeman, G.G. Moisen, T.S. Frescino, Evaluating effectiveness of down-sampling for stratified designs and unbalanced prevalence in random forest models of tree species distributions in nevada. Ecol. Model. **233**, 1–10 (2012)

16. W. Gao, Opportunistic peer-to-peer mobile cloud computing at the tactical edge, in *Military Communications Conference (MILCOM), 2014 IEEE* (IEEE, 2014), pp. 1614–1620

17. A. Glikson, S. Nastic, S. Dustdar, Deviceless edge computing: extending serverless computing to the edge of the network, in *Proceedings of the 10th ACM International Systems and Storage Conference* (ACM, 2017), p. 28

18. A. Graves, A.-R. Mohamed, G. Hinton, Speech recognition with deep recurrent neural networks, in *2013 IEEE International Conference on Acoustics, Speech and Signal Processing (ICASSP)* (IEEE, 2013), pp. 6645–6649

19. K. Habak, M. Ammar, K.A. Harras, E. Zegura, Femto clouds: leveraging mobile devices to provide cloud service at the edge, in *2015 IEEE 8th International Conference on Cloud Computing (CLOUD)* (IEEE, 2015), pp. 9–16

20. T. Higashino, A. Uchiyama, A study for human centric cyber physical system based sensing–toward safe and secure urban life–, in *Information Search, Integration and Personalization* (Springer, Berlin, 2013), pp. 61–70

21. A. Holzinger, M. Plass, K. Holzinger, G.C. Crisan, C.-M. Pintea, V. Palade, A glass-box interactive machine learning approach for solving np-hard problems with the human-in-the-loop (2017). Creat. Math. Inform. **28**(2), 121–134 (2019)

22. N. Japkowicz, S. Stephen, The class imbalance problem: a systematic study. Intell. Data Anal. **6**(5), 429–449 (2002)

23. S. Kosta, A. Aucinas, P. Hui, R. Mortier, X. Zhang, Thinkair: dynamic resource allocation and parallel execution in the cloud for mobile code offloading, in *2012 Proceedings IEEE Infocom* (IEEE, 2012), pp. 945–953

24. Z. Kou, L. Shang, H. Zeng, Y. Zhang, D. Wang, Exgfair: a crowdsourcing data exchange approach to fair human face datasets augmentation, in *2021 IEEE International Conference on Big Data (Big Data)* (IEEE, 2021), pp. 1285–1290

25. Z. Kou, Y. Zhang, L. Shang, D. Wang, Faircrowd: fair human face dataset sampling via batch-level crowdsourcing bias inference, in *2021 IEEE/ACM 29th International Symposium on Quality of Service (IWQOS)* (IEEE, 2021), pp. 1–10

26. Z. Kou, L. Shang, Y. Zhang, S. Duan, D. Wang, Can i only share my eyes? a web crowdsourcing based face partition approach towards privacy-aware face recognition, in *Proceedings of the ACM Web Conference 2022* (2022), pp. 3611–3622

27. Z. Kou, L. Shang, Y. Zhang, Z. Yue, H. Zeng, D. Wang, Crowd, expert & ai: a human-ai interactive approach towards natural language explanation based covid-19 misinformation detection, in *Proceedings of the 18th international joint conference on Artificial intelligence (IJCAI)* (2022), pp. 5087–5093

28. M. Kuhn, K. Johnson, Remedies for severe class imbalance, in *Applied Predictive Modeling* (Springer, Berlin, 2013), pp. 419–443

29. K. Kumar, Y.-H. Lu, Cloud computing for mobile users: Can offloading computation save energy? Computer **43**(4), 51–56 (2010)
30. A. Kurniawan, A.W.S. Learning, *IoT: effectively manage Connected Devices on the AWS Cloud Using Services Such as AWS Greengrass, AWS Button, Predictive Analytics and Machine Learning* (Packt Publishing Ltd, 2018 Jan 29)
31. N.D. Lane, S.B. Eisenman, M. Musolesi, E. Miluzzo, A.T. Campbell, Urban sensing systems: opportunistic or participatory? in *Proceedings of the 9th Workshop on Mobile Computing Systems and Applications, HotMobile '08, New York, NY, USA* (ACM, 2008), pp. 11–16
32. F. Laws, C. Scheible, H. Schütze, Active learning with amazon mechanical turk, in *Proceedings of the Conference on Empirical Methods in Natural Language Processing* (Association for Computational Linguistics, 2011), pp. 1546–1556
33. E.A. Lee, J.D. Kubiatowicz, J.M. Rabaey, A.L. Sangiovanni-Vincentelli, S.A. Seshia, J. Wawrzynek, D. Blaauw, P. Dutta, K. Fu, C. Guestrin, et al., *The Terraswarm Research Center (TSRC) (a white paper)*. Technical Report UCB/EECS-2012-207. EECS Department, University of California, Berkeley, 2012
34. X. Li, D. Caragea, H. Zhang, M. Imran, Localizing and quantifying damage in social media images, in *2018 IEEE/ACM International Conference on Advances in Social Networks Analysis and Mining (ASONAM)* (IEEE, 2018)
35. M.J. Litzkow, Remote unix: turning idle workstations into cycle servers, in *Proceedings of the Summer USENIX Conference* (1987), pp. 381–384
36. Y. Ma, T. Chantem, R.P. Dick, X.S. Hu, Improving system-level lifetime reliability of multicore soft real-time systems. IEEE Trans. Very Large Scale Integr. VLSI Syst. **25**(6), 1895–1905 (2017)
37. J. Marshall, D. Wang, Mood-sensitive truth discovery for reliable recommendation systems in social sensing, in *Proceedings of International Conference on Recommender Systems (Recsys)* (ACM, 2016), pp. 167–174
38. A. Mtibaa, K.A. Harras, A. Fahim, Towards computational offloading in mobile device clouds, in *2013 IEEE 5th International Conference on Cloud Computing Technology and Science (CloudCom)*, vol. 1 (IEEE, 2013), pp. 331–338
39. S. Nath, Ace: exploiting correlation for energy-efficient and continuous context sensing, in *Proceedings of the Tenth International Conference on Mobile Systems, Applications, and Services (MobiSys'12)* (2012)
40. J. Ni, A. Zhang, X. Lin, X.S. Shen, Security, privacy, and fairness in fog-based vehicular crowdsensing. IEEE Commun. Mag. **55**(6), 146–152 (2017)
41. B. Nushi, E. Kamar, E. Horvitz, D. Kossmann, On human intellect and machine failures: troubleshooting integrative machine learning systems, in *Association for the Advancement of Artificial Intelligence* (2017), pp. 1017–1025
42. B. Nushi, E. Kamar, E. Horvitz, Towards accountable ai: hybrid human-machine analyses for characterizing system failure (2018). Preprint. arXiv:1809.07424
43. R.W. Ouyang, L.M. Kaplan, A. Toniolo, M. Srivastava, T.J. Norman, Parallel and streaming truth discovery in large-scale quantitative crowdsourcing. IEEE Trans. Parallel Distrib. Syst. **27**(10), 2984–2997 (2016)
44. L. Pournajaf, D.A. Garcia-Ulloa, L. Xiong, V. Sunderam, Participant privacy in mobile crowd sensing task management: a survey of methods and challenges. ACM Sigmod Record **44**(4), 23–34 (2016)
45. M.T. Rashid, D. Wang, Covidsens: a vision on reliable social sensing for covid-19. Artif. Intell. Rev. **54**(1), 1–25 (2021)
46. M.T. Rashid, D.Y. Zhang, Z. Liu, H. Lin, D. Wang, Collabdrone: a collaborative spatiotemporal-aware drone sensing system driven by social sensing signals, in *2019 28th International Conference on Computer Communication and Networks (ICCCN)* (IEEE, 2019), pp. 1–9
47. M.T. Rashid, D.Y. Zhang, D. Wang, Socialdrone: an integrated social media and drone sensing system for reliable disaster response, in *IEEE INFOCOM 2020-IEEE Conference on Computer Communications* (IEEE, 2020), pp. 218–227

48. S.J. Russell, P. Norvig, *Artificial intelligence: A Modern Approach* (Pearson Education Limited, Malaysia, 2016)
49. M. Satyanarayanan, P. Bahl, R. Caceres, N. Davies, The case for vm-based cloudlets in mobile computing. IEEE Pers. Commun. **8**(4) (2009)
50. E. Saurez, K. Hong, D. Lillethun, U. Ramachandran, B. Ottenwälder, Incremental deployment and migration of geo-distributed situation awareness applications in the fog, in *Proceedings of the 10th ACM International Conference on Distributed and Event-based Systems* (ACM, 2016), pp. 258–269
51. L. Shang, Z. Kou, Y. Zhang, D. Wang, A multimodal misinformation detector for covid-19 short videos on tiktok, in *2021 IEEE International Conference on Big Data (Big Data)* (IEEE, 2021), pp. 899–908
52. L. Shang, Z. Kou, Y. Zhang, D. Wang, A duo-generative approach to explainable multimodal covid-19 misinformation detection, in *Proceedings of the ACM Web Conference 2022* (2022), pp. 3623–3631
53. L. Shang, Y. Zhang, Q. Ye, N. Wei, D. Wang, Smartwatersens: a crowdsensing-based approach to groundwater contamination estimation, in *2022 IEEE International Conference on Smart Computing (SMARTCOMP)* (IEEE, 2022), pp. 48–55
54. L. Shang, Y. Zhang, C. Youn, D. Wang, Sat-geo: a social sensing based content-only approach to geolocating abnormal traffic events using syntax-based probabilistic learning. Inf. Process. Manag. **59**(2), 102807 (2022)
55. W. Shi, S. Dustdar, The promise of edge computing. Computer **49**(5), 78–81 (2016)
56. W. Shi, J. Cao, Q. Zhang, Y. Li, L. Xu, Edge computing: vision and challenges. IEEE Internet Things J. **3**(5), 637–646 (2016)
57. J. Shu, S. Kosta, R. Zheng, P. Hui, Talk2me: a framework for device-to-device augmented reality social network, in *2018 IEEE International Conference on Pervasive Computing and Communications (PerCom)* (IEEE, 2018), pp. 1–10
58. N. Sinha, K.E. Pujitha, J.S.R. Alex, Xively based sensing and monitoring system for iot, in *2015 International Conference on Computer Communication and Informatics (ICCCI)* (IEEE, 2015), pp. 1–6
59. H. Su, D. Zhu, An elastic mixed-criticality task model and its scheduling algorithm, in *Proceedings of the Conference on Design, Automation and Test in Europe* (EDA Consortium, 2013), pp. 147–152
60. A.L. Thomaz, C. Breazeal et al., Reinforcement learning with human teachers: evidence of feedback and guidance with implications for learning performance. In Proceedings of the AAAI Conference on Artificial Intelligence, pp. 1000–1005 (2006)
61. C. Urmson, J. Anhalt, D. Bagnell, C. Baker, R. Bittner, M. Clark, J. Dolan, D. Duggins, T. Galatali, C. Geyer, et al., Autonomous driving in urban environments: boss and the urban challenge. J. Field Rob. **25**(8), 425–466 (2008)
62. Y. Wang, J. Lin, M. Annavaram, Q.A. Jacobson, J. Hong, B. Krishnamachari, N. Sadeh, A framework of energy efficient mobile sensing for automatic user state recognition, in *Proceedings of the 7th International Conference on Mobile Systems, Applications, and Services* (ACM, 2009), pp. 179–192
63. D. Wang, T. Abdelzaher, B. Priyantha, J. Liu, F. Zhao, Energy-optimal batching periods for asynchronous multistage data processing on sensor nodes: foundations and an mplatform case study. Real-Time Syst. **48**(2), 135–165 (2012)
64. D. Wang, T. Abdelzaher, L. Kaplan, R. Ganti, S. Hu, H. Liu, Exploitation of physical constraints for reliable social sensing, in *2013 IEEE 34th Real-Time Systems Symposium* (IEEE, 2013), pp. 212–223
65. D. Wang, L. Kaplan, T. Abdelzaher, C.C. Aggarwal, On credibility estimation tradeoffs in assured social sensing. IEEE J. Sel. Areas Commun. **31**(6), 1026–1037 (2013)
66. D. Wang, M.T. Amin, S. Li, T. Abdelzaher, L. Kaplan, S. Gu, C. Pan, H. Liu, C.C. Aggarwal, R. Ganti, Using humans as sensors: an estimation-theoretic perspective, in *Proceedings of the 13th International Symposium on Information Processing in Sensor Networks, IPSN-14* (IEEE, 2014), pp. 35–46

67. D. Wang, L. Kaplan, T.F. Abdelzaher, Maximum likelihood analysis of conflicting observations in social sensing. ACM Trans. Sensor Netw. **10**(2), 1–27 (2014)
68. D. Wang, T. Abdelzaher, L. Kaplan, *Social Sensing: Building Reliable Systems on Unreliable Data* (Morgan Kaufmann, Burlington, 2015)
69. D. Wang, T. Abdelzaher, L. Kaplan, R. Ganti, S. Hu, H. Liu, Reliable social sensing with physical constraints: analytic bounds and performance evaluation. Real-Time Syst. **51**(6), 724–762 (2015)
70. D. Wang, B.K. Szymanski, T. Abdelzaher, H. Ji, L. Kaplan, The age of social sensing. Computer **52**(1), 36–45 (2019)
71. Z. Xu, H. Gupta, U. Ramachandran, Sttr: A system for tracking all vehicles all the time at the edge of the network, in *Proceedings of the 12th ACM International Conference on Distributed and Event-based Systems* (ACM, 2018), pp. 124–135
72. D.Y. Zhang, C. Zheng, D. Wang, D. Thain, X. Mu, G. Madey, C. Huang, Towards scalable and dynamic social sensing using a distributed computing framework, in *2017 IEEE 37th International Conference on Distributed Computing Systems (ICDCS)* (IEEE, 2017), pp. 966–976
73. D.Y. Zhang, Q. Li, H. Tong, J. Badilla, Y. Zhang, D. Wang, Crowdsourcing-based copyright infringement detection in live video streams, in *Proceedings of the 2018 IEEE/ACM International Conference on Advances in Social Networks Analysis and Mining 2018* (2018)
74. D.Y. Zhang, Y. Ma, Y. Zhang, S. Lin, X.S. Hu, D. Wang, A real-time and non-cooperative task allocation framework for social sensing applications in edge computing systems, in *2018 IEEE Real-Time and Embedded Technology and Applications Symposium (RTAS)* (IEEE, 2018)
75. D.Y. Zhang, Y. Ma, C. Zheng, Y. Zhang, X.S. Hu, D. Wang, Cooperative-competitive task allocation in edge computing for delay-sensitive social sensing, in *2018 IEEE/ACM Symposium on Edge Computing (SEC)* (IEEE, 2018), pp. 243–259
76. D.Y. Zhang, L. Song, Q. Li, Y. Zhang, D. Wang, Streamguard: a bayesian network approach to copyright infringement detection problem in large-scale live video sharing systems, in *2018 IEEE International Conference on Big Data (Big Data)* (IEEE, 2018), pp. 901–910
77. D.Y. Zhang, D. Wang, N. Vance, Y. Zhang, S. Mike, On scalable and robust truth discovery in big data social media sensing applications. IEEE Trans. Big Data **5**(2), 195–208 (2018)
78. Y. Zhang, D.Y. Zhang, N. Vance, D. Wang, Optimizing online task allocation for multi-attribute social sensing, in *2018 27th International Conference on Computer Communication and Networks (ICCCN)* (IEEE, 2018), pp. 1–9
79. D.Y. Zhang, Z. Kou, D. Wang, Fairfl: a fair federated learning approach to reducing demographic bias in privacy-sensitive classification models, in *2020 IEEE International Conference on Big Data (Big Data)* (IEEE, 2020), pp. 1051–1060
80. Y. Zhang, L. Shang, R. Zong, Z. Wang, Z. Kou, D. Wang, Streamcollab: a streaming crowd-ai collaborative system to smart urban infrastructure monitoring in social sensing, in *Proceedings of the AAAI Conference on Human Computation and Crowdsourcing*, vol. 9 (2021), pp. 179–190
81. Y. Zhang, R. Zong, Z. Kou, L. Shang, D. Wang, Collablearn: an uncertainty-aware crowd-AI collaboration system for cultural heritage damage assessment. IEEE Trans. Comput. Soc. Syst. **9**(5), 1515–1529 (2021)
82. Z. Zhou, H. Liao, B. Gu, K.M.S. Huq, S. Mumtaz, J. Rodriguez, Robust mobile crowd sensing: When deep learning meets edge computing. IEEE Netw. **32**(4), 54–60 (2018)
83. Q. Zhu, H. Zeng, W. Zheng, M.D. Natale, A. Sangiovanni-Vincentelli, Optimization of task allocation and priority assignment in hard real-time distributed systems. ACM Trans. Embed. Comput. Syst. **11**(4), 85 (2012)

Chapter 9
Conclusion and Remaining Challenges

Abstract In this chapter, we summarize the techniques, theories, models, and solutions reviewed in previous chapters. We also discuss a few remaining challenges and exciting research directions for future research in the field of social edge computing. We expect the interests in social edge computing from different research communities (e.g., distributed computing, IoT and cyber-physical systems, social computing, AI, human-computer interaction, privacy and security, etc.) will keep on increasing and more fundamental and interesting research work will be carried out in future.

9.1 Conclusion and Summary

This book presents a new paradigm—Social Edge Computing (SEC), that leverages the collective power of billions of edge devices as well as the power of the crowd to jointly empower edge intelligence by revolutionizing the computing, learning, and training of the AI models. The contributions of this book can be summarized threefold: (1) the book presents a set of novel resource management system frameworks and task allocation algorithms that enable heterogeneous IoT devices owned by end users to collaboratively provide *computing* power for executing AI models on resource-constrained edge devices. (2) The book then presents several human-machine interactive learning frameworks that leverage the crowd at the edge to provide *intelligence* to troubleshoot, calibrate, and eventually improve the AI at the edge. (3) Finally, the book introduces a federated learning-based edge learning framework that allows the crowd together with their devices to provide distributed *training* for AI models to optimize their performance under the human-centric constraints such as privacy. Through extensive evaluation of real-world edge computing applications, it is shown that SEC is able to achieve impressive performance gains in various performance metrics including service responsiveness, energy efficiency, model accuracy, user privacy, and data imbalance. In this section, we briefly summarize the contents and key points presented in each chapter of the book.

In Chap. 1, we started the book with an introduction to the emerging research field called *Social Edge Computing (SEC)*. It is an interdisciplinary research field that is situated at the intersection of social sensing, edge computing, IoT/cyber-physical systems, social computing, and AI. We identified a few key characteristics that help define SEC and pointed out several fundamental challenges of SEC that are centered around the human-centric idea. We also outlined the organization of this book at the end of the chapter.

In Chap. 2, we summarized a few main technical enablers and fundamental motivations for research in SEC. To show the real-world implications of SEC, we also presented a set of emerging applications of SEC such as disaster and emergency response, collective traffic monitoring, crowd abnormal event detection, automatic license plate recognition, and crowd video sharing.

In Chap. 3, we reviewed a task allocation framework, CoGTA, that addressed the rationality challenge in SEC. The CoGTA provided a principled framework that allows the individually owned edge devices to effectively compete for the computational tasks in SEC in a cooperative way while respecting the rational nature of edge devices and inter-dependency and heterogeneity of the computing tasks.

In Chap. 4, we considered an important issue in SEC: the pronounced heterogeneity where the edge devices owned by individuals often have heterogeneous computation power, runtime environments, network interfaces, and hardware equipment. In this chapter, we reviewed HeteroEdge, a new supply-chain based resource management framework that provides a uniform interface to abstract the device details and allocates computation to heterogeneous edge devices.

In Chap. 5, we investigated the time dimension of the SEC paradigm. Specifically, we reviewed a new collaborative real-time AI framework, EdgeBatch, to expedite the execution of AI models in SEC by fully utilizing the data parallelization feature of AI models. In particular, the EdgeBatch scheme develops a new task batching solution that can identify the optimal size for GPU-intensive AI models to optimize the tradeoff between the end-to-end delay of tasks and energy consumption for edge devices.

In Chap. 6, we explored the human and AI interaction and integration challenges in SEC. The SEC paradigm brings about the opportunity to incorporate human intelligence from the crowd into AI models at the edge. In this chapter, we reviewed two novel human-AI integration frameworks, CrowdLearn and iDSA, which leverage the crowd intelligence to troubleshoot and boost the performance of AI-based solutions in SEC applications.

In Chap. 7, we further studied a human-centric issue in SEC: privacy. In particular, we reviewed FedSens, a new federated learning framework that is designed to address the data imbalance problem in health-related SEC applications with explicit considerations of participant privacy and device resource constraints. The FedSens is one of the seminal works that addresses the privacy and data imbalance issue under the same principled framework.

In Chap. 8, we recommended a few directions of related work for further readings. These directions include social sensing, edge computing, distributed system, IoT middleware, human-AI Systems, active learning, and learning with imbalanced data.

9.2 Remaining Challenges

We hereby discuss a few promising remaining challenges for future research directions of SEC.

9.2.1 Security Against Malicious Crowd

Security in SEC is an important concern, both for the benefit of the crowd participating in the application and for the application itself so that the services rendered are not sabotaged. Unfortunately, the unique design of SEC in which data originates and is processed on privately owned edge devices does not lend itself to conventional security systems (e.g., authentication in order to access a resource). Care must be taken, therefore, to ensure that (1) peer-to-peer APIs in SEC computing architectures are designed such that private information cannot be stolen by malicious attackers; (2) it is difficult or impossible to "game" the system by contributing incorrect sensing measurements or computation results in order to obtain the incentives without expending effort; (3) the system is resilient against attempts to sabotage or "poison" the results of the application for malicious purposes, even under sophisticated attacks (e.g., collusion attacks); (4) the system is resilient against denial-of-service attacks such as intentionally delaying tasks in order to harm the QoS. SEC is particularly vulnerable to the attack vectors highlighted above because it relies on privately owned and therefore untrusted devices to provide the bulk of the data collection and processing for the system.

9.2.2 Robustness Against Churn and Dynamic Context

In SEC, edge devices are often individually owned and managed, and therefore suffer from churn [4, 5], causing inconsistent availability by devices in edge computing. The inconsistency of edge device availability is aggravated since devices routinely kill tasks for power savings, or are opportunistically contributing compute power and then must stop in order to serve their primary purpose [11]. Furthermore, in the case of mobile computing systems, the main criterion ineligibility of a device to perform a task is the location of that device. Should the device move, then it may become unable to serve its function and must be replaced by a device in a more favorable location [2]. To solve this problem in a way that is both scalable and reliable, the SEC introduces buffering into multi-stage streaming applications. In such systems, tasks are broken into multiple stages where different devices perform an operation at each stage of a computational pipeline. If a device along the pipeline unexpectedly quits and must be replaced, then the replacement can be "filled in" by the devices adjacent to it in the pipeline. Furthermore, this pipeline design lends itself to taking fine-grained advantage of heterogeneous edge computing hardware since each stage can be matched to a specialized computing platform.

Another challenging issue in SEC is that edge devices have volatile statuses and their willingness to participate in applications may change dynamically over time [3]. We refer to this challenge as *dynamic context*. Consider an environment sensing application where edge devices (e.g., mobile phones) are used to collectively monitor the air pollution of a city. Each edge device is tasked to monitor a particular area. An edge device (or its owner) may change the compliance of task execution due to (1) changes in the battery status of the device, or (2) changes in the physical location of the device with respect to the monitored location. Failure to capture such dynamics may lead to a significantly suboptimal resource allocation where the costs of edge devices to complete a task are prohibitively high.

9.2.3   Uncertainty Quantification in SEC

Another direction for future work lies at the intersection of the uncertain data challenge and black-box nature of AI models in SEC applications. In particular, the current AI-based solutions mainly focus on improving the accuracy or performance of their models and ignore an important aspect of the output results: uncertainty quantification [8]. For example, in the intelligent traffic risk sensing application, the estimation confidence of a location being risky is critical (e.g., a location of a high traffic risk level with low estimation confidence can easily lead to false positives in the traffic alter system) [9]. As another example, in the disaster damage assessment application, the assessment confidence of the damage in a location is important for the response teams to make decisions on how to prioritize their resource allocations [10]. The uncertainty quantification is well studied in statistics and estimation theory [6, 7] but is largely missing in the current AI solutions due to the lack of interpretability and the black-box nature of the AI models [1]. An open research question in this direction is: how to provide a rigorous uncertainty quantification of the results generated by the AI models in SEC applications without knowing the ground truth a priori?

9.2.4 Blurring Human-Machine Boundaries with Social Edge Graph

The human-in-the-loop design of SEC enables the integration of human intelligence (e.g., context-awareness, cognitive skills, reasoning abilities) with the processing and sensing capability of physical devices. We envision that the human component of SEC can be further modeled as an "edge node" in which the human can perform inference or make decisions in the edge computing framework just like a physical device. Consequently, the physical devices (edge devices) and the crowd can be naturally represented by a uniformed "crowd-edge graph" consisting of edge nodes representing both humans and machines. With such a graph in place, the state-of-art theories in graph-based models such as knowledge graphs can be possibly adapted to perform graph queries and traversals in this crowd-edge graph to answer questions such as (1) which supply chain of nodes should be used to perform particular tasks? (2) where to perform inferences and where to acquire the knowledge to answer a particular query? (3) what is the optimal combination of human nodes and edge device nodes to accomplish a given task in SEC?

References

1. J.E. Dayhoff, J.M. DeLeo, Artificial neural networks: opening the black box. Cancer: Interdisciplinary Int. J. Am. Cancer Soc. **91**(S8), 1615–1635 (2001)
2. M.T. Rashid, D.Y. Zhang, D. Wang, Socialcar: a task allocation framework for social media driven vehicular network sensing systems, in *2019 15th International Conference on Mobile Ad-Hoc and Sensor Networks (MSN)* (IEEE, 2019), pp. 125–130
3. M.T. Rashid, D.Y. Zhang, D. Wang, Dasc: towards a road damage-aware social-media-driven car sensing framework for disaster response applications. Pervasive Mob. Comput. **67** 101207 (2020)
4. N. Vance, M.T. Rashid, D. Zhang, D. Wang, Towards reliability in online high-churn edge computing: a deviceless pipelining approach, in *2019 IEEE International Conference on Smart Computing (SMARTCOMP)* (IEEE, 2019), pp. 301–308
5. L.M. Vaquero, F. Cuadrado, Y. Elkhatib, J. Bernal-Bernabe, S.N. Srirama, M.F. Zhani, Research challenges in nextgen service orchestration. Futur. Gener. Comput. Syst. **90**, 20–38 (2019)
6. D. Wang, T. Abdelzaher, H. Ahmadi, J. Pasternack, D. Roth, M. Gupta, J. Han, O. Fatemieh, H. Le, C.C. Aggarwal, On bayesian interpretation of fact-finding in information networks, in *14th International Conference on Information Fusion* (IEEE, 2011), pp. 1–8
7. D. Wang, T. Abdelzaher, L. Kaplan, C.C. Aggarwal, On quantifying the accuracy of maximum likelihood estimation of participant reliability in social sensing, in *DMSN11: 8th International Workshop on Data Management for Sensor Networks* (2011)
8. H. Zeng, Z. Yue, Y. Zhang, Z. Kou, L. Shang, D. Wang, On attacking out-domain uncertainty estimation in deep neural networks, in *Proceedings of the Thirty-First International Joint Conference on Artificial Intelligence* (2022)
9. Y. Zhang, Y. Lu, D.Y. Zhang, L. Shang, D. Wang, Risksens: a multi-view learning approach to identifying risky traffic locations in intelligent transportation systems using social and remote sensing, in *2018 IEEE International Conference on Big Data (Big Data)* (IEEE, 2018), pp. 1544–1553

10. Y. Zhang, R. Zong, Z. Kou, L. Shang, D. Wang, On streaming disaster damage assessment in social sensing: a crowd-driven dynamic neural architecture searching approach. Knowl.-Based Syst. **239**, 107984 (2022)
11. X. Zhu, C. He, K. Li, X. Qin, Adaptive energy-efficient scheduling for real-time tasks on dvs-enabled heterogeneous clusters. J. Parallel Distrib. Comput. **72**(6), 751–763 (2012)

Index

Printed in the United States
by Baker & Taylor Publisher Services